Czermakiana

Czermakiana

A Viennese's Life-long Infatuation with America-on-the-Wane

Herbert Czermak

Teaching History and Literature to American Students, and English to Our Own.

A Selected Autobiography

LPP
library
partners
press

ISBN 978-1-61846-146-9

Czermakiana

With assistance from Thomas O. Phillips
Cover photo courtesy of Marianne Hofer
Cover design Eve Gietka

Produced and distributed by
Library Partners Press
Wake Forest University
1834 Wake Forest Road
Winston-Salem, North Carolina 27106

LPP library partners press

www.librarypartnerspress.org

Manufactured in the United States of America

"Die Wirklichkeit von der wir sprechen können, ist nie die Wirklichkeit an sich, sondern eine gewußte Wirklichkeit oder sogar in vielen Fällen eine von uns gestaltete Wirklichkeit"

WERNER HEISENBERG

"The human observer has to take his bearings from the point in space and moment in Time at which he finds himself; and he is bound to be self-centered because this is part of the price of being a living creature"

ARNOLD TOYNBEE

"MY FRIEND, HERB": REMEMBERING HERBERT CZERMAK

Perhaps logically for any sort of memoire, *Czermakiana* represents only a glimpse of Herbert Czermak's extraordinary biography. Growing up amid the Viennese rubble of WWII; using his great ear for languages to educate himself in multiple countries and cultures; drafting on his incredible curiosity about the world both to travel and to absorb deeply: Herb Czermak studied and lived the world.

Herb was born in Vienna, Austria, amid the growing tensions of nationalism. With the onset of WWII, he and most members of his family isolated in the tiny village of Hardegg, a family ancestral home adjacent to the river Thaya on the Czech-Austrian border. Herb's memories of those times included the terrifying sweep of soldiers: retreating Germans, advancing Russians, advancing Americans, sometimes literally minutes apart. With the end of the war, Herb's family returned to Vienna. Since their apartment was situated in the American sector of the quadrated city, Herbert began to acquire English, the second language (there would be others) that would serve him so well. Indeed, his interest in and mastery of English extended to college topics, graduate study in the United States, and a lifetime of friendships on this side of the Atlantic.

Throughout his years of education and the establishment of a career in teaching, Herb was ever a free-spirited traveler and cultural sponge. His adventuresome curiosity opened up sights and sounds throughout the world. (It was a good joke and a truism that he was bettered traveled in the US than I and many other an American.) His African adventures alone – some of which are documented here – are the stuff of derring-do and cultural exchange on the fly. He was a great teacher, commentator, colleague, and friend because he had seen and experienced so much of the places of the history (not just European history) he taught. He was a keen reader of all manner of western and non-western literature and philosophy and also contemporary commentary.

Not long after Wake Forest University acquired and developed semester programs at Flow House, in Vienna, in the late 1990s, Herb signed on as the European history professor. Almost two decades of students had the benefit of his lively erudition, his clever point-counterpoint of happy pedagogy, his wide-ranging cultural and political intellect. With house resident manager and literature teacher Prof. Gunter Haika, Prof. of Art Bea Ottersboeck, Prof. of Music Ulrike Anton, and others (not to forget the Flow House irreplaceable house assistant, Snjezana Kraljic) Herb was the conduit for Wake Forest students and faculty members to the best of Viennese and Austrian history, music, art, literature, ideas, and culture. He was a fantastically interested and interesting human being, blessed with a deep if sideways sense of humor.

Herb died in late 2022, survived by his longtime partner, Marianne Hofer, and his son. The Czermak-Hofer home in the Hernals area of Vienna – its top floor views looking out stunningly southwest to the Viennese woods and northeast to St. Stephens Cathedral and the heart of downtown was a happy meeting ground for faculty and student visits, meals, recitals, and Scrabble games. (Herb could rarely be beaten in Scrabble, regardless of the language in play.) To this writer and many others, Herb Czermak and Marianne Hofer are ever friends of Wake Forest, and to all who love the arts and literature, who appreciate the vital need to understand the tides of history. As you read *Czermakiana* you will affirm and appreciate the courage of one person to tell of his own remarkable life.

THOMAS O. PHILLIPS

WINSTON SALEM, NORTH CAROLINA

DECEMBER, 2023

About to lose the race against leukemia, the refusal of white blood cells to maintain the immune system, I dismissed the idea of finding a US publisher. Enough American teachers and students who have gone through or heard about junior-year-abroad courses taught by Europeans over the decades might well have been interested in the genesis of an Austrian prof. Hence this unusual title, and hence English as a medium.

HERBERT CZERMAK

CONTENTS

MY THIRTIETH BIRTHDAY

It was on the eve of my thirtieth birthday that my mother surprised me with a cryptical comment. "Sit down, I have to tell you something about papa that I have never told you before." My father had died when I was ten, and I barely remembered him because he was serving with an anti-aircraft unit far away in northern Germany for five long years. Of course, I knew that he, descendant of an ethnic German (*Sudetendeutsche)* family in southwestern Bohemia and as such susceptible to the nationalist view of the world had been a member of the Nazi party. Mother, who loved music and art, still complained after all these years that he had often refused to attend a play or movie, explaining that the whole world of entertainment was "one big Jewish *chuzpe."* But why now, twenty years after his death? "That´s easy to explain," mother went on, "since you returned from America, you have been a lot more interested in political issues and of course about papa´s views. Anyway, I thought you would want to hear this now that you are plunging yourself into History as a second field after studying literature in the US. It happened shortly after Hitler joined his native Austria to Germany in 1938 that papa came home one day from his position in the bank, surprising me with the question whether I would like to move to a big villa in the upscale nineteenth district. Wondering what this was all about, I was waiting for an explanation and finally asked him whether some relative had made him the sole heir. Smiling but eager to hear my reaction, your father explained that he had been offered this opportunity by his boss for ´distinguished services rendered`. Still no clue on my part, though I had a hunch it might have something to do with the Nazi takeover, I brought up the admittedly vague chance of having won in the lottery we played every so often. Laughing this away, his facial expression changed, his patient explaining lost its casual tone, and he told me what *aryanization* meant. Of course, you and the people you know are aware it meant that Jews were expropriated in favor of so-called "real Germans." So, my vague feeling had been right, though I had never heard the term but, my God, what was he going to decide? I simply burst out, 'Are we going to do it?' And then, my dear son, your father put his arm around me and reassuringly said 'of course not.'" By then I was the same bundle of nerves my poor mother must have been back then. Both of us sat back, she relieved to have finally clued me in, and both of us happy that papa, defying the demon within him, had chosen to stay in our two-and-a-half-room apartment. I went through my years studying history with this redeeming piece of the puzzle that my father was in many ways.

BETWEEN AIR-RAID SHELTER AND A CHILD'S PARADISE OUT IN THE COUNTRY. MY EARLY INTEREST IN LANGUAGES AMIDST THE CHAOS OF NAZI COLLAPSE AND VICTORIOUS SOVIET FOOTPRINTS

Our childhood was totally wrapped around mother and Marie. Looking for a trustworthy maid and a good cook in the 1890s, grandpa had found her forsaken by her husband who dragged them into abject poverty in Bohemia and eventually drunk himself to death. Her sense of humor and her hands-on approach to household chores had become part of my grandparents' lives and those of their daughters. Long before putting up with Paul and me, she had been everybody´s darling. While mama spent most of the day in the family-size printing shop, Marie was humming endless melodies while ironing. How easy it was to like her funny Czech accent!

One morning, dipping her hand into a pot of water and sprinkling it on the next shirt, she started singing the heart-breaking words of "Little Johnny traveling out into big wide world all by himself / his mother crying, now that her Johnny´s gone." I still remember my tears until mama calmed me down, "It's just a song, silly, and I´m here with you always." Just as vivid is my memory of Paul that day, half listening to Marie´s tragic story but hardly looking up from the wooden locomotive he was pushing along the stripes of the carpet fitting his narrow gage.

It was eerie squatting down in the dimly lit basement among all the other tenants. Waiting out yet another air-raid, some were straining their ears to catch any outside noise, while we children, scared and confused, were asking silly questions. When we surfaced into the total darkness after the alert, we could see houses burning beyond our immediate neighborhood. “What are these long white beams crisscrossing the pitch-black skies?”—"Searchlights, boys, looking for the English and American enemy bombers,” mama explained, “much like what papa is doing now so far away.” Since there were more and more alerts, the regime was advising the Viennese to move out into the countryside. More and more, they needed empty apartments for families bombed out, and people were requested to leave their homes to these unfortunates. Those unwilling to comply would be evacuated by force anyway.

The village of Hardegg on Thaya River was the ideal place to escape to. My grandparents had spent many years summering there, and my parents had met as teenagers on the premises of the medieval castle. Mother knew many of the villagers from childhood and staying with her former playmates would be no problem at all. We boarded the train at the North Station, from where during these very months thousands of Jews were taken to Prague and then east into concentration camps, as I was to learn decades later. Country life was paradise for us children, especially the orchard teeming with bees, beetles, and butterflies in grass feeling as high as we were. Looking after a huge sow, two goats, four hares, two geese, and lots of chickens and ducks was the old landlord’s job but helping to feed them Ah, the first touches of nature for us city boys like stepping into chicken shit and enjoying the warm goo oozing out between my toes!

One week we saw grandma sewing pillows, little ones for us and bigger ones for everybody else. The whole village was living in fear of the power dam upstream being blown up by either our own withdrawing troops, the Czech Communists gradually taking over, or the advancing Soviets. The water flooding the narrow valley would probably drown us all, and our only hope was to run uphill with grandma's pillows to sleep on. Known as *hamstering,* trudging for miles with mama to scrounge up some bread, , a little cheese, and a few eggs from peasants in surrounding villages was exhausting but Paul and I sometimes snuck away into the fields and returned with a few cobs of corn.

One sunny day our elementary school teacher did her part to help the war effort by taking us picking blackberry leaves "so that our soldiers, fighting the Bolshevik enemy during the awful Russian winter, can have hot tea. The *Führer* expects all of us to contribute our part." Who were these enemies beginning with *B,* and how could our tea leaves reach the far-away front? One afternoon when I was alone with grandpa, who was dozing away but evidently still catching snippets of the news on the radio, he suddenly mustered enough strength to wind himself out of the armchair and turning to me, spoke the strange words, "Das Schwein ist tot!" Amazing, for he had not uttered a word in days! Half scared but also curious, I remember running away to tell mama that grandpa had just announced our pig was dead. She calmed me down, assuring me that Susi was all right in the pigsty. When we were much older, she sometimes told us the story whenever early April pulled around. Though in his dotage, he had correctly understood that *Franklin Delano Roosevelt* had died.

What angered me decades later was that so many older people kept insisting that Roosevelt was really Rosenfeld and obviously Jewish. "Correct, he was Jewish, but whether his Dutch name had come from the German is irrelevant. What counts is that he could not even be classified as Jewish according to the abominable 1935 Nuremberg Race Laws."— "Maybe. But he was the driving force behind the U.S. breaking its professed neutrality and pulling it into war against us."— "Correct again. What should he have done, watching Hitler taking over Europe and persecuting minorities, especially Jews?"— "Many experts argue that if it hadn´t been for America entering WW II, unemployment would have wrought disaster over there."—Probably correct again, but all the more reason to do something about Hitler AND mass unemployment." On and on it went and still does, the political jousting between pro-German and pro-Allied loyalties.

On rainy days we loved to play the *Eagles´ Air War Game*, first deciding who gets to pilot the red planes by playing "stone, scissors, and paper." The Germans were always the red, and red was supposed to win. Paul lucked out and flew the red eagles, and in his mind the blue were doomed to crash. Three 15 mm plastic heavy bombers and three smaller interceptors for each. "Mine are not JU 88, they are ME 264 bombers," brother was showing off. He knew more about weapons than I did, and when I tried to tease him about what these letters stood for, he shot back, "that´s for *Junkers* and *Messerschmitt*, *Dummkopf*!" He even knew from our gung-ho *HJ* (*Hitler Youth*) neighbor that a specially equipped version of the ME 264, the *Amerikabomber,* was supposed to reach New York from occupied France and return safely. On either side of the blue Atlantic were three red and three blue battleships mounted on cardboard buttons. The ships were firmly anchored, could neither attack nor hide, but were wide-open targets as were the two flak positions on either side. When we quit playing war at the time agreed upon, baby brother Paul ignored the verdict of the roll of the dice and simply announced that "thanks to superior maneuvering, the red bombers destroyed one English ship while only one of our interceptor was lost." Not only was he beside himself that his elder brother's good luck had beaten him, but he also resented my mock English military voice questioning the German victory in red. Family jealousies and nationalist sentiment!

Remembering the funny looking sign from our years in Vienna, a sign called a cross of sorts in German (*Hakenkreuz),* we recognized it in all the flags, emblems, or the photos papa sent in his rare letters. It was pretty to look at and one day the neighbor´s son, twice our age, showed us the huge white swastika painted on the granite wall across the river "probably on Hitler´s fortieth birthday." All we kids were interested in was how anyone could possibly have reached the middle of that steep rock wall. How could he possibly move in all directions to draw this enormous funny-looking cross? Giggles until our savvy neighbor solved the mystery. "Without a well thought out plan, this wouldn´t have worked, but my dad and his colleagues selected the strongest and gutsiest members of the regional *Hitler Youth.* Each was given a particular section to plan and prepare for before they went to work. Of course, those comrades coming down from above used ropes and even steel cables, a bit like *abseiling* in the Alps. The bottom portion of the *Hakenkreuz* could only be reached from the riverbank, and for that they hauled in a special ladder. What always counts is capable individuals, self-discipline, working together in a team, all right?" We liked the fellow despite his stern tone because he let us ride the rubber-tire scooter his dad had shipped from Paris! Smooth sailing compared to our wooden wheels. The grown-ups knew, but none of us children asked what his father was doing there.

Nobody in my family ever spoke a foreign language, but I went word-hunting with a piece of paper, a pencil, and great enthusiasm to the point of getting on most people´s nerves.

Mama supplied a few English words she remembered from her youth like *swing time, foxtrot, and film star* now, less usable now in Hardegg, and the *pullover* I was wearing. Learning about my passion, one neighbor greeted me with *bon giorno* and then talked about *bella Italia.* I was fascinated that every language used our German word *radio.* With Russian nobody could help me, but some suggested it was written with different letters anyway. Correct, as we were to find out in a few months. I remember one Russian soldier spelling *drug* (friend) for me in two alphabets. Too confusing.

Except for occasionally hearing a politician blaring over our little *Volksempfänger* (people´s receiver) or wondering what exactly the call of the cuckoo clock signaling enemy bombers approaching meant this time, we were still children enough not to worry about the real war. Only when we could clearly see the long white bands set off against the blue sky and trailing behind tiny black spots, we sensed that those might be bombers of a real game. Why was everybody looking up, pointing in the direction the planes were headed, and crossing themselves, mumbling or swearing? Airplane expert Paul suddenly observed, "They must be American because they say everything is much bigger over there, houses, cars, and even candy. Why not their bombers?" In a letter written from father's North German flak unit that I found many decades later, I read "Tell the children that we are going through the *Eagles' Air War* up here too" and, without frightening them, add that ours is for real!" Then his terrible question "What will become of the children?"

During another one of those allied raids, a few days before the war officially ended, a tall black SS-uniform lifted me up, pointed into the sky and gently kissing me said in a Prussian accent I could barely understand, "Ven sis Schwein shoot down here, ve vill all be dead!" Part of a unit withdrawing west, he knew about the many dozens of petrol barrels stored camouflaged under the trees in our garden. Only a few days later in April 1945, the whole village stood watching endless military trucks trying to escape the advancing Russian front. Unforgettable, even for us children, the white painted slogans of "Four more weeks to final victory!" or "The A-bomb is underway!" Half starving soldiers, many with bandaged arms or legs, all in tattered uniforms and eagerly catching the few loaves of bread or apples we threw up to them. Wondering what the big stove with a pipe mounted right behind each driver was, we learned that for lack of gasoline charcoal was now the ersatz fuel spreading a ghastly biting stink. Except for a handful die-hards, nobody was in the mood to mention preparations for the Führer's fifty-sixth birthday coming up.

Roughly around this time, long treks of exhausted old people, mostly women and a few children, were pouring over the steel bridge before the Czechs removed the wooden beams from their side. At the old customs house, which served no purpose after the *Sudetenland* regions of Czechoslovakia had been occupied by Germany in autumn 1938, Czech border guards now searched each refugee, yanking rings, bracelets, or watches from them. They were ethnic Germans *(Sudetendeutsche)* and afraid of getting caught in the last ferocious clashes between advancing Soviets and withdrawing Germans. As we later learned, they were justly scared of being beaten up, arrested, or killed by the Czech Communists who were taking over now. Too hungry, sick, weak, or just too old to move on, they made for pitiful street scenes in the middle of withdrawing German troops. I remember two women dying by the roadside and nobody around to know what to do with them.

"Can´t you greet decently by raising your right arm to a clear-cut *Heil Hitler*?" the woman I met on my way from school screamed at me. Running home to tell mama I was happy that she smiled, adding it was perfectly all right to wish people a *Guten Morgen* instead. The Russians were approaching fast, which had some well-known local Nazis worried. They sensed that the day of reckoning was approaching and that sooner than expected many a political or family feud would be settled by finger-pointing and slander. Unbelievable that the butcher's wife could drown herself in the shallow brook behind their shop and that the photographer and his wife had tried to end their lives by swallowing potassium cyanide, suddenly a household word in the village. While nobody saw the husband again, we children spent breath-taking minutes peering at the pale and motionless woman laid out on a cot. Silly as we were, we imagined her blinking with one eye and claimed to have seen her lips move, though rumors had it that the doctor eventually did bring her back to life.

Suddenly a lot of noise and men shouting through the night! Six or eight soldiers, each with a rifle (*pushka),* were pouring into the room, a sergeant addressed mother in the pretty good German he had picked up during their long advance west, "I am downstairs and when problem, you tell. Soldiers sleep, very tired." Her arms around us, mother had offered to clear the big bed for some of them, but before we knew it each had found a few square meters on the floor. Peeking from under our sheets, we began to feel safer by their regular grunting and snoring. In the morning we saw that the other rooms were just as packed with exhausted soldiers, all of them so different looking. Years later mama often told us how relieved she was at this first encounter with the enemy, the one enemy people were most afraid of. If this unit had arrived here only three hours earlier, that is three hours *before* armistice, we might well have perished, all of us. There was only one road from Moravia, now still German occupied, across the river through Hardegg and leading to the flat lands toward Vienna. Trucks, tanks, and all sorts of military equipment came thundering over the bridge. A memorable instance was the shortcut a *T-34* tank took, plowing right through the neighbor's house jutting out into the road. Amazing, but our older Parisian scooter friend seemed to know that "the *T-34* was the toughest Russian tank against our superior German *Tigerpanzer.*" As I learned many years later, it was exactly this smaller but sturdy *T-34* geared to endless Russian roads vanishing in mud that had defeated the bigger sophisticated *Tiger.*

Little did I know only two days ago that another soldier would lift me up again soon, this one grinning "Gitler kaputt!" *Kaputt* was a household word in our lives with tools and gadgets, and the other word, I figured, sounded like *Hitler.* Another *Ivan,* as everyone referred to them, just as drunk as his buddy, broke the same news to Paul, holding him up crying and his little feet kicking. Imploring the fellow not to drop him on the stone slabs below, mother noticed his buddy staggering back from the pigsty with a bucket of red wine. "No, please not, my children are babies, don't drink wine" she kept begging him with different words and in different accents to make him understand. Laughing her off, he kept repeating "Babushka, Russkij baby drink *vodka*!" and held a dirty mug right to our little mouths. Trying to slip out of this messy situation, mother was wringing her hands until the two staggered away. A mild version of what was to happen in the weeks to follow. Once during the night, gunshots directly below us, followed by yelling in Russian. Scared silly, we waited for—what? Perfect calm until morning. What had happened? An alarm clock had gone off in the middle of the night and the soldier sleeping next to it fired at what he probably took for a Nazi weapon.

For us children everything was exiting, a welcome change from playing board games, picking mushrooms, and catching butterflies. Drunk or sober, the soldiers were nice to us kids, but girls quickly learned to hide. I remember two aunts, their faces somehow made older or *uglified*, with shawls slung around their heads and wearing dirty rags, squatting in remote corners of the stable and the attic for days on end. One early morning mother and her friend had gone picking blueberries and collecting wood but stayed out much longer than promised. "Imagine, three trucks full of soldiers were getting ready to picnic just across from where we were. Not too far away, we could watch them eating, drinking, and singing to ukulele music! Suddenly, two of them got up and began to walk toward us. What to do? Duck even further, whisper even lower, and pray to the heavens! It´s funny for you to hear this, but you have no idea how relieved we were when we saw them taking a leak and rejoining the others. Surely the longest picnic we ever saw."—Over the following weeks, all sorts of trespasses, thefts, robberies, or threats at gun point occurred—all terrible and some perhaps even understandable under the circumstances. Probably because they had never seen watches, these soldiers from far beyond European Russia were just stealing or yanking watches off civilians, some with two or three tied around their wrists. This became a joke all over in due time. Not funny yet, just frightening.

One afternoon a blast from the riverbank scared us even more than the grownups were already. Paul and I ran down and saw hundreds of fish floating downstream, all belly up. They had done some fishing, Russian style, with a grenade. Collecting as many as they could, they brought them over to the women in the house, "You, good cooks, you do fish for hungry soldiers. You also hungry, you have fish." Slicing open the trout, yanking a little balloon out from the inside, chopping off head and fins, then the chore of removing the scales. Another lesson of living in the country for us children.

The victors were just as starved as we were but had the advantage of living off the land. They had slaughtered a horse down by the bridge one sunny afternoon and were in the middle of carving it up. A few Hardeggers watching them were surprised, as I certainly was, when a Russian waved the only man over and told him to take the rest of the meat. Within minutes, our landlord was back with a wheelbarrow. It took some time for a few helping hands to heave the huge chunk of bloody horse meat into our wooden contraption. Eat horsemeat? They never did around here, but we were hungry. Little did we know that within half a year we would taste our first horsemeat out of cans packed in the USA.—At school one morning the teacher didn´t come back from a short break, and when some of us children went next door, we found her weeping, her green summer dress torn, urging us to go home and leave her alone. We enjoyed those unexpected days without school and learned about the details much later when were old enough to understand.—One incident Paul and I certainly remember was the fellow alternately cajoling and forcing our aunt Ida to climb on the truck with him. He was so drunk that he promised the Soviet officer whom we had called to help that he would take Ida back to Russia! More than adamant and potentially dangerous, he even started to wrestle with the officer who was trying to reason with him until two higherups brought him to his senses. Scared but happy that this scene was over, we watched his sober comrades hitting him over the head a few times and dragging him away. Though he never showed up again, poor Ida was under shock until this unit moved on a week later. If Marie had been here, she could sometimes have helped with her native Czech, though letting on to *Ivan* that she could keep track of their Russian talk might easily have taken a dangerous turn.

Watching a couple of soldiers prodding the ground with different length rods, Paul and I were scared they might detect some of what we had buried. A couple of old gold coins and a few rings or bracelets in little steel cases, for instance, or the little brass telescope I had been given on my fifth birthday with the order to keep it safe. If they had found father´s Nazi party badge or documents stamped or postmarked with swastikas, it would have caused problems. One day two of them detected something, did a lot of shoveling, and in the end came up with a sewing machine. "*Singer*. Good American machine, *karashó*, we take to Russia" one of them declared while the other, more realistic, seemed ticked off at the sweat wasted.

When the Soviets stumbled on a warehouse full of food rations which the Nazi mayor had refused to issue to the starving villagers, it was the Soviets who saved his neck. It would have been the perfect moment to kill him and his ilk, who had watched the population go hungry for a reason nobody understood. Maybe they had just waited for an order from above that never came in total chaos. We children never quite understood what had happened when the miller´s mother came in sobbing and explaining the details of her misery. A teenage classmate of her son had reported to the Soviets that her fifteen-year-old son Alfred was hiding a gun somewhere in the old wooden mill. "They were just here, searching for a weapon all over the place and came up with an old rifle from World War One that he had kept hidden all these years. Why?" and she broke out crying again, "did he do that? Only because nobody could take away his toy. My old invalid husband and I pleaded with the Russians not to arrest Alfred, that they had only found a boy´s treasure, just an old unusable gun, without ammunition at that." They shoved Alfred up a truck with a

Cyrillic license plate painted on all sides, leaving the millers behind.

Much later, as I began to listen to stories of witnesses and to read books about the war on the home front, I began to be especially interested in Soviet misdeeds against the civilian population committed after hostilities had ceased. Could it be that there was something to the rumor of a four-week free-for-all that Stalin had granted his victorious boys and for which a certain Ilja Ehrenburg in Moscow was allegedly responsible? It was only decades later that I came across a highly relevant page in a highly relevant book. In his celebrated The Battle of Stalingrad, English historian Anthony Beevor cites an encouragement by one Ilja Ehrenburg that had actually reached Soviet troops fighting their way into Germany. "Do not count the days; do not count the kilometers. Count only the number of Germans you have killed. Kill the German—thus sounds the prayer of your mother, the cry of your Russian soil. Do not waver. Kill." Ehrenburg was a successful writer awarded the Stalin Prize but evidently also a political heavyweight. If he could compose such merciless propaganda against the German enemy, why doubt that he could be the origin of what happened to German civilians after ceasefire? I came across material dealing with this subject many years later again when I read a book by Milovan Djilas, distinguished Yugoslav fighter against the Nazis and a friend of Marshal Tito. In Conversations with Stalin, he spends quite a few pages on the unpardonable behavior of the Soviet troops who had helped Yugoslavia defeat the Germans. The situation had deteriorated to such an extent that Tito, already wary of Stalin's intention to throw Yugoslavia out of the Communist International, sent Djilas to Moscow to complain. Mass rape among friendly nations? Stalin´s answer to Djilas tallied pretty much with what Ehrenburg must have thought if he was behind the decree that may never have existed in writing. According to Djilas, the dictator downplayed the seriousness of his troops´ behavior on friendly soil as "rewarding the boys."

None of these indelible impressions are supposed to mean that Austrians are free to choose between having been liberated from Nazi tyranny or Soviet barbarity.

RETURNING TO WAR-RAVAGED VIENNA, BUT THE AMERICAN ZONE. OUR SHORT-LIVED REUNION WITH FATHER.

Mama and grandma looking after grandpa, who was really too old to be transported, we went on a day-long bumpy tractor ride back to Vienna. Squeezed in between chairs and a table, sacks of potatoes, crates of vegetables and fruits, or sitting on top of a valuable pile of wood, Paul and I sensed that we were close to the city when we saw the first ruins and felt the zigzagging our tractor had to do to dodge bomb craters. Arriving in the rubble of what once was the house next door, we could not see much else in the unlit street but heard the hydrant spilling water into the cold October night. While mama was helping her old parents off the tractor and the farmer was unloading the precious firewood, Paul and I stood guard, eagle-eyed. Scurrying past in the dark, strangers were grabbing a log or two but there was nothing we could do about it! Venturing upstairs into the dark house, I made it to the second floor and turned right as I had been told. Scared to see a snoozing Russian soldier, his black boots sticking out into the corridor, I raced back down. "Three flights up, I said!" I often saw the heavy blonde living in the flat where the military boots had scared me and wished her a good day. When many years later mother clued me in, we had a good laugh over the big black boots.

Our "new" apartment was in the same district as the one we had to vacate for a bombed-out family two years earlier. There was no way our grandparents could live by themselves anymore in these days of scarcity, and so being forbidden to move back into my parents' home was less of a blow. Forbidden because father, a member of the Nazi Party and by now sending censured letters from a British POW camp, was ineligible for reclaiming his own apartment. Nor was he allowed to return to his position at the bank until the procedure known as *denazification* cleared him of his one crime, that of having joined the only Party. Necessary though this ideological reeducation no doubt was, it was considered a misnomer by some because it was unlikely that any serious follower could be cleansed of Nazi ideology as instantly as he could be deloused.

The only important thing was that the bombs had missed us and that we had enough to eat thanks to the good fortune of living in the U.S. zone. This became crystal-clear to me only much later, though Paul and I were already developing a sense of longing for everything that looked, sounded, or tasted American. Mama often told us how they had virtually been starving for two years after World War One because none of the victor nations had planned ahead for the civilian population. Now we could buy lard, that age-old Austrian specialty, and if it was suspiciously dazzling white, the rosy-cheeked woman behind the counter explained that it was American. Mama tasted it, and we loved to spread it on the equally white mushy American bread. We still had potatoes and jars of plum preserves from Hardegg, but when it came to fresh vegetables, we could only get two sacks of tomatoes and cabbages my uncle was growing in his once beautiful rose garden in the British sector. As a city fire commissioner, he had rescued his old *Ford Eiffel* and drove us to the zoo, where some animals had visibly lost weight and others were back in their makeshift cages after escaping during air raids.

A big hit during those meager early years were the so-called CARE packages. Discovering things that nobody had ever seen like powdered egg, powdered milk, horse meat, and silver hake, Paul and I felt like explorers among all those strange words. A couple of reams of what mama explained was the smoothest toilet paper ever, for in Hardegg we had taken to using Nazi and later course-grained Russian newspapers. Hidden in tough wrapping was a bar of something called *Hershey,* splotchy white all over and hard as a stone. Having no idea what chocolate tasted like, it surely gave our teeth a rare workout. There were several small bags with s u g a r and s a l t printed on them and something to drink, called *Coca Cola.* The perfect mystery was a green pack, smaller than the stony chocolate. Opening it, we saw five green flat sticks, same color and same words. Mama knew a few words more than I did by now, but she had no clue. We had a great time teasing each other about monsters like W r i g l e y—how could you pronounce a *W* before a rolling *r?* S p e a r m i n t also remained a mystery until mother figured it out by smelling it. We did solve the word g u m because, as wise apple Paul cracked, "it´s only a bit shorter than our word *Gummi.*" C h e w successfully defied us even after we tore one open from the silvery stuff around it, debating whether to eat it—it tasted sweet—cut it up and use it as sugar, or boil it first? Perhaps a type of putty, impossible to get to repair all the shattered windows? It was only days later that we learned what the word meant and why it had been supplied to the soldiers all the way across the sea. Paul and I took to chewing until everybody, even Marie, told us we looked like monkeys.

As mother later often described the scene, there was no telling how we would react. A soft knock at the door, followed by something she had never said before. "You want to open, see who´s there?" Seventeen months younger after all, Paul was hovering behind. Another knock and I dared to open slowly, inch by inch. This man who stood there was—who? Spotting a ring around his forehead and watching his steadily trembling bald head, I felt like nailed to the floor. Not until he moved a bit closer, smiling, did I begin to imagine having seen him before. We did slowly warm up to him, but not before I, cuddling up to mama, whispered "Is this our real papa?" Then father held us up high, the first born first, then Paul, then both of us on one arm each, squeezing us real hard. Noticing us staring at the ring around his trembling head, we heard his voice for the first time, "The ring is from the helmet, a very heavy cap that I had to wear during the dangerous bombing attacks." Sighing and ducking to help us understand, "And the trembling is what the awfully loud explosions of the bombs did to many of us. Papa cannot stop it, it`s always there. But I was lucky they didn´t hit me," and he lifted us up again even more exuberantly. Children united with their father, this time for good and not just for his rare ninety-six-hour furloughs, and what are they talking about? The war.

I have often wondered whether my fledgling fascination with language didn´t get a further boost when I sat on father´s lap, looking at a book title he slowly read out loud and explained to me. *I Learn English,* a fellow with a kilt, a funny hat, and a bagpipe on the cover. I loved them all. Mother often told us that emotionally he had certainly come to grips with defeat sometime during those awful years fighting the *Royal Airforce* and that he never believed there was any truth to Hitler´s order "beginning at 4:20 a.m. Germany will *retaliate*," implying that on September 3, 1939, neighboring Poland had attacked Germany first. He had even been interrogated by the *Gestapo* because in a chat with neighbors he had carelessly pointed out friendly and enemy countries in his beloved atlas and insisted that Germany could not possibly win the war. Unforgettable during that first peacetime Christmas with papa, a wooden board with two teams of queen, king, and their retinue varnished black and yellowish. No dice? Who can move where, and how far? Awfully hard to remember, but father put it all in terms of warfare so that it was easier for us to follow. He knew how we had enjoyed the *Eagles´ Air War Game*, so this was a little similar. Hard to foresee by the enemy, the knights did their strange jumps while the bishops carried messages to and from the royals; the castles standing firm against the enemy and the rank and file, the eight pawns, deciding the right moment of attack and hanging back to defend the home country. Days of happy excitement.

Partly because he was not allowed back into the bank and partly because the small family printing shop needed somebody badly, papa began to tread the pedal of the old machine. I remember him in a heavy black winter coat under a wide-brimmed hat on the unheated premises, rhythmically swaying back and forth with the machine. We sometimes went to watch him plodding away while answering our questions but also noticed that he was getting weaker by the month. Mother kept the worst from us—tumor of the kidney at a time without adequate medication or even food. He passed away at 49 years of age, a few weeks after he had learned of being reinstated at the bank. A week later, the shock of seeing him in an open casket, his black coat set off against his sallow complexion and the pallbearers carrying him off in the snow.

THE CHALLENGING WORLD OF *GYMNASIUM*. FALLING IN LOVE WITH EVERYTHING AMERICAN. FIRST STEPS TOWARD ENGLISH AS A CAREER. MY "SECOND BROTHER" PETER ENTERS OUR LIVES.

The many new challenges of *Gymnasium* made it a bit easier to overcome the wounds of the past. English soon became my favorite subject, though my teacher, an elderly lady was adamant about sticking to BBC standards. This made no difference to anybody else in class, but it did to me because the GIs and everything they spoke, sang, ate, drank, played, read, or stood for had bewitched us within the year. It is hard to describe the enthusiasm with which we watched them during their morning drill, their tight-fitting uniforms and special shape caps appealing to us so much more than those of the French across the street. Always eager to keep us happy after these awful years, mother even sewed two such military caps for us, one patterned after the British style with the royal insignia for Paul and another for me with the shiny *U.S.* up front. Sometimes we could watch them marching to music entirely new to us whose ears were attuned to good old Austrian marches and the more precise Prussian ones. These GIs—no idea what those letters stood for—seemed to march with a certain bounce, each step a wee bit behind the basic beat. Paul and I and many classmates were sure they were marching to the music of *Glenn Miller*, a hero to us and to many adults who had either never heard anything like it or had secretly listened to jazz on shortwave radio. It was easy to see GIs throughout our American-occupied zone, but I still lacked enough English and a bit more courage to communicate with any one of them except by smiling. A welcome extra chance to observe more Americans was the Christmas party they put on for us pupils. A huge banner with *Merry Christmas* and *USFA (Forces in Austria)* the tall *Tannenbaum* chock full of candy we had never seen, let alone tasted, and lit by electric candles when much of Vienna was still struggling with streetlights. A military choir did American Christmas songs, their unfamiliar tunes and sometimes animated beat a real thrill followed by a little gift for each of us, handed out by two Negroes beaming with the good tidings.

Two memorable encounters changed that first impression a bit. One day on my way to school the crazy notion got into my head to finagle a stick of gum from the first black man I had ever approached and for some inexplicable reason even dared talk to. Practicing the three magic words, I mustered up enough gumption for a clear *chewing gum, please.* "He cracked up laughing", as I would have expressed it years later, reached into his pocket and handed me a stick of what we had almost thrown away out of sheer ignorance a year ago. Told later that the GI was not supposed to let anything interfere with standing sentry in front of the requisitioned *Manner* chocolate factory, I felt proud that he had broken the rules for me. This chewing gum raid egged me on with my English, and I tried to appease the teacher by learning her vocabulary without neglecting my own Americanisms including their pronunciation. "We don´t say *guys* and we don´t end our truly English sentences with prepositions. You are not supposed to slur your words beyond recognition, and you do need the originally French "*u*" in colour, honour, and labour. Yes, there is there is no *-f* in the spelling of *lieutenant*, but you will remember I told the class the other day that English spelling is difficult when it comes to logic." Even if she never got around to writing a straight *A* into my report card, she was a kindly and knowledgeable lady. An ethnic German, balancing her heavy limp with a silver-headed cane, she had been brought up in war-torn Yugoslavia and probably went through some circle of hell. As I remembered from the ethnic German refugees stranded in Hardegg, their pronunciation of German sounded frightfully correct to us, and her immaculate British English was beautiful to listen to, even to me. She not only suffered listening to the *Awful American Language* of her American-infected pupil, but it was everywhere by now, gaining ground fast. We did agree on one thing, namely that *Esperanto*, the artificial language invented by a few idealists half a century ago, had no chance against our English.

Within a few years Paul and I had become jazz fans who could not convince mother, let alone grandmother, that rolling cascades of hammered piano keys called boogie-woogie was great music, and that one *Louis Armstrong* did really have a voice! One unexpected success I landed with the daily *luncheon matinee* request show on *Blue Danube Network* was that the announcer actually read off my request. I had told my first ever girlfriend to run home from school like I did to catch the whole program, just in case. *Sugar Blues Boogie* by trumpeter *Billy May*, sure enough, here it was, though I barely caught the funny way he pronounced our names. Hero in English class after that, though only a small consolation for flunking math. More and more sophisticated to differentiate between pop and jazz, Paul and I gradually founded a whole club of listeners, some bringing in *V(ictory)*-discs that they had somehow acquired on the black market to play on an old gramophone running on a pickup arm with exchangeable needles. *Mary Lou Williams* caught my fancy early while Paul became a gung-ho *Count Basie* fiend. It wasn´t just the music. We drank Coca-Cola, and those of us who had succumbed to smoking saved up enough pocket money to buy American cigarettes. To buy *Pall Malls* on the black market! *Wherever Particular People Congregate.* The interesting question we were not asking ourselves yet was whether our mix of basic English and GI lingo made us sensitive to the music, or whether the intriguing beats and riffs drove us toward *cooler* English. Anyway, funny to learn that *What´s first, the chicken or the egg?* was the same in German—or was it English first?

Slowly but steadily life in Vienna had settled into living with the American, British, French, and Soviet soldiers. If I had grown up across the street, I would have had to learn French. Not that I would have minded that, but it would certainly have steered my future into a different direction. *Bon jour, au revoir, monsieur, madame* and *mademoiselle* had been in my earliest collection of foreign words and with the French in several Viennese districts now I became aware of the origin of so "many German words" like *appetite*, *café*, *bistro*, *restaurant, hotel* or even *trottoir*, the sidewalk to get to them. Their uniforms were blue, and some of their soldiers wore *berets.* These looked *cool* and becoming more fashion-conscious, some of us began to wear them. If we adored jazz, so did the existentialist French philosophers we were beginning to study at school, *guys* like Albert Camus. Our teenage headgear code soon split into *the Ami* camp, the rest divided between friends of the *beret* and the clods still cultivating the German caps. The British also wore berets, but they somehow couldn´t get it right, none of the chic of the blue French pulled down sideways at just the perfect angle. By then Paul was referring to the English berets as hanging down like Marie´s pancakes over the plate.

The Four in the Jeep became a household word describing the daily sight of four soldiers, one of each, cruising through the city to nip potential trouble in the bud. Not just any soldiers, but the toughest MPs. The driver and his copilot could talk to each other fluently, we assumed, but the Russian and Frenchman in the back may well have had a rough time. The most memorable experience I witnessed was the US squad proceeding to action at the skating rink, a time-honored establishment where champions had won medals in decades long gone. One Saturday afternoon, a routine gathering of local boys and a few *Amis* was underway up on the balcony, some of them plastered (my new favorite word) and all of them raising hell one way or the other around a couple of girls. Wrestling, screaming, a knife. Out of nowhere, two Negro military police, broad white belts and MP helmets popped up and without discussing anything with anybody involved, grabbed two GIs, banged their heads together and dragged them downstairs. Wow! Impressive, because that sort of entertainment used to go on every weekend and none of the Austrian police, probably still unsure about their new role in a democratic Austria, dared put an end to it.—My other experience was a lot more personal. Forever learning and practicing new words, I decided to find out whether the word *fool* was really so bad. It was probably by design that I singled out that one GI struggling badly to stay on his skates. "You fool" I said sort of half muffled because I was scared. He must have been at least four years older, and for that reason alone I might have been too daring. I watched him flailing his arms, taking forever to stop. "Whatdidya say?" he demanded. Smiling a bit to defuse the situation, I called him a *fool* again, whereupon he did something I have admired ever since. "Take that back!" I didn´t. "You take it back. This time I`ll count to three. That´s how we do in America." He stood up bravely now, eager not to be insulted by a young foreigner and one who could skate well at that. I had understood every word, his face alone signaled action, but instead of apologizing now that I knew *fool* was offensive, I hesitated for a few seconds but said nothing. Faster than lightning, a quick jab right on my diaphragm made me gasp for air. He staggered on and I staggered to the nearest bench. We had both accomplished our mission.

Without fully understanding the slogans painted on the walls beside the *elevated*, I remember "Rettet (Save) die Rosenbergs!" and "Acheson, Go Home!" The vast majority of Austrians, however, had no sympathy at all for Communism and we listened to the daily Russian fifteen minutes of *The Hour of the Allies* only for the Tchaikovsky music. The American counterpart began with a song nobody knew but which was easy to like, "I come from Alabama with my banjo on my knee O Susannah, don`t you cry for me!" Where was Alabama? That was easier to solve than to find out what the man had on his knee. Of course, the American program praised democracy to the skies, but what else could people possibly believe in after the catastrophe of Nazim and the new dictatorships next door in Hungary and Czechoslovakia? After Stalin´s death in 1953 paved the way toward the conclusion of the State Treaty within two years, Austria was obligated to permanent neutrality. The diplomatic yardstick to follow was best summed up in the words of later Socialist Chancellor *Bruno Kreisky*, "As much trust as possible toward the United States, as little distrust as possible toward the Soviet Union."

Viewed from many years later, it was clear to me that all my teachers reflected the exceptionally challenging decades before, during, and after their own studies. The Latin teacher insisted that without Latin grammar, learning a foreign language would be a lot more difficult, if not impossible. From what I knew about English then, both from class and spoken on

Blue Danube Network, English was fascinating because it rarely required us to understand its rudimentary grammar. All right, our German word order often stood in the way, but the rest was merely learning *new words and idioms galore!* My supposed gift for languages just didn't work in Latin, a form of torture like math!—The History teacher was phenomenal when it came to explaining why the Romans had lost their empire after so many successful centuries, but he was more of a philosopher when it came to dealing with ancient Greece and an ardent defender of the Enlightenment against what he termed the intuitive *belly thinkers*. More importantly, he confided to me much later how incredibly difficult it had been during his time as our teacher to get his hands on quality literature about "the wars" and their terrible results. I had always felt he had been "on the right side" and agreed with him that too many people, lucky to have been born too late, felt called upon to *swing the Nazi club* from the moral high ground. I was also old enough now to understand that he was one of my earliest intellectual pillars.

One day mother surprised Paul and me with the idea of an affordable summer camp in the British occupied southernmost lake district, where we would have enough to eat, strike up new friendships, and learn how to swim. Friendships were indeed quickly struck in this newly found paradise, especially the one with the only Lutheran in a Catholic camp at a time when this was considered rather unusual. Peter quickly became popular for his outgoing ways and soccer skills rather than the absence of *Holy Mary* in his world. Plagued by nostalgia for faraway places, we soon went on a hitchhiking tour. "What kind of tour did you say?" –"Simple. We hike, that is, move by letting some car pick us up and take us along." Firming up our friendship with each new experience, we loved the stretch over the Alps with two GIs in a car they called *Chevvy*. Unbelievable, the driver was plugging something into the dashboard to shave during the better portion of the trip. America must really be incredibly modern! The last lap back to Vienna was with Soviet soldiers in a pickup, sitting on top of watermelons—just as funny as watching the *Ami* shave.

We did get some serious religious education in the sense that the camp's director, *Herr Helmut,* took us to old Gothic churches with windows of elongated saints being pulled toward heaven and ghastly gargoyles to keep away evil and spew rainwater. "Captured in France, I was taken to the U.S. a year before the war ended on a ship full of other POWs. The crossing was dangerous, not only because our submarines were still a hazard, but because a group of die-hard Nazis, certain that Hitler′s secret weapon would turn around the war, threatened us. It got so bad that we had to ask the crew to help us, which they did by locking the fanatics up. My year in Colorado felt like the first holiday in many years except for the backbreaking job of collecting Colorado beetles on potato fields." Maybe you know that the Nazis claimed the Americans had dropped them to destroy our harvests. I think it's rubbish."

Wavering a bit between focusing on English as spoken and written today and English literature, I passed the admissions exam to the *Institute of Translation and Interpretation* to learn from a professor there that I had done well but needed to improve my pronunciation. Good grief, was I going to have one of those intolerant British English fiends again? To my relief she explained that unlike in German, the "*g*" is to be pronounced separately *as, i.e.,* in *EnGlish* so that one can hear it. *FinGer*, not fi*ng*er. Young enough to have ben to the US already, she was *right down my alley*, a new idiom I had just picked up. More interested in the humanities than in law and economics, I expanded my GI stock of words learning whether a church was Roman or only Romanesque and whether studying Romance languages might be as Romantic as they sounded. *False friends*, the horror of language learners, were plentiful. No, in English *eventually* does not mean *possibly* as it does in German, and an entrepreneur may become an *undertaker* only in a worst-case scenario.

The US-financed library across the opera fascinated us, not merely because we could delve into every possible aspect of life in America but especially because of its *open shelf* system.

Everybody had access to it, and even Peter's younger brother, an idealistic Communist intellectual, grudgingly admitted that borrowing books that easily was good even if they were probably all written from a capitalist-imperialist viewpoint. Browsing through LIFE and studying the *journalese* of TIME was my daily linguistic nourishment and watching films on *Abraham Lincoln* (born in a log cabin!) via *Teddy Roosevelt* (always carried a big stick) to FDR (won the war by talking to the nation in *fire-side chats*) were unheard of novelties. A regular sight was the so-called *bookmobile*, a caterpillar-like lending library disseminating American books that the average population either should or would like to read. Most of us studying English wanted to go to America for obvious reasons, some of us more so than others. It was difficult to accept that the so-called *Fulbright* scholarships we kept hearing about were a lot easier to come by in higher semesters. By now Paul and I had made several friends among the older American Fulbright students, some independently wealthy but all endowed with a wholesome pack of dollars. Invited to restaurants we knew only from passing by and treated to opera tickets for seats rather than standing room, we had joined a privileged club. Most were piano students, and some spoke German well enough to confront mother with the idea of a *Hausmusik* evening at our place. How excited she was to meet her first real live Americans, and pianists at that! She was as happy as could be listening to melodies she recognized from *Porgy and Bess* and various renditions of Viennese folk music. What fun it was to teach our guests a few Viennese terms and to fill them in on the details of the lawsuit between the two leading confectionaries over who made the original *Sachertorte.* Eight years had elapsed, and still we thought of how wonderful it would be to have father chit-chat with cultured young *Amerikaner.*

THE MAN WHO PAVED MY WAY TO *PARADISE.* ARRIVING AND ENJOYING BEING *COKED AND DINED* IN MISSISSIPPI AND DRINKING MY WAY INTO ORANGE COUNTRY.

Then one of these *Fulbrighters* called and suggested I come and meet his friend visiting from Holland. I met organist Conrad M. and his buddies to attend concerts with them, eagerly picking up new idioms in the process and having fun teaching them Viennese lingo and lore. Asking whether I was interested in coming to the U.S. was a question the visitor kept repeating over three days until I, shrugging my shoulders in disbelief, wanted to know what he actually meant. "Of course, I am. You know what I am studying. In a later semester I´ll probably qualify for a scholarship, maybe a Fulbright like yours."—"No, no, I mean sooner than that. We can help you, all you have to do is say that it´s not just a whim of yours (I had to ask him about that word) but that you are a hundred percent serious." Puzzled but still curious, I was listening to his plan. "I am the organist at a Methodist church in Mississippi—look it up on the map!—and we have connections to a Methodist college in Florida. With the help of my church community, we'll get you a type of work scholarship." Learning what that meant, I was still dumbfounded. "But there´s nothing my mother or I or anybody else can contribute!"–"Look, I am not expecting you to understand how this will work in every detail, but this is America, and where there´s a will, there´s a way. I am sure you have heard this proverb in your language before." We had

Conrad over at our place, mother was impressed by this project, his exquisite manners, and the patience it took him to teach me how to tie a bow tie, the quintessential mark of an American gentleman, as he jokingly explained. He left me four of them, different colors and design each, and I was proud to show my new skill off to Peter, Paul, and my new friends. Conrad left after three days, and I sort of buried the whole idea. Within a few weeks I learned much to my surprise that "I shouldn´t count my chickens before they are hatched," another colorful idiom I wasn´t sure I had used in the right context. Every single week, a long envelope arrived, two green 15-cent stamps with the Manhattan skyline and pages meticulously handwritten in capital letters. Each repeated Conrad´s project, adding ever more details to the still vague dream and eventually discussing my departure. I was so grateful to my mother for not merely having no objections, but for supporting this admittedly unusual idea. Except for a few politicians, businessmen, musicians, and a handful of *Fulbright* students nobody had ever gone to America, not counting the shiploads of desperados before and after the wars. Nobody had ever heard of a no-name youngster about to do just that, simply because he was "nuts" about everything American. Many a well-meaning friend argued, "You don´t know anything about this fellow and his church community and nothing at all about America, except what those GIs left us." Mother´s answer was something along the lines of "I trust my son completely. If he wanted to goof off or play around with girls, he could do that right here and I wouldn´t know. We already have a photo album of this beautiful college, and even if it´s Methodist—we have no clue what this really means—it can´t really be that dangerous."

Picking up my ticket, the real thing with the *Union Jack* on several slips, one for the leg to Scotland, then the important ones to the United States of America, was pleasantly nervewracking, the woman behind the BOAC counter commenting in a decidedly British accent that she had never printed out a ticket for "such a young globetrotter." The countdown had begun, from heart-breaking farewells to imagined worst case scenarios. Marie was not surprised. On New Year's Eve, her old magic around pouring clumps of melted lead into ice cold water had worked. Holding the congealed lump up against the wall at just the right angle, she had detected the contours of a boat, sails all set. We had all seen it, but I alone wanted to believe it. My brother, my mother, her "third son" Peter, and Herr Helmut were watching the turboprop taking off. What was really going through their heads? What was really expecting me?

Never having been on a plane before, I asked my neighbor whether he thought the blue flames shooting out of the right wing were standard procedure. Laughing it off, he turned out to be quite interested in my apparently most unusual forthcoming adventure and explained what a *collect call* was, which that lovely Irish Fulbrighter had urged me to place on arrival. A chauffeur sent by Conrad´s painter friend picked me up at Idlewild and took me to her sophisticated apartment on FDR Drive, as I learned the next day. Having fastened my emotional seatbelt for all kinds of surprises and shocks, I never found much time to unfasten it during the three days until my flight south. It had been one thing to see films of skyscrapers but to walk between them was literally staggering. My host had fun watching me looking up those canyon walls and trying to figure out headlines, billboards, and traffic signs. The many black people, especially uptown! Sitting in a show in Radio City Hall, I surprised myself and my host by pointing to the couple three rows ahead. "Excuse me, but isn´t that *President Truman* and his wife?" My hostess just could not believe that at my age and from so far away I could possibly recognize him. An experience

I was to go through often: many foreigners, friend and foe alike, tended to know so much more about America than the other way around. It wouldn´t be me, though, if I hadn´t found an excuse of sorts, “We are so much smaller and less important than you are!” I would certainly return to the *Big Apple,* but how come that funny name? But now off to the South, which I had read and been told was different in so many ways.

Scheduled to touch down in Gulfport, where Conrad was expecting me, the plane was rerouted because of heavy fog to the city whose name spelled jazz to me. Coming in over vast stretches of dead trees and bayous was like something out of Rudyard Kipling´s *The Jungle Book* we had read at school. My debut Greyhound ride took me across my first Confederate state to my second one, spelled with a total of four *-s's.* Here they are! Conrad M, his elegant mother and an even more elegant lady friend, a leading church member. “Mah name´s ” A first sample of a

Southern accent. Introductions, hugs, compliments. A first drive along the Gulf Coast, rows of simple wooden houses, stately homes in other areas, then quite unexpectedly poor shacks, many with tin roofs (there IS a *Tin Roof Blues!*), awfully hot, though *muggy* is the word. Off to an official visit in my herringbone jacket and tie. The mayor himself, pleasantly outgoing, walks me to his office, where he signs a document with my name on it and hands it to me with a big smile. “For the distinguished services rendered...”— *“Golly”*—don´t use God´s name for everyday matters!—“how do I deserve that?” The other accents are not as tough to crack as the mayor´s, and so a first chit-chat over a big bowl of gumbo—isn´t that in the old song *Jambalaya*?—is soon underway in an atmosphere of good humor, riddled with questions on both sides and language gaffs on mine. It is true, they really do say *y´all* even though I am all by myself! Taking me to his home in a yellow sedan,

Conrad points out some old-time furniture, two oil paintings by his New York painter friend, and—surprise—a kitchen that does not at all look like what we call *Amerikanische Küche* in Europe. A giant fan mounted on the ceiling above my bed will help me sleep in this muggy climate. He is obviously a bachelor, spends much of his time with his mother, and plays mostly classical music on an old upright surrounded by subtropical flowers. Taking good care of me, he tells me all he knows about college life.

The even bigger highpoint is the garden party at the church with about two dozen people welcoming me. Judging that they are pretty much in their Sunday best, Conrad and the fellow who will drive me to Florida in long-sleeve shirts, jackets and ties, the women in long pleated skirts, teenage girls in petticoats. Aware that probably nobody except Conrad had ever seen a European, I listened to the lady in charge introducing me, "Here is Herbie, a real live European!" Judging by their accents, I am around smalltown folks, cordial, outgoing, and visibly proud of what they have helped bring about. The entire congregation, at Conrad´s doing, donated money over the year to pay half of my tuition. But now the conversation is much more about me, my family, and my country. "Herbie, what y´all gonna have to dreenk?" with the voice rising toward *dreenk*. Not aware yet of this no-no, "Maybe a glass of red wine, please." Absolutely shocked, this friendly matron, upset not only about my request but maybe also about her own reaction, "We don´t drink alcohol, there are so many cold beverages over there, Hawaiian punch, coke, Pepsi, 7-up, iced tea, orange squash, grapefruit juice, and root beer." A younger lady with a bun and a bit upset about her friend´s somewhat brusque manner, gently takes her arm, admonishing her, "Ethel, don´t be so haaarsh on him, he´s from different culture!" Of course, I know that many Protestants over here don´t drink, but is it that serious? Looks like I have a lot to learn about where the devil, shrewd as he is, really hides. No insult intended, we are both going back to discussing what is customary and what is not. My second blunder during that memorable reception is only offensive to my taste buds. Curious whether it is perhaps some weaker brand of beer, something wholesome with herbal roots, I am opening a root beer. Learning later on campus that just about every European tends to fall into this trap, I vow to make this mistake only once. A welcome service with the whole congregation attending in the wooden neo-Gothic church gives me a chance to express my sincere thanks. Lots of "The Lord be with you!" wishes on my way out. Walking past the black usher I suddenly hear him saying, softly, "Want you to know I also donated a dollar for you!"– The week until departure to Florida is passing in no time. Meeting the church member who is going to drive me to the Frank Lloyd Wright campus and a wealthy couple driving us to New Orleans in an open black Mercedes for a sumptuous meal in the legendary French Quarter. Two local fellows stationed at the nearby Biloxi airbase manage to smuggle me inside, put me on a jet, fasten my seatbelt, and are having fun turning circles and watching me turning colors. Another couple from the church takes me to a fancy restaurant built on the premises of the old slave quarters. A strange feeling indeed to enjoy savory Southern cooking on these unholy grounds, but I have already spent quite some time learning local history, and not only about the *do´s and donts* of today.

The long drive along coastal Alabama and the Florida panhandle is uneventful except for the hilarious episode at the Florida state line. Why are we stopping at all, it is not a real border, perhaps only to "shake our legs"—lovely expression!— or to while away the hours of the officer on duty? Little do I know how important state lines are in traffic or legal matters, that the forty-eight states often have their own laws. A lesson not easy for many Europeans to grasp, it is the UNITED States, though we talk about *its* and not *their* history. “Florida Orange Juice. The world´s best. Drink all you can.” A glass with a small fountain next to this invitation makes me wonder how serious the offer is. After five or six glasses I am forcing myself to have one more—and that does it. “Your friend´s mighty thirsty,” the officer is grinning at my driver, “where´s he from?” Telling him that we don´t have any orange juice at all, and if so, then imported as canned concentrate turning your stomach upside down, I am taking him up on his offer to have a few more.

MY FIRST YEAR AT *FLORIDA SOUTHERN COLLEGE*. FASCINATING, CHALLENGING, PUZZLING, AND CONFUSING.

The first days on campus are one uninterrupted fascination with the beauty of the architecture and the surprises of college life. I have studied the catalog Conrad sent me, but reading about living in a dorm, four small rooms to four students in one compound and actually living in it are, as they put it here, "two different ball games." So is lining up at the cafeteria, picking up a tray, grabbing the right cups and plates, pressing the right *faucet* (no, not *tap*!) for the beverage, and handing the cashier my meal ticket. In hindsight, my second day on campus turned out to be decisive in more ways than one. Called to the Dean's Office, I had to clarify a few details for an important man. It so happened that I had great trouble understanding his accent, somehow different from that of "other folks" around here. Long, drawn-out vowels, diphthongs where I wasn't expecting any, terms I had never laid my ears on, and slurring it all a bit—embarrassing! As I learned later, he was from rural Alabama. Holding a sheet that looked like a copy of my Viennese educational background, he declared, "Ah see you've come to us to do some *Phys Ed* here." Once he explained that abbreviation to me, I gladly said, "No sir, this must be a misunderstanding because I've come here to improve my English and hopefully finish my degree"—"Oh, ah see, that's better 'cause", and he sized me up, smiling, "it says heah you went to a *gymnasium* ova thea." Fumbling for a way to explain what type of school I had attended, I was relieved to see that clearing his throat he recognized his mistake and corrected himself. “That´s o.k., ah just rememba that´s what y´all call your haagh schools.” And to put us both at ease a bit, he advised me to take some waterskiing or canoeing for half a credit each. The concepts I learned this morning were most important for my daily survival—*transcript, liberal arts, credit points, audit,* the difference between *undergraduate* and *graduate* among them. More than half of the courses on my transcript from Vienna were accepted toward the sum total of credits I needed, which made me a *junior.* Had I started here from scratch, I would have been a *freshman* and the second year a *sophomore.* Learning the etymology of that, *wise fool,* fascinated me language buff but also made me a bit sad. After all, I was a whole year ahead of all the wise fools and still felt as though I knew precious little about what was awaiting me here.

“Hey Paul,” I wrote home, *“they don´t call out to anybody here without that hey, so this is why my hey! What I want to tell you, though, is that many students really do sport that crew cut you´re so proud of. Funny clothes, such as knee-length shorts striped or checkered, you know, named Bermudas after the islands south of here. Most of the fellows long white pants, never shorts the way we wear them, only the girls in shorts, some in short shorts, wow! Some on the college team wear numbers on their shirts, probably the position within the team, many with the red logo of the school to show their team spirit. When it comes to talking jazz, I haven´t found anybody yet who knows much about it, in fact they are just as bad as ours, confusing hit songs, jazzed up pop songs, or commercialized jazz numbers with the real thing. You can tell Peter and the rest of them we should be proud of our Vienna, city of music! Something else you´ll think is funny. There´s a pool right here and my swim trunks are a sensation, less than half the length of theirs. But what killed some of the guys was seeing me with my bathing cap on! They gave me a hard time, some of them calling*

me a sissy. Once they told me what that meant, I just laughed with them, shaking my head. Trying to explain that we have to wear them for hygienic reasons because most men have longer hair didn´t help much. "When in America, do as the Americans do," right? Girl students are officially referred to as coeds, which to me sounds like an insult to the prettier ones. It´s so formal, an abbreviation of co-education, you get it? Because it´s difficult to land a date without a car, one of my roommates took me along on a blind date. This scared me because he is a theology student and with his fiancée, that´s the girl he wants to marry, tend to help people. Was I going to date a blind student? He didn´t explain but assured me it would be fun, so I went along and the four of us had a great time. The rule of the game is simply that the boy and the girl are not supposed to know each other. My date, an attractive refugee from Cuba, and I had a great time, but I guess this game could well end up a flop. The four of us went to what they call a drive-in movie, which means dozens of visitors watching the movie on a huge screen from their cars, popcorn and coke bottle ready to go. We attended a double feature, that is, two movies in a row, which gave me a lot of time to practice my Spanish. Don´t laugh, you know me, one of two respectable brothers."

Lining up for lunch that same second day began with another shock but ended on an upbeat note. "You are obviously not from here" the distinguished looking man in a dark blue suit, his white hair meticulously parted, had addressed me. He was standing in line behind me like every student. "I can tell from your clothes and the way you´re trying to choose your food." When I said I was from Vienna, I heard the most puzzling comment on my hometown I had ever heard. "Vienna! Well, I hope you are nor as arrogant as some of the Viennese I have met." Ouch, what do I do with this totally unexpected comment on my second day at school? He must have spent some time in Europe as a young man because his German was still pretty good. He went on asking how I was paying for my tuition, and l explained that while half of it I was paid for by my sponsors in Mississippi, I may well end up peeling potatoes in the kitchen or helping the gardeners for the rest. By then we had picked our food and drinks and were wandering off to an empty table. Sitting down, he introduced himself as the Head of the Department of Psychology and spoke these remarkable words, "If you´d rather work for me, let me know as soon as you can." Dumbfounded, I started counting my blessings, but could not figure out what he might have meant by this strange initial observation.

The longer I was living in America, however, the more I thought I understood. There is a certain type of Viennese, and even at my age I had met a few, whose comments, judgments, or just haughty manner of presenting themselves can be very offensive. Each by itself maybe not worth mentioning but they all have to do with this *idee fixe* that Vienna is somehow the hub of culture, that America may have a great civilization, but certainly no culture. In fact, pondering what the psychology professor had said, I thought of a name we had come across in *gymnasium,* that of *Oswald Spengler,* the Viennese author of *The Decline of the West,* who pioneered this dichotomy of *Kultur* versus *Zivilisation*, the former dealing with the humanities and the latter limited to the sciences and technology.

Within a few days I was working at the Department of Psychology in an old wooden house without air-conditioning but otherwise an *el dorado*, where I did four hours every afternoon. Interesting how one remembers ridiculous details, but my daily respite from the stifling heat was to spend the nickel set aside for an ice-cold cup from the coke machine. Taking my time sipping it, I had a few minutes every afternoon to study the names and dates chiseled into little squares of the sandstone walls. Dismissing the idea that they might be famous faculty or athletes, I correctly figured them to be donors, probably alumni. Impressive. Correcting aptitude tests, collating sheets of exam questions, or devising simple geometric forms—circles, squares, triangles, oblongs—which I put into envelopes, one each, for testing purposes. Dr. L was conducting an experiment against a well-known colleague at Duke University, demonstrating that the number of blindfolded students giving the correct geometric form in a sealed envelope would never surpass random chance. Even more fascinating was his explanation of how hypnosis worked. We had learned a few terms in *gymnasium*, but here I was about to witness actual experiments. In one session, Dr. L proved to me that even under optimal conditions—a neutral, quiet room without any distraction whatever—I was not a "good sleeper," meaning I subconsciously put up too much resistance against being hypnotized. Not disappointed at all, I was infinitely more excited the day he had his entire class eating apple pie. Stuffing pieces of crumpled-up paper into their mouths, the students were told not to swallow the pie. Unbelievable! Here they were, about three quarters of them, munching away, their eyes wide open and in no way in a trance. When he told them to stop munching, they did, removing their pies and waiting for class to continue. Back in our office, Dr L was telling me about his fascinating past as a specialist in hypnosis. Just as I was asking him more details, there was a knock at the door and in came a student claiming he had an appointment now. "Ah, our *post-hypnotic* message" the boss said, thanked the messenger, sent him away, and then explained yet another aspect of this mysterious process to me.

One incredible experience seemed to chase the next, especially during the first months when the New World had to offer truly new adventures. Smiling at his plan for the evening without spilling the beans—why *beans?* I have no clue—Dr. L drove us to a weird assembly, not just weird in student lingo, but downright eerie. The stage in something like a ceremonial hall was decked out in an array of pungently smelling flowers, some in long-necked vases, others in heavy clay pots radiating the grim features of ancient genuine or quasi-Mexican deities.Sounds of soothing music pervaded the atmosphere already pregnant with a numbing fragrance. A man in a maroon velvet suit, a red rose in his lapel, dark glasses, and a cane was standing by an open upright. Introducing the purpose of our gathering, the maestro let us know that this was a particularly promising evening for establishing contact with the deceased, always on condition that someone in the audience was willing to respond to a message he would pick up. Dr. L was as new to this place as I was but had assured me that whatever might be happening, it was easy to explain. Puzzled that the impresario first pointed at me and announced a message from a younger man who had just died somewhere far away, I was trying to gather my wits. Concentrating on the message supposedly meant just for me of all those present, I had to admit to myself that it could indeed tally with the anticipated passing away of my twenty-eight-year-old cousin. Conveying the dead man´s cordial greetings and enthusiasm over my good start in America, where he had always wanted to study, the transmitter of messages regretted that he could only vaguely decipher my name but that it ended in something like -*bert.* A few chords on the piano to grant us, in this case me, a respite to formulate a reply. Animated whispering among those present. Revealing Hubert´s imminent death of incurable cancer to the crowd, I added that it was his name, not mine, that ended in *-bert.* Not a bit bothered by my intended correction, he insisted that the difference between sender and addressee of a message was as clear as an open book to experts. Judging that in his mind he had landed a victory in the eyes of most visitors, I watched him pricking his ears to receive another message, pounding the keys again to summon concentration. On the way home, Dr. L had a ball with my naiveté, first reminding me that, no matter how Americanized I thought I was by now, sensitive observers could tell I was from far way, never mind details. I had not been to the barber yet over here, a good example. The *esoteric*, our name for him now, may well have had a spy mingling with the crowd, a few telltale words of German we occasionally exchanged would be worth a lot to him. Besides, did I forget that we were all asked to sign our names? A minor point perhaps, but statistically there is a pretty good chance that someone of the roughly a hundred people present would know (of) a young man deceased recently or about to die.—Still a shocking experience. When I saw Hubert only about a month ago, we both knew he would not live to hear me rave about America.

By now we had become as close as we would probably ever be, I proud to work for him and he possibly beginning to see me as the son he never had. Occasionally, he took me down to the baseball diamond to watch and explain a complicated game, and a slow one at that. "No, a homerun is not the same as homecoming" and giving it a few good chuckles, "we'll probably see one here today, it just means that a batter can complete the whole circuit of bases including the last one, the home plate. You remember homecoming last October when former graduates poured back to campus for the basketball game that our *Moccasins* won hands down. Anyway, baseball is more for people like you and me, football is too rough to my taste and watching basketball perhaps too much of a strain on our eyes." Every now and then he drove me home in his vintage maroon Buick with those little portholes on either side, and his wife and daughter jokingly wondered whether I would give them the honor of staying for supper.

One day he had a special surprise for me. We drove to a huge tent set up way beyond the town limits with close to a hundred people pouring in, all whites. Dr. L explained that this type of event was called a tent meeting, that the preacher and attendants would be praying out loud whenever the spirit got ahold of them, and that I had certainly never experienced anything like it. The musicians were a five-member family from Kentucky, which guaranteed down-to-earth faith played on original instruments. Folks were still pouring in when we found two seats near the exit with a close-up view of the tall poles supporting the giant roof. *The Kelly Family* it read across something resembling a pulpit, and for a reason I was to discover later, a long bench was set up right across the open space where the altar would be in a church. Leading an opening prayer that was punctuated by blasts of music, the minister lost no time getting to the point of this three-week meeting scheduled for central Florida. The music was slow and familiar enough to the congregation to sing along, but soon the whole atmosphere was getting more emotional. Mrs. Kelly at the Hammond organ, the children playing guitar and banjo, but especially the tall head of the family alternately playing the trombone and whipping up a storm with his sonorous voice, were on their way to salvation. As I had trouble sucking it all in and following the minister´s words advising the crowd to do penance for their sins, I pulled myself together long enough to watch Dr. L watching me. It was fascinating to see him in operation, the clear-headed analyst observing the reaction of his student assistant and the reactions of the swaying crowd around us. Following a loud blast from the trombone on the pulpit, a scraggly looking fellow in T-shirt and jeans suddenly started climbing up the nearby pole, waving and screaming on is way up and crowning his ascent with the remarkable shriek of, "Closer to God!" That, no doubt, he was. They were now fanning each other´s hysteria, the crowd, several believers writhing on their seats, and the savior of his own soul on top of the pole. The emotional climax was yet to come, as Dr. L had intimated beforehand. The minister quit preaching sense of sorts but invited us, his voice alternately cajoling and caressing the sinners, to step forward and confess. "Kneel down on the mourner´s bench and don´t hide any of your sins. The Lord knows you, and he knows you well, but he also knows you want to rid yourselves of your burden." By now sinners were weeping and wailing around us, swaying back and forth, some rolling on the sawdust ground. My boss was right—I had never seen anything like it! Hearing about *holy rollers* and experiencing hysteria of this dimension were downright frightening! All I could think of was, "Don´t budge an inch, don´t follow the cajoling messages of the minister, just ignore the tears of the folks in front. Soon Dr. L and I were the only ones still sitting, the rest shouting and huddled together on the *mourners' bench.* Now was the right time to confess, and so I did—to my boss. It had been really hard work not to surrender. Learning by working for a psychologist.

School was certainly different from what I was used to, much of it in a positive sense. Small classes, all teachers ready to answer questions, silly ones included. Specific assignments, usually a syllabus allowing for some planning ahead. One thing I could have done without were the *quizzes.* You couldn´t ignore them either, because most profs included them in the final grade. Back home I was used to sitting in on classes I hadn´t even registered for, just to see what my buddies were doing or out of curiosity. Serious cramming right before the only exam at the end meant that one really remembered the material. I think it was in *History of the Confederate States* that

I was a bit careless copying a few dates or names out of a copybook and was caught by the teacher. She gave me a hard time about it but let it go at a warning. The following weeks I noticed that some of my classmates weren´t quite as friendly as usually, one really snubbing me. When I put two and two together and asked her about her strange behavior, she said "We have something called the *honor code* at FSC, and cheating is just not done." A theme I was to encounter often, "the tricky European versus the honest American." In politics this age-old difference appears as "the realistic European versus the naïve American." Notwithstanding the moral flaw I had revealed during the exam, I learned an awful lot from an excellent and generous teacher. That *Erwin Rommel* had studied *Robert E. Lee´s* deployment tactics made my day as a history fan, and I added *ante bellum* as a perfect example to my collection of foreign loan words hitting the subject´s nail on the head.

My classes were interesting for different reasons. I had wanted to go to America *now* because I thought it was stupid to have to do German shorthand as a student of English translation. At least passing American shorthand would make more sense and, only kidding myself, would surely be accepted back in Vienna. I had never really wanted to return to Vienna after just one or two terms, nor was American shorthand any more intellectually challenging than ours— practice every single day, just for fifteen minutes, but regularly! The teacher gave me an undeserved *D.*

The professor teaching *The History of the English Language* was offering a most demanding overview of the language across the centuries, which even those admired who could not quite keep up with the former Yale scholar. He won the admiration of every one of us when he came to class one morning with a quarter of his jaw missing. The same impressive posture, the same analytical mind radiating the same fascination for his subject, the same beige corduroy jacket with matching bow tie. When his condition deteriorated, his wife began to translate what she alone could understand of his explanations. Asking me to do my studying at their home for several evenings a week to see what her dying husband might need, she found a student greatly honored by her offer and the few dollars coming with it.

I fondly remember the ornithology professor because she advised us on which birds best to see where and when in their natural habitat. That´s why people flock to Florida. With a puzzled yet understanding smile she criticized the subject of my paper, pointing out that I was the only one who had ever chosen to write on *The Hawk and the Ibis under Several Egyptian Pharaohs* instead on something like the various local birds´ behavior under changing conditions. She told us a lot about the alligators in some of the twenty-odd lakes within the city limits, warned us not to swim at dusk or at night, even though swimming in the same lake in broad daylight was not really a heroic deed. By the time a boat full of students tried to teach me how to waterski, they couldn´t really scare me much–or could they?—with their "Hold on, don´t crash, there´re gators in the lake!" In broad daylight they lie buried in the reeds, maybe even asleep. What if an unplanned spill had landed me precisely there? It was much safer and just as spectacular to watch one crossing from one lake to another at night, a huge lengthy lump lying in the middle of the road blinded by the headlights.

The course called *Comparative Religion* caught my Catholic imagination but spread itself too thin to my taste. What did fascinate me, though, was that there is allegedly only a quantitative difference between organic and inorganic life, between various degrees of consciousness. When it came to choosing a foreign language, an obligatory subject, I couldn´t imagine anybody would question my choice, *English.* "English is not a foreign language here, you´ve got to pick something else." —"O.k., in that case, put me down for German."—"But you are from Vienna and you people speak German, don´t you?"—"Yes, of course we do, though many Germans don´t think so." Thinking that this was a funny little disagreement, I had my mind set on Spanish anyway. Very few spoke Spanish anywhere in Europe outside of Spain, and I was already looking forward to being an exception back in Vienna. There was not much tourism from Latin America either and it was only after Franco´s death that Spain opened up. Quite literally, I had my fingers on the pulse of history because my teacher named Castro had just escaped from Cuba before her namesake took over at New Year´s. The way so many students saw this issue touched a sore spot with me, who had grown up fifteen miles away from Hungary and fifty miles from Czechoslovakia. The markers off the Florida Keys a few miles further away read "Ninety miles to Communism." Endless discussions with students indicated that, on balance, many were not at all against Castro's ideals and Romantic ways of how to achieve them. The situation was pretty much the opposite with their parents. Youthful idealism against grownup realism.

Both the student body and the faculty reflected the age-old concept of America as the haven of persecuted foreigners, a vital difference to the Soviet Union as I pointed out in many a bull session. The large greenhouse was run by a very shy man, a famous expert in his field, who had fled the Bolshevik revolution half century ago. The German professor had come with her old mother only a few years before I did. Fleeing from the Red Army via the American zone in Germany, she spoke *English vis a typical Cherman eccent* but took us foreign students to ride the incredible glass bottom boats of Silver

Springs and to the *Ringling Museum* housing original European paintings of centuries ago. What an eye opener! A Hungarian student, who had landed here a few months before I did, was giving lectures about how he had wriggled into Austria through the Iron Curtain. The most remarkable example, though, was my roommate.

Paul's mother was the head of the Yugoslav Methodist Church and for this reason he had been allowed to leave Communist Yugoslavia to study theology after the college president had intervened with President Tito himself. When we moved in together, Paul's English was virtually nonexistent, but he had his future in the US all worked out and his first goal was the B.A. Every night when I came home from selling sandwiches on campus and brought a left-over *Cuban* or *P&J* for my hungry roommate, we put our European heads together, talking about what we liked and what we could do without. He was working hard behind the scenes on having his bride come over and marrying her on campus, and a truly moving celebration it was! Paul was incredible: a strong believer in the values America stood for, he was a lot more critical of certain social aspects we could not see around our lily-white campus. The only blacks we ever saw on campus were the wonderful *Bathoon Cookman Choir*, heavenly black music, but far away from the worlds of jazz and pop I had been brought up on by our beloved *BDN.* Of course, he knew we were living south of the *Mason-Dixon Line,* and of course he had heard–not seen—that slowly, far too slowly for him, "the times they were achangin.". Always eager to pursue his ideals, he suggested the two of us do something nobody else was interested in, to attend the Sunday service at a black Methodist church on "the other side of the railroad tracks," where simple wooden houses were standard and hardtop roads the exception. I was all for it, though without much of his missionary zeal. Not that we minded, but having no car, we had to walk the two miles to the little church. Little children dressed up in white, their moms every bit as elegant and several under wide-brimmed hats, all of them eager to have their photos taken. It wasn't just Paul′s Methodist contacts, these people genuinely welcomed us, the only whites in sight. Then the preacher, welcoming and telling us in yet another accent what being Christian was all about. What exceptional color slides for my growing collection!—Walking all the way to the white Catholic church on the tenth anniversary of my father′s death brought back memories of the funeral on a cold winter day and mother′s spells of grief during the first anniversaries. Walking over square stone slabs past all the subtropical splendor on a bright morning gave me plenty of time to ponder where I, in so many ways supposedly like father, would go from here.

Two of us rooming together had the idea to drive over to a so-called "wet county," just for a few beers. That division into dry and wet counties was *mindblowing*, my latest verbal acquisition! No such separation between the more and less privileged drinkers in my country! I had no real problems keeping up with my assignments, though reading English was still not quite so easy. They tried hard, wanted to get to know me better. Anyway, I turned them down. Maybe next time, my guardian angel saying *no* again. The next morning the entire campus was in shock. On the way home, their car had crashed into a freight train, the impact so terrible that not all parts of their bodies had been recovered yet. It was exactly three weeks after my family had watched me taking off for my wonderful new world.

That tragedy welded us together even faster. Al, whose family had moved south from New England, was an *econ* student and was to play a major role in my life here in a year from now. In a way I envied Frank, the funny theology student, who at our age was obviously engaged to be married. Then there was Phil, the Korean veteran, who had the nerve-racking habit of packing his cigarettes tight by pounding them against his watch while talking about his GI Bill. We sort of respected him, and I certainly took him at face value when he suddenly yelled, "Herb, there´s a trapezoid under your bed! Quick, look at it!" Throwing myself on the floor and crawling under the bed, I saw nothing but heard giggling above. Surfacing, I realized Phil had really pulled one over on me. I had learned about all sorts of animals here, but didn´t remember that name. "Go check it in the dictionary!" Phil kept it up, and when I found out what a dangerous animal the trapezoid was, they had more laughs for the rest of the day, and I with them.

Despite what some of us may have been afraid of in Vienna, religion was in no way important at this Methodist school, let alone interfering with my Catholic upbringing. Mother was religious but attending mass, preferably in a beautiful old church with stimulating sermons was the extent of our religious lives. Yet I had, out of my own free will, submitted a request to the bishop, asking permission to read any material required of me in this possibly strange new world. Certain books were still "on the index" then. Why had I bothered when even the Church was about to ditch this leftover from the Middle Ages? Just an obedient boy, or one trying to find his direction in a potentially confusing world? Of course, my request had been granted, though I never needed it. Most students probably were not even Methodist and if they were, neither they nor I were eager to discuss the finer points of John Wesley's world. The only *must* was the weekly convocation in the ultra-modern chapel, its bright red upholstering the reflection of the school colors, with an impressive goateed Scottish minister pouring forth his ideas on the Holy Spirit in an enchanting accent and audibly rrolling his *r´s.*

Though slowly becoming part and parcel of campus life, I was still puzzled by things. I wasn′t quite sure, for instance, whether the so-called cheerleaders were supposed to somehow further our education or to make sure that we were becoming fully aware of our already amply budding manhood. Agreed, catching a glimpse of nice legs under a flapping short white skirt or of a shapely body bouncing for a home victory was quite appealing, as was peeking at a VPL that my roommate spelled out for me as *visible panty line*. All this whipped-up quasi-sexual excitement, while everything concerning real sex was officially tabu. Housemothers–what a ridiculous title!—ran a tight ship checking on their *coeds'* moral well-being, *pinups* were half-secretly swooned over in our dorms, sex symbols like Marilyn Monroe or Jane Russell adored, but movies with explicit sex were X-rated or not shown anywhere. Petting was something to be avoided, and campus police were looking after our moral well-being, allegedly even shining searchlights into the orange groves after sundown. I was sometimes envious of these fraternity guys or football cracks with their dates, lining up for supper suntanned from an afternoon on the beach. Poor boy, I wasn't here for *Phys Ed,* had no money and no car. "Watch out, he′s from Europe, these guys are fast!" was something I often heard and, when applied to me, I felt like saying, "Wish I were, but I′m just very average, Romantic and harmless, more like "Could I have a chocolate sundae with you in broad daylight?" After two years here I had to agree that, on average, Europeans and Latin Americans on the one hand, and North Americans on the other were from different planets.

Another surprise was typically American in a way, and it concerned me directly. Time and again the same three fellows went out of their way to greet me with *Heil Hitler,* the blondest one clicking his heels. Thinking it was a silly joke, I ignored it until I saw a Nazi flag hoisted in front of their fraternity. I couldn´t believe it. Was I the only one on campus to know what this stands for? Not that these fellows were stupid, in fact one of them appeared shocked to have to teach me that *Hitler´s* real name was *Schicklgruber.* Thanks, buddy, for this bit of information, which we had certainly never heard at school, but please stop this! When I threatened to take this to the Dean´s office, they quit. At that time, I already knew that in this country freedom was interpreted to include even Nazi symbols. Things were a little different with Communism, not because that was less dangerous in the 50s and 60s than the Nazi cult, but because too many people still thought Communism and Socialism were pretty much the same. After all, *USSR* stood for *U*nion of *S*ocialist *S*oviet *R*epublics.

Communication with home was something I had to really work for and gladly did in the sense that a meaningful letter took some time. After all, I wanted to let them know about so many things like stopping by the campus post office to see whether there was something in *Box 178* and the overflowing joy if there was but blaming it on our inefficient Austrian mail system if there wasn't. Peter wrote that he was preparing for the Olympics in Rome, Paul that he was surprised I was living among moccasins, which he thought were just Indian leather footwear. And mother in her hard-to-read handwriting, "Paul was beside himself when he saw the basketball shorts you sent him and did some badly needed translating of your newspaper clippings. One thing he didn´t get, though, was your X-mas wishes. We ended up laughing when we figured it out. We are sorry to hear that you don´t have much contact with Conrad anymore and don´t quite understand. He did everything for you, and you promised not to disappoint him."

The deteriorating relationship with my sponsor had begun to really bother me. Gradually his letters became fewer, and when I asked him what the reason was, he replied that he was terribly disappointed because I was not doing well at school. I couldn't believe it! Aware of how fond he was of Vienna, I had even brought over a small gift, realizing I would need something for him some time soon. Why not discuss this with Dr. L., who dealt with interpersonal problems anyway. When I told him that Conrad had practically ceased writing altogether, claiming that I was doing poorly at school and misbehaving on top of it, he asked me what my reply had been. "I wrote that he could ask anybody on campus that this must be a misunderstanding, that I was fully aware of my promises, that I would never let him down."— "The people who know you here would certainly stick up for you, if he should ever choose to find out. You mentioned the little gift from Vienna, would you mind telling me what it was?"–"Two little brass frogs, a bigger one and a smaller one, solid Viennese handicraft."-"Why do you think you chose just that?"—"There was absolutely nothing mother and I could contribute to all his idealism, and I thought he would treasure something reflecting my gratitude. Father frog, son frog, sort of. You know I grew up without my father, maybe that was also part of it."—I noticed a smile around Dr. L's face. "Oh, he treasured it all right, it´s just that he may have interpreted it differently! Tell me, did you ever have the feeling that he was getting too close to you—you know what I mean?" What an eye opener, I thought. "No sir, it never even entered my mind, and it would have if he had made a single wrong step because some of the people around him were queer, some openly and others less so."—"This is extremely helpful to know, though it is not enough to prove anything. Yet I am reasonably certain we are on the right track. You have described him as a morally superior person and a sincere Christian Scientist on top of it. This means that he could never allow himself to come any closer to you than he was. Aware that you are not of his sexual orientation, his advances could not possibly lead anywhere.

Poor man, he is trying to break away from you! He can´t tell you the real reason because in his book, inventing a white lie like 'Herbie, the poor misbehaving student' is less of a disappointment to you. He realizes how terrible confessing his love would be for your young psyche." I saw Dr L in our office every day, and he implored me not ever to answer any of his letters, it would only hurt both of us even more. "I've had quite a few entangled cases coming to see me recently, but this stands out in a way." And as the paternal friend and competent counsellor that he was, he never brought it up again. Nor did I ever bring it up in Vienna until many decades later when it was distant history.

GO WEST, YOUNG MAN MY ROOMMATE INVITED ME. I DID AND WAS IN FOR SOME STRANGE EXPERIENCES

A long summer ahead, full of ideas of what to do, but no money. Roommate Phil suggested that I drive right across the continent with him all the way to *Tarzana.* “What’s that name? Anything to do with the fellow jumping around on trees?”—“Well, yeah, it´s named after the jungle hero in the movie, but forget that, you’ve seen enough jungle here in the Florida. Every day you’ve let us know one way or the other that seeing the country is what you really want to do. So come on, you can stay with my family, the whole basement is yours, I already told them you might be coming. A summer job’s a good idea, but we’ll cross that bridge when we get to it.” So off we drove in his old jalopy but instead of going west we went east first because we wanted to see Cape Canaveral. Apart from the space center, I was impressed by something he took for granted, namely that without being checked seriously we could get close to launching pads, enter several hangars where preparations were going full tilt for an adequate answer to the Russians. Only half a year ago they had shocked the country and me by successfully launching *Sputnik.* Having done his service in Korea, which had meant fighting against Soviet heavy arms, Phil was not amused at all. He didn’t care for a cartoon showing Ike in a wheelchair with a golf club looking up at the Russian triumph, nor did he find the joke I told him about a Soviet and an American satellite funny. “Passing each other in space, the American sneezes and the Russian wishes him *Gesundheit, mein Herr,* whereupon the other answers, *Danke schön, mein Herr.*” That both sides had brought German space scientists into their countries after the war kept us going for a while.—I had of course read and heard about the empty spaces, enormous distances, and vast flatlands in the South and Midwest, but to actually experience them in over three days was something altogether different. More and more Spanish names. *Amarillo* gave me a real linguistic kick, the many shades of yellow of this parched land coming together in the city's name. The scenery in New Mexico was getting a bit wilder, and while the name *Santa Fé* presented no language barrier, unpronounceable *Albuquerque* sure did. We falsely agreed it wasn´t even Spanish, maybe *Apache* or *Comanche*. But even Spanish names could look and sound bizarre—it was once named after the tenth Viceroy of New Spain. That *Arizona* comes from *arid zone* didn´t bother Phil, who was by now more interested in the worsening condition of his flivver, as he called it now. Suddenly a fascinating sight for me, once a devoted reader of the popular *noble savage* adventure novels by nineteenth-century *Karl May*. A family of Indians squatting by the highway, no need to add *Red* like our old English teacher did and nothing noble about their appearance. "They're probably Návajo" Phil commented, putting ‚the emphasis on the first syllable, which immediately made the language purist in me cringe. "It´s Navájo, second syllable stress, my Cuban Spanish teacher told us, and even if Cuba is far away from Arizona, she'd know for sure."—"Maybe but remember correct is that which the majority believes and uses, and that's English here." We were on another vast subject for the next hundred miles.

Driving into the *Mojave Desert* at sundown was the most spectacular experience yet, but it also meant the collapse of our car. Not even "Phil of all trades" could get it going, and we had no choice but to wait for the bus into metropolitan L.A. His mechanic would haul the wreck into the garage tomorrow, only about four hours away, no big deal. Until then, staring into the sands faintly glowing with the flashing of headlights and enjoying the brightest starlit sky ever. So different from muggy Florida.

Making me feel at home in no time, his lovely family knew a lot about Central European cooking, even the Bohemian yeast dumplings filled with poppy seed that our Marie used to make. After a few days, the question often asked whether I was typically Austrian, and my answer that I was not necessarily typically Austrian, but probably a fair sample of a Viennese. Still excited about my idea born out in the desert a few nights ago, to try my luck for a summer job at a dancing school, I took this stroke of genius to my host family, mother and daughter all for it and dad smiling good-naturedly. "Heavens yes, you are from Vienna, so why don't you give it a try?" Not really a pro, but I could certainly teach the Viennese waltz, turning to the left, the real thing! They knew the name *Arthur Murray* and Phil´s father, by now also excited, gladly drove me the little distance, about forty minutes. Everything was always further away than I thought, even after a full nine months in the *Sunshine State,* but why should it be different in the *Golden State?* The first time at the dancing school my name came over the mike in a manner that left me uncertain whether it was mine, but within a few minutes a very professional looking man surprised me with "Why don´t you come back tomorrow with a *real name.* I can´t pronounce it right, and nobody would like to practice with a name that doesn´t sound good around here." At home we had a good laugh, but before the family came up with a better sounding name, I had thought of just the right one. Back in Vienna, the name of another American student had really appealed to me phonetically, *Alistair McDuffy.* Definitely Scottish, all vowels present, no harsh sounds, and probably easy to tackle for people here. It went over well and before I knew it,

I was in a full practice session that lasted all afternoon. This schooling for all the new instructors was supposed to last a whole week, six hours a day. Exciting it was, though extremely strenuous, covering six or eight dances, none of them the Viennese waltz. In the meantime, I was foxtrotting, tangoing, rumbaing, sambaing, and cha-cha-cha-ing my way across the floor, the last three a veritable gym lesson. On about the fifth day it happened. Customers were allowed or encouraged to try their luck with us rookie instructors, our names to be announced on the P.A. system. "Mr. McDuffy, please report to door # 5 for your first partner today." Concentrating on my regular practice, I had to be reminded by a colleague that my name had been called. There it went again, "Mr. McDuffy, this is your third call, please..." *Good Golly* (I loved that euphemism!), I had forgotten to respond to my new real name, was now running to meet whoever. Already waiting for me, the boss informed that he could not keep anybody who had a rough time with the faster dances, but especially somebody who had trouble remembering his new name. Shaking my hand, he wished me a good summer, and I did not have to bother my wonderful host family about driving me to *Where Dance Dreams Become Reality*, their logo.—What to do? By coincidence Phil and I drove past a restaurant called *Peppi´s* one evening, and again I felt that certain itch—Vienna´s got to do something for me out there in San Fernando Valley! Peppi, a jovial old Viennese, listened to my situation and told me to start tomorrow at 6 pm, eight-hour shift, fairly decent pay. When he added that I would work as a bus boy, I told him I couldn´t even drive my friend´s Chevvy, let alone a bus. I guess I did all right the first three weeks before bad luck caught up with me again. My job was to clear the tables for the next customers and to take little plates of butter and dips as well as pitchers of ice water down two carpeted steps. Candlelight, soft spoken atmosphere, laid back music they called it here. At first, I felt funny walking to my job and back, not because I was afraid of being held up but because there was nothing remotely resembling a sidewalk. And sure enough, twice a patrol car pulled up behind me, wondering what I was doing walking on the highway. "Better get a license sometime soon in this country" the cops told me instead of taking me to my job. I had had a hunch all along that those two steps in the dark would eventually do me in, and one night they did. Stumbling and dropping the whole tray, I felt awful when a couple of sympathetic guests jumped up to my rescue. Peppi just stood there, apologizing to his guests, but not acting angry. Walking home that early morning I had plenty to think about, agreeing with my mother´s frequent complaints that I was born a scatterbrain. The week after that I ran out of good luck again, this time for good. From across the street, I could already see that *Peppi´s* Viennese oasis had died an unexpected death of a disease I could only guess. Not a single light on and several boards nailed across the entrance didn´t look like a temporary breakdown. Long after I had returned to Florida, I was to receive a summons to appear at court in Tarzana. Absurd, considering the importance of my position as a bus boy! My lovely hosts took care of it one way or the other but now took me to several spots they wanted me to have seen before leaving. The huge Hollywood Bowl was one of them and driving along Sunset Boulevard along rows of eucalyptus trees was another.

I took the *Greyhound*, almost popular in Europe even then, to San Francisco where I had only two days and one night. The four hours on the bus stood out in my memory for quite some time. "Do you play chess?" a fellow on the bus turned to me. "I´ve got a travel board here with me. I ´m not really very good at it, but we could kill time this way."— Just an average player myself, I had nothing against it at all, in fact made up my mind to beat him. Sicilian opening, clever arrangement of his central pawns, he did know the game. Getting both knights jumping together and guarding each other, castling as soon as possible were on my mind. Gee, I hadn´t played since Vienna. Then he made a totally unexpected move by jumping over my queen, taking her off the board, and asking whether I was conceding defeat. It took me a while to gather my wits and then told him there was no such option in chess, that he was playing checkers instead. "I don´t know where you are from, but that´s the way we play it in the US." Who had the last laugh on whom?

Forever eager to absorb as many impressions as possible and to go through as many new experiences, I spent longer than necessary to walk across the giant *Golden Gate Bridge.* Lucky day, no fog, only spectacular vistas. *Alcatraz* over there, I knew it means *pelican.* Was it really true that a couple of exceptionally shrewd and strong prisoners had escaped in these supposedly shark-infested icy currents? I remember tasty food on *Fisherman´s Wharf* and almost hanging from one of those historical cogwheel trams climbing up a steep hill. Fairly good modern jazz in an atmosphere reflecting the music, especially the elegant black velvet walls. Higher up so that I had to stand on tiptoe, a small notice in English and Hebrew, *Se Habla Yiddish.* Funny, interesting, elegant, unusual, crazy, all of these. It was obviously my day for unusual and funny notices. Before going to bed in the inexpensive but clean YMCA, I thought a hot shower would relax me after a long day. It did but before it did, I spent some time laughing at the notice on the shower cabin. "Should you drop a keg of soap, don´t bother to pick it up." Was there something to the rumors I had heard about these hostels after all?

The bus trip diagonally across the continent made me feel the distances were even longer than I had remembered them on the way west. Spectacular scenery across the Rocky Mountains, though hard to believe that Colorado alone had fifty peaks higher than our highest in the Austrian Alps, all looking less rugged than ours do. Granite versus limestone? Awakened by the driver´s voice in the middle of nowhere informing us that, having crossed a state line, the air conditioning system could now be turned up higher. Still having no feel for Fahrenheit, I soon realized I would need to put on my sweater to survive in the middle of the desert in Utah. Funny and worth remembering because in those days nobody in our income bracket in Austria had ever even seen an air-conditioner. Learning to enjoy the chilly desert.

Getting to Florida involved changing buses, which gave me enough time to wander down to the harbor in New Orleans, hopefully as colorful as the one in Frisco. Too bad, neither time nor money to catch more than a couple glimpses of the *birthplace of jazz.* Suddenly an unexpected brush with the real America. A uniformed officer, customs I suspected, stopped me, brusquely asking for my papers. Looking at a passport he had never seen, he demanded I open my suitcase right there on the sidewalk. Turning my foreign clothes upside down, he gave me my passport back, said I was O.K. but that with my long hair and funny cardigan I looked like one of those characters coming in over the Gulf.

MY SECOND YEAR TO GRADUATION. "YOU CAN'T GO HOME WITH A B. A." MY ROOMMATE INSISTED, PLUNGING ME INTO A DECISION-MAKING PROCESS.— FORLORN, BROKE, BUT MAKING IT IN *THE BIG APPLE*

Eventually reaching my campus with exactly $ 1.75 to my name, I had something to remember and write home about. Luckily, the fellow running the sandwich business on campus wanted me again for the nightly rounds from dorm to dorm, men´s dorm to men´s dorm, that is. Two baskets, one of five kinds of sandwiches piled up high, the other full of half-a-pint cartons of regular and chocolate milk. All along I had planned to save enough money to fulfill mother´s secret dream, to be able to afford a *frigidaire*. All our teenage years Paul and I had done what we all had to do twice a week, namely wait for the horse-drawn buggy with the huge blocks of ice. The coachman would ring his bell, we would run down with two buckets, lug them back up full, then chop the blocks up with a hammer or screwdriver and finally jam the chunks into an ice box. Amazing that I could even think of such a project, but after saving sandwich dollar after sandwich dollar I could go about sending the money for her birthday. Such was the power of the dollar in those years! She had a hard time believing that her son had not struck it rich somehow. Anecdotes galore of "the rich uncle in America" were still alive in so many European minds, a leftover from immigration in the 20s and 30s.

John, a new acquaintance –everybody here would call him a friend—was an insurance salesman whose life was combining making money with enjoying the wilderness. We often went all afternoon along vast patches of purple water lilies on dirt roads that had no names and stopped long enough for John to lure garfish closer before shooting them at close range. Exciting indeed for a European big city boy! Even I could tell an egret from a heron by now, and ospreys were birds of prey. If I wasn´t sure about alligators because we didn´t see any, I was taught a lesson the day we came across what John explained were gator hooks. Submerged in water holes and marked by buoys, they had been laid out to catch alligators, chances were, illegally. Working hard to pull a thick rope leading to a buoy closer to our chartered boat, I suddenly felt an incredible commotion under the surface. Within seconds now, the gator started going wild because I was hurting him. "Pull him a bit closer, get his muzzle up on the boat but not the whole body, he´s likely to whack a hole into our side. Get your camera ready, I´ll hold on to him." With a couple of close combat shots in the camera, we dropped him to survive for a few days until a poacher would relieve him of his suffering.

Having dinner at John´s home always meant discovering a bit of wilderness for me, like the day we went canoeing through the cypress swamp across the road. Behind curtains of Spanish moss, a dark mysterious scene of black cypress stumps, their rugged contours set off against the sun in the distance so that canoeing was reduced to zigzagging at a snail´s pace. The mere thought of tipping over scared me to death especially since John had told me about water moccasins. "Every so often you hear about one dropping into a canoe, not funny at all. That´s why I told you to put a hat on, and that´s why I brought along my gun. It´s just that we want to be on the safe side. No gators ever seen in here, they´re in the pond behind the house." Amazing how they had learned to live with these critters, lots of *do´s and don´ts* to be sure. The two children playing in the garden knew exactly that the good snake was long and did not look like much and that the bad coral snake was much shorter but very beautiful. It took a bit of courage, I had to admit, to take a dip in that little bay with the gators John had mentioned. I had gone through a similar test of sorts waterskiing on the lake by the campus, but this here was raw jungle. "You were not really having a good time in there, we watched you nervously looking left and right and speeding up your funny breast strokes to get out faster," half the family agreed laughing. "We all cool off in broad daylight sometimes, but nobody in his right mind would do so at dusk." Telling Paul about all these creepy-crawlies—loathsome new word!—was yet another step toward letting him find out for himself someday, maybe next summer.

More unique jaunts throughout the state. To Cypress Gardens to watch the Aqua Maids each do one of their amazing stunts on one ski; to an outdoor arena, where *Mike Osceola* of the largely defunct Seminole Indians was showing his skills wrestling down a live alligator; to Tarpon Springs to see Greek immigrants sticking to their background, selling sponges; to Tampa to marvel at great old and new Spanish architecture; or to the Atlantic coast to St. Augustine to look at the oldest fortification in the USA (1513) established by *Ponce de León* in search of the Fountain of Youth.

"You can´t go home with a B.A." Al protested, "that´s just the basis for an advanced degree." Telling my roommate that I appreciated his *top-drawer* advice, I added that didn´t have anybody to pay my tuition from now on. "Look, you have been through this incredible experience of a whole church community putting you through school and the psychologist and the sandwich man doing the rest, so why don´t you just write to several graduate schools. Your whole background is fascinating and different from what we call *run of the mill.* It won´t cost you more than the postage."

I´ll never forget the weekend I wrote a dozen letters to different universities, asking for their criteria of admission and financial aid. What made my situation worse was that I wasn't even sure whether I would prefer to go on in English, my original reason for coming to the States, or in Political Science or History, my other budding fields of interest. Luckily, none of the positive replies asked me to be specific about my major. Waiting for several weeks was enervating, but at long last two positive letters arrived. One from *The American University* in D.C. and the other from the *University of New Hampshire.* Trying to find meaningful advice proved to be impossible, everybody arguing that only I could make such a big decision. Which would be better in Austria, English or Political Science and History? Which would open more opportunities if I stayed in America? I knew practically nothing about the academic levels of these two schools, only that one was a private and the other one a state school. Judging from the vantagepoint of a later generation, I did something ostensibly insane. Trying to convince myself that I had absorbed enough American self-confidence to make my own decision about my own future, I began to mull things over day in and day out –History and Poly Sci in D. C., or English Lit in New Hampshire? A big city boy, I began toying with the idea of choosing the countryside with a comparatively small New England school near the cultural hub Boston, right by the ocean, and close to the mountains. After weeks of tense waiting, great relief and time enough to await the details. "Just come up in the first week of September," the Chairman of the English Department wrote. There´ll be some form of financial aid for you and certainly a job on campus to make ends meet." This permeating optimism and incredible nonchalance!

It was a much better idea to describe the details of my graduation to mother and Paul rather than to dwell on the uncertainties of this summer, let alone my future. Wonderful photos of me in my red FSC gown, the mortar board with the tassel on the left now I had been "knighted to be a bachelor" holding on to the degree itself. An emotional farewell dinner with Dr. L and his family, a few beers in a wet county with my roommates, and then I was off into a new chapter, a wild one.

Hard to comprehend even for myself, in many ways I was now the sole trailblazer of my own future. Hardly ever fully aware of this, I didn´t mind. After all, "to make it in America" was the ultimate achievement. Several classmates had told me about the cheapest way of going north, namely driving people up in their own car. Good thing I had taken my roommate up on his offer to teach me how to drive, though unfortunately I never took the exam. "Older couple needs experienced driver to take them to New Jersey in their own Cadillac Fleetwood." I couldn´t believe it: the FSC sandwich man driving a Cadillac! Meeting this older couple was not too pleasant because they gave me a hard time about my only recently acquired driving skills but fortunately did not want to see my license. Having spent occasional nights in much smaller cars on assorted excursions before, I had no qualms suggested spending the night in their roomy front seat rather than waste money in a motel. At first, they refused but then unwilling to pay my single, they grudgingly agreed. We parted without much of a good-bye, and I made my way to find our FSC Hungarian refugee, the wooden-legged student of economics. He had urged me to visit him here if I needed anything or felt lost in the big city. He wasn´t just joking when he described the apartment he was renting as "too small to change my mind in." Neither of us had much to hold on to and neither knew how to get over the summer away from "our campus," but we reached an unlikely compromise. For some reason he had often commented on my grey pre-war flannel jacket, and I had no problem giving it to him if he let me spend a few nights nights in his big white bathtub. Maybe his melodic Hungarian accent or our Austro-Hungarian background had smoothed the way until I would find something a bit more promising. Any summer job would have to do now because I was down to a sandwich and a subway token per day.—Drugging myself into believing that I would cope with this rock bottom situation, I went to the employment agency to get a social security number without which nobody can survive in the US. While standing in line, my eyes came to rest on a terse ad, "Brooklyn radio factory, unskilled, night shift." Without anything more promising in sight, I signed up for it, my security number maybe laying the groundwork for success. The first time it took me almost two hours to find the old company in a shabby building, the foreman the only person I felt I could even talk to. "The metal back of each radio set you´ll find over there, the fellow next to you will see to it that the shelf is never empty. You just stand each one up like that, curved side toward you, and push it against this motor drill at the two clearly signed marks. That´s all, you ´re a smart guy, I can tell." What the hell was I getting into! Beginning at 10 pm, I left at 6 am, exhausted. Too tired to see much during the day and trying to stay awake during this awfully boring work, I was nevertheless proud I had to weed out only five panels within a week because I had put them up against the drill lopsided. After two years in the country, I thought I had heard a lot of swearwords and enough dirty language to wrap them in, but the linguistic education I was exposed to here topped it all. The ethnic mix was New York alright, two blacks, two Puerto Ricans, an older fellow with an Italian accent, and the white foreman with a Brooklyn one. Apart from my pay slip, this was the kind of experience I was after in a way. Slowly but steadily, I had been toying with the idea of quitting to start living above ground again when the foreman wanted to have word with me. Confronting me with my five panel rejects in just a week and contrasting this to zero rejects in two weeks of one Spanish fellow, he suddenly switched his reproachful tone and said something I would never forget. "I knew right away you couldn´t last. Take this from me, you are not cut out for this type of work. To show you I have nothing against you, here´s what I suggest. If I sign this slip to the effect that you could not go on because of a breakdown of sorts, you won´t have to pay the commission, o.k.?" We were both relieved and shaking hands with me he wished me well as did the likeable *wop*, the Italian. "I've got to stay. I have a son and the one thing I want is to see him going to college." Impressive. What next? Stretching my legs a few nights in the Hungarian's bathtub would not really get me anywhere.

Going through the classified ads again, my eyes stopped at the only offer for an outdoors activity in neighboring New Jersey. "Private summer camp, two four-week sessions, above-average pay, room and board included." Spending my last small cash on a phone call and my slightly bigger cash on a bus trip to rural New Jersey, I considered myself lucky and even a bit proud of slowly approaching my ideal of an American self-made man. Of course, I could have asked my mother to wire some cash to Florida but sending money for a fridge and then begging for help? The director and his wife showed me the premises with a pool, my own room, the quarters of the dozen pupils, then introduced me to an older camp counsellor. If the pay wasn´t really "above-average," I still felt I had landed a lucky strike. What nobody had told me was that the pupils were of different age, from seven to fourteen and, hard to deal with, from a spoiled brat to an almost juvenile delinquent. Half of them pretended to pick up some basic Spanish with me, the rest not really eager to learn the basics of their native English. One day I had yet another run-in with little Circus, an unbearably nasty and psychologically unstable boy. But today he overdid it, and I was at my wit's end. Squirting water at me from his toy gun and refusing to stop, his spoiled brat nature came out when he gave me a smirk, "You can't do anything to me 'cause my daddy´s rich, and he is paying a lot to the school." That did it. I slapped him on his cheek backhand and, good luck for him and bad luck for me, he started bleeding. Screaming, he ran down to the director´s office, and I expected to be dismissed right away. Defending myself seemed hopeless when I was lectured by the boss that "in this country we do not hit children in the face." While her husband had stepped out briefly, his wife tried to console me, "Mum´s the word, but my husband used to teach until he had to give it up. He has such a temper, and that´s not good for the owner of a school." Three weeks out in the countryside, only one week lost, enough money to tide me over until New Hampshire, and yet another facet of America behind me. *Learning by Doing.*

NEW HAMPSHIRE—THE PERFECT MIX OF AMERICA, ENGLAND, AND OUR OWN STYRIA. SIGNING UP FOR FABULOUS COURSES, EARNING MY FIRST SPURS TEACHING, MAKING LIFE-LONG FRIENDS.

That charming Irish American student who had left Vienna making sure I call her *collect* once I landed in the New World was in for another such call. Now that I knew what *calling collect* meant, I needed it more than ever. Now married, she and her husband drove me up to Durham as if we had just parted last week. One sunny afternoon we crossed the state line into what would become my real American home. The only adult around on Sunday happened to be a dean of something or other, who showed me to my dorm. "Hi, my name′s Bill, we′ll be sharing this room in the basement. I snore, but I can tell you the real noise comes from the heating system." Bill really taught me how to drive to get the license, cost four dollars, something to write home about. He took me to the beach in Maine, where my loose European ways got me in trouble right away. Opening the car door to put on my swim trunks, I saw him close to panicking and pointing to people about half a mile up the beach. We spent a few hours discussing his Puritan and my Catholic background, concluding that my permissive behavior and his ridiculous reaction probably did have a quasi-religious basis. Bill took me to his home for my first Thanksgiving here in the land of the Pilgrim Fathers and told me details about how they could not have survived without the Indians, that the real problems came much later with mass immigration.

I wasn´t sure whether I was the victim of some sort of a hallucination when at a meeting for all the new students an exuberant man introduced himself as Donald S, Professor of Music, announced that he was going to dedicate the following tune to a young man from Vienna somewhere in the audience, and sat down to play the *Blue Danube Waltz.* Fortunately, I had never gone through a single spell of homesickness, excepting a few minutes under the Christmas tree, but this musical assault almost did me in. Eager to meet that same evening, we poured out the stories of our lives to each other. A jovial native New Hampshirite, he had studied piano in Vienna long ago and had fallen in love with it hook, line and sinker. Of the many musical events he took me to, one stood out—the first-ever American performance of Anton Bruckner´s *Eighth Symphony* at Symphony Hall in 1958, Karajan conducting. Disgusting how little I knew about our own musical background, how amazed I was when he explained that Bruckner was considered too Germanic over here, and how proud I felt that in his book the acoustics of Vienna´s *Musikverein* ranked even before those of Boston´s *Symphony Hall.* Within half a year he was to take lots of little stories of my years in the US back to Vienna, mother fully adopting him as something like our anecdotal *uncle from America.* Their first meeting was crowned by an experience we all interpreted as another bridge between the Old World and the New. Their postcard from Vienna described how they had watched *Echo,* America´s first answer to *Sputnik,* in Prof S´s company from the hills above the city. One day he was to invite me to something typically American, an outdoor piano recital on the premises of *Tanglewood* with hundreds of music lovers lying, sitting, squatting on blankets but all listening attentively. Something to write home about—would anybody ever sit on the lawn and maybe even sip refreshments while listening to classical music?

My first steps the next morning felt like bathing in a sea of red maple trees. Reporting to the head of the Department of Languages, I found myself talking about my forthcoming job.

"Wonderful that this has worked out because we have more beginning German students than ever," and with his sense of humor the Spanish chairman added, "You wrote you were from Vienna, but surely you can bend to German standards so that they'll understand your accent"—"But, sir, I have never taught a course in my life."—"This is not a good answer, Herr Czermak" his Spanish accent giving my name its correct pronunciation for a change "because we all have to start some time. Besides, you will want your monthly check, right? Wednesday at 9 am right here, you'll have about fifteen students."—There they were—all of them beginners. Big smiles, skeptical faces, shuffling legs. The older students, physics or chemistry majors, had to meet a requirement called "German reading knowledge," the remainder of an era when studying science was considered a primarily German domain. Equipped with a textbook of grammar rules, I felt like delving into a foreign language myself. Tables full of conjugations, how awful compared to the few irregular English verbs! Amazing how complex the declensions, definite and indefinite articles systematically arranged in front of sample nouns! Who will ever remember the adjective endings? I suddenly had to explain according to rules in the book what I had been saying naturally all my life! My nervousness gradually let up and things fell into place by the time I set up the final exam. For the first time ever, I found myself on the dealer´s side of the objective true-false and multiple-choice questions. Can I really flunk this straight-*A* physics student, or award this gorgeous coed with an *A* because she claimed she needed it? Justice vs leniency. Little did I know that this was my greenhorn initiation into my life´s career.

No longer wavering between English and History, I was finally beginning to study English literature. Prof. N′s way of breaking the ice was already special when instead of cracking a hackneyed joke, he quoted lines relevant to the topic. Disciplining himself to stick by the program as planned without deviating too much, his sonorous voice teaching us novel terms, he hit it off with us undergraduates right off the bat—another baseball idiom in daily conversation for me. Dark tousled hair and in short sleeves, he came across as the type you would want to go fishing with while discussing *The Old Man and the Sea.* First appealing to me in his class, the poetry of *Robinson Jeffers,* high priest of venerating the raw beauty of the Californian coast, intrigued me with its pessimism of modern civilization and how to combat it. I eventually decided to write my M.A. thesis on his poetry—hard work but typing every onion skin page of it was a raw pleasure. Prof N was going to pass me with flying colors but to make sure the second reader would do the same, he helped me rephrase my final arguments to perfection. How happy I was to be able to reciprocate of sorts when he asked me to translate a passage of his forthcoming book into German. Would there ever be a student—professor relationship like that in Vienna?

Another course, *New England Renaissance,* first captured my curiosity because the concept of Renaissance implied that something flowering earlier was reborn. A course on the *Pilgrim Fathers*, the *Puritans* and their theological penetration of early New England. If many present-day names like *Mystic River*, Salem, or *Great Works* pointed in that direction in my mind, it was this course that convinced me that there were American poets worth reading beyond *E. A. Poe,* whose raven′s *Nevermore* still resounded all the way from *Gymnasium* days. I vaguely remembered a certain *Paul Revere* on horseback, but now I was near where *Longfellow* had put that historic ride into verse. My greatest discovery, however, one that would last a lifetime, was *Emily Dickinson.* I had never read poems summing up their essence in terser language and in unique images at that, reminding me of a quotation by philosopher *Martin Heidegger* that "Poetry, not philosophy, can best illuminate for us what concepts have concealed." One of my earliest trips from campus was to her grave in *Amherst*, and half a lifetime later I had her unique epitaph chiseled onto the marble of our family grave in Vienna. "That such have died enable us / the tranquiller to die / That have lived certificate /of immortality." Probably the only *Emily D.* poem in all the graveyards of the Old World! Wanting to take another course with the man who had guided us through New England poetry with so much enthusiasm and his half Irish sense of humor, I ended up reading a lot of *Browning.* Not quite my cup of tea but good for religious discussions from different angles. As had already happened so often in Florida, whenever nobody could answer the question asked, the professor would turn to me, "Well, maybe our European friend knows." Usually he did not, but that afternoon he was sure he did. The words *noli me tangere!* sounded awfully familiar, but I had no clue. Rather than keeping my mouth shut, I answered into the dead quiet, "I´m not sure, but it was somebody important." Serious until now, the professor broke out laughing, "You´re damn right, Herb, it was Jesus Christ!"—*Shakespeare´s Contemporaries* proved to be another prolific excursion into a world I knew nothing about. Tall and quiet-spoken, his mind roaming through the vast fields of past religious, political concepts, and conflicts with great ease, Prof S. would be remembered for an unforgettable session one winter morning. The campus snowed in, some students arriving on skis, attendance reduced. Like a snow man himself, Prof. S. appeared with earmuffs on, sat down on the rostrum, peeled his lute out of a case and accompanying himself on the strings began reciting *Shakespeare´s* Sonnet # 60: "Like as the waves make towards the pebbled shore, / So do our minutes hasten to their end; / Each changing place with that which goes before, /In sequent toil all forwards do contend " Memories are truly made of this.

English Romantic Poetry was taught by Prof H, the funniest and funniest looking genius on campus. His foreign English accent was tough for me, but incomprehensible for some of my rural classmates. Unnecessarily curious one morning whether anyone in class would recognize the embroidered badge on his *Oxford* blazer, he was looking around in vain expecting the correct answer. Jed´s answer, we had planned it a few minutes earlier, from the back row, "Sir, from *Cambridge*." If anybody had thought the difference between these two famous English universities was not worth mentioning, we were taught a lesson. Beside himself, his long strands of hair lashing against his triangular face and the huge bib-like tie threatening to cover the famous badge, he just stuttered and stammered his way to a painful "Heavens, no! From *Oxford*, of course!" His slight speech impediment did not in the least take away from his excellent lecturing, except when he started confusing Shelley with Keats and ended up with Sheets and Kelly. One Monday morning, a queasy looking Prof H got as far as the rostrum to announce, "class is dismissed." No Puritan streak in him.

It could not have been a coincidence that falling in love with New Hampshire coincided with falling in love with *Sweet Diana*, also a popular tune at the time. A brunette country girl, not at all beautiful in the sense of a Greek statue, just overwhelming. Maybe all my trials and tribulations would finally be over? All we had ever talked about in religion class in high school was the notorious *Sixth Commandment* and still afraid of violating it, I wanted to know what Bill thought of this bind I was in. Instead, I learned from my perplexed buddy that in America *the Sixth* deals with murder, not my sex problems. Was it the *Tenth* then that forbids us to covet the flesh, not the meat, as I could well distinguish between these two by now? The wide beaches and those great camping trips with my friends Karl and Norma, but only one couple sinning! In a moment of manly resolution, I made up my mind to get what they called a *rubber* here, which to that day had meant nothing more innocent than *eraser* to me, a relic of my British English schooling. Embarrassed to ask for something as suspicious as that, I had found out that it went by the name of *Three Trojans.* Shrewdly hiding it among several everyday names of tablets, ointments and cremes, I asked for a *Trojan* as if it was the least important item I had almost forgotten. "You mean *Three Trojans*" the woman made sure she had correctly understood my half-mumbled order. Was I ever glad to get out of that drugstore!

Jed took me to a lecture at the *American Alpine Club*, which I attended mostly because I found it interesting that an American mountaineering organization should have adopted the name of the Alps. He was already a well-known mountaineer, familiar with many peaks in the country, including in Alaska, as of now the fiftieth state. Fortunately, both of us had other interests beside how to climb mountains and *abseil*—fantastic, a German verb! The name *Presidential Range* fascinated me for historical rather than mountaineering reasons but taking the old steam cog railway climbing the supposedly second steepest incline (37%) in the world on *Mount Washington* was well worth it. One of our common interests was foreign policy, and so one day Jed walked me over to his neighbor in an upstate New York village for a most memorable talk with one *Walter Lippman.* One of his publications was *Cold War,* but of course I had no idea how well known the man really was. Working out of his home, connected to every important office in the country by state-of-the-art equipment, he was easy to talk to. His basic point about the European situation was that, whether we liked it or not, the U.S. would have to respect the "Soviet sphere of influence." When I said Austria was so lucky to have escaped being within their sphere of influence, he signaled understanding but added, as if to allay my fears, that the *Iron Curtain* would soon be history. It was to last exactly thirty more years. Aware that I had spent two years on the *Frank Lloyd Wright* campus, Jed took me to New York to get a feel of what most Europeans believed to be the real America. Getting a few good looks at the *Guggenheim Museum* going up was an all-time first for both of us. I had touched base (my latest linguistic acquisition, helping me to understand baseball a little better) with the city twice before but never had time or money enough to venture out as far as *The Cloisters.* What an experience to suddenly stand before medieval altars, tapestries, crosses, and stain glass windows! There, an altar from our Carinthia! This oasis of tranquility and contemplation in the middle of the quintessential soul of our times, *E=mc2.* Dedicating this sublime world to those seeking consolation after the crash of 1929, chief capitalist *John D. Rockefeller* had opened this part of *The Metropolitan Museum of Art* nine years later when Hitler had already rounded up a few thousand enemies in Vienna.

The Cat, short for *La Cantina,* was the pub three miles away from campus where we sometimes went for a few beers when alcohol on campus was still a distant dream. The place was packed with students eager to solve problems such as who was going to date whom, or who would write a letter-to-the-editor of the *Manchester Union Leader* for criticizing a faculty member for Communist sympathies. The booth I sat in that night was discussing where the human species had come from, the meaning of life for us and future generations, and other such light subjects. The lively debate becoming less focused by the pint, our attention was attracted by an old man at the counter sipping his beer all by himself. On their rounds the owners, possibly twin brothers, sometimes stopped to bring him another glass. "Sorry, but would you mind telling us who the old man is? He was here last time, and he acts as if he belongs here" we wanted to know. "No problem. That's our dad, he'll be ninety-four soon. He is blind. Even if you wanted to talk to him, no way, he has never learned the language." The unexpected answer got us right back to our subject, the meaning of life. When we came back the following week, there was an obituary on the door and the notice "closed for two weeks." We agreed that the owners, no matter how much they might have loved their dad, were probably relieved in some ways, and that certainly ninety-four was a Biblical age to reach. Ready to resume our almost regular sessions, we returned after the mourning period to see the lonely old man sipping beer at the bar, but only one of his sons serving. What a shock! Wasn't it in Milton's classic *On His Blindness*, where his daughter wrote down her blind father's words ending with *"Who best bear his mild yoke, they serve him best. They also serve who only stand and wait."*

"Dear mother, Dear brother, dear Peter!—I imagine the nicest present I could possibly give you on your birthday, mother, is telling you that I have finally become so much part of American life that I never even think of my Austrian citizenship except once a year to have my visa renewed. My definition of the Granite state—Florida was the Sunshine State and California the Golden State, remember?—is "the perfect mix of England, America, and our own beloved Styria." Maybe my two first years were a necessary steppingstone, sort of morphing

from a late teenager into an early adult. Though life up here is of course different in many ways, especially the climate and the food, it is equally true that everyday campus life is pretty similar. The same concepts, the same mix of students of different age groups and backgrounds, the same basic college system, the same vocabulary, barring a few exceptions. I also know now beyond the shadow of a doubt which degree I am pursuing in which field. If one of our smart-aleck friends should make comments like, "But he already knows pretty good English, why is he staying on?" I hope you´ll know what to answer. English in graduate school now means doing an awful lot of reading older and more recent English and American literature. Five fabulous professors, none of them with the "I do the talking, you be quiet" attitude. You would love the scenery, Durham is right on the Atlantic, so close that I can walk it in ten minutes. It´s also only over an hour to mountains about as high as ours south of Vienna. Hiking is big here, except you´ve got to stick to clearly marked trails, it´s all private but we do have something called poison ivy that gives you bad burns. You asked about mushrooms the other week, and I can tell you there are chanterelles galore on the islands where we anchor on our sailboat trips, but that´s further north in Maine. Nobody courageous enough to eat them with me, those great pioneers they like to be!—Three political episodes you´ll love to hear, one serious, the other half serious, and the third one funny. You may remember that the country is getting ready for the elections in November. I was invited to a meeting for foreign students by one of the candidates of the prominent Democratic Kennedy family. Fairly young, impressive, a great sense of humor as part of his Irishness, they say. Some of the Democrats present believed he would be our next President. Let me tell you that I won a spelling contest among foreign students on this Indian name Massachusetts. A banana split was my prize. Last week we had a famous Soviet politician on campus, Mrs. F, Minister of Cultural Affairs. I don´t know whose idea it was to single me out as her guide on campus, maybe because she felt more at ease speaking German. You cannot imagine some of her questions regarding my life here, but I know you can guess my answers. As I told you, this semester I have been living in the basement room of a small private house right on campus free of charge. All I have to do is keep the door free of snow and empty the trash can once a week. When the Minister heard that, she told me how foreign students were treated in the Soviet Union. Asking her whether they were as free as I was here to go anywhere with anybody at any time, she replied that in a free county like the USSR that was understood. When she tried another tack, asking me whether I didn´t miss the cultural opportunities of my beautiful hometown, my answer was that studying English language and literature and to experience a different culture were my main goals. Proud of the fact that higher education was of course free in her country, she wanted to know how much my parents were paying. I told her that my tuition was paid for by UNH and that I was teaching a course for my room and board. Needless to add, I had plenty of time during this absurd conversation to heap praise on the free shelves library system, on the uncomplicated relationship between students and professors, and on the easy reach of Boston, a smaller and younger competitor of Vienna with all its museums and concert halls. I never found out, nor cared to ask, why she had chosen to come to UNH. I should have told her point blank that this university system was paradise. The following funny political interlude did not upset life on campus but was still interesting to a handful of "beautiful dreamers," a famous tune here from some musical. Interested in this sort of thing, I went to hear Gus Hall speak, the Chairman of the American Communist Party. He was a tougher critic of literally everything here than even our Soviet guest. Used to such fruitless discussions from Vienna, I soon left. Hall is running for public office. How long can a society tolerate ideologies trying to saw off the branch it is sitting on? Should I have done Political Science after all? Dein amerikanischer Sohn."

Telling the difference between all those confusing three-letter abbreviations was quite a hassle, now MTA in Boston, IRT in NYC, the BLT sandwiches I sold, and the first VPLs I detected on cheerleaders. Reading Hawthorne´s The House of Seven Gables was a much more profound experience than visiting it, but together they propelled me into a past reality, possibly merging with my reality of New England now. Donald said he knew what I meant because it had worked on him the other way round. Having studied and performed Mozart before visiting Vienna and then playing him on site there, these two experiences together had transported him to what he felt real eighteenth-century Vienna must have been like. Similar with Emily Dickinson. First reading her poems, then reading and learning about her, and eventually visiting her grave made me feel I had caught a glimpse of Amherst as it once was. Yet I had begun to develop a yearning, hardly noticeable at first but picking up over the months, for spots reminding me of the Old World. Nothing special, just a rickety outdoor table with two chairs and an old farmer serving homemade blueberry pie—simple, no ads, no come-ons, just the way I thought all New Hampshire must have been long before the old steam engine took me past clusters of white and yellowish clapboard houses into the heart of Boston and back at sunset. My two souls perennially sparring away.

Teaching *Remedial English* the second year was challenging in a different way. Embarrassing indeed to have to explain some high school level English grammar point to a brilliant engineer. Must be a mistake, I thought, but it was not—one morning a brand-new copy of *Webster's New Collegiate Dictionary* with my name embossed on it was waiting in my office, free of charge. It is a rich country indeed!

Florida had begun to feel strangely distant within these two years. Was it that everything I had to cope with there was new, or just that I was two years younger then? While I had not felt a gaping hole leaving FSC, I already sensed that leaving the cradle of my most formative two years would be like throwing away the proverbial emotional blanket. We all knew some of such obvious victims, the fellow running the sandwich shop lingering on for no cogent reason other than "being around," the starry-eyed English major who was going to write "the great American novel," the totally uprooted Korean veteran who never took any classes and had no clue what to do next, or the brilliant student from South Vietnam in his elegant suit and tie, who recited French poems to whoever cared to listen to him. Lacking one more course, I chose Prof S′ *Milton,* and coming to the first class we learned that *Ernest Hemingway* had put a bullet through his head.

"BROTHER DEAR, BE MY GUEST FOR THIS SUMMER!" THOROUGHLY ENJOYING THE WILDERNESS OF NEW ENGLAND AND FLORIDA WITH PAUL. THE CUBAN CRISIS BUILDING UP.

I had first asked Paul last year whether he would be interested in visiting my American home, meeting our pianist friend Donald S again, traveling on four-lane expressways, hearing jazz where it was born, trying some of the twenty-odd flavors of *Howard Johnson's* ice cream, temptations of this kind. Now already crossing the state line into New Hampshire, we stopped for a moment to take photos, two brothers in bliss. We had lots of linguistic fun, Paul listening to my translations of American idioms yielding blatant nonsense, and I hearing his Viennese accent after years of exposure to mostly immigrant hodge-podge German. Traveling with Donald in what I thought was the most elegant car imaginable, his sleek yellow Studebaker, was a daily treat and listening to him brushing up his rusty German and to Paul testing his English in real life were truly entertaining. Nobody had written to me about it, just as well, but Paul shocked—no amused—me by repeating comments he had picked up at the neighborhood pub or our reverberating Viennese corridors to the effect that "young Czermak must have had a reason for going to America, maybe gambling, some trouble with the police. Nobody knows, but surely young people don't just run away just like that." We had fun going over a few suspects spreading such gossip, none of them educated enough to keep the penal colony in early Australia apart from America. After this revelation, Paul's description of the first Viennese supermarkets, the first TV sets in cafés to watch soccer and skiing events, and the one political meeting that had turned Vienna upside down in early June was a welcome change. He was raving about the young and elegant Kennedys vis-à-vis the rotund older Russian couple, but of course we realized that complex issues like Cuba and Berlin would not be decided by body mass index. Stopping by markers of Indian massacres, learning how to disarm lobsters without hurting himself, or climbing around the rocks by old lighthouses were all-time firsts for Paul. On one of our jaunts along the magnificent Maine coast Donald pointed out several square concrete towers, fortifications against our German U-boats. We knew that the U-boats had been very successful against British and American ships until their code was cracked, but what we did not know was that they had torpedoed such a frightening number of ships so near the coast.

Of course, music always played a major role in Donald´s world. He showed us his office, sat down to illustrate a point that Paul could follow better than I could, and complained that jazz was becoming a field among many in the Department of Music. "But this is the one genuine American music," my amateur musician brother protested. "That may be, but it is primarily of black origin, and secondly, there are many Americans who do listen to what we call classical music, which also includes American composers. Don´t get me wrong, I have nothing against jazz, it´s just something essentially different." Much to our surprise, he offered to take us to a jazz club, and we were lucky that Dave Brubeck was at *Basin Street East* at the time. While we had heard his LPs, Donald knew only his name. The evening was a revelation with Paul in Seventh Heaven, I fascinated on a lower circle of heaven, and Donald admitting that he did not think it was possible to move in and out of the most complex rhythms with Brubeck's ease and creativity.

Returning to Florida was our last trip together to show Paul some of the wildlife including literally getting eaten up, not by gators or water moccasins, but mosquitoes. He had never heard the story. During my own first few days in Florida, my roommate had bet me one whole dollar that I would not be able to stand two minutes of greedy mosquitoes at sunset without ducking under. Greenhorn that I was we went to the beach at maximum supper time for the little buzzers, a towel ready to rescue me. Watching his watch and watching me jumping and flailing my arms, he won the bet seventy seconds into the contest. They had a great time teasing me, swollen face and itching all over, and so did Paul, asking whether I had not remembered the mosquitoes by the Danube. Like me two years ago, he was comparing little tame Central European samples with their ferocious New World cousins. John E, my hunter & insurance broker, welcomed us on the very afternoon their children were told to stay indoors because a gator had ventured out of the bayou across the road. Within a few days Paul could tell an egret from a heron and, not bad, an eagle from an osprey. We even found a place where they served barbecued rattlesnake and of course we ate it for the record, John watching us from his hamburger. During the first longer trip to St. Petersburg, I noticed right away that the laid-back atmosphere of that retirement center had changed. Troop movements on shore, ship movements offshore. We were aware of the Cuban crisis building up only three months after the disastrous failure to overthrow Castro but had not kept up with the details. On our drive all the way to the Everglades, we also saw more naval activity than normal, as John commented. Huge posters signaling "90 miles to Communism." Little did we know that within fifteen months we were to escape an infinitely bigger disaster by the skin of our teeth. If it did not strike, we should be grateful to three courageous men, as I was to learn later from several documentaries: to Soviet *Colonel Penkowski,* who was executed for tipping off the CIA about the exact positions of the missiles on Cuba; to *JFK* for verifying the Colonel's tip and ordering the blockade of the island, and to *Vasili Arkhypov,* second man in command on a Soviet submarine, who chose not to fire a nuclear torpedo without the express order from Moscow, which probably for a technical reason he could never receive.

One day we went past *Lake Okeechobee* all the way to the *Tamiami Trail,* the only west-east connection through the swamps. Not a language nut like his brother, Paul was still interested in these strange sounding Indian names and wanted to know what they meant. John explained that the Trail obviously had something to do with *Miami* meaning "big water" and that judging by its enormous size, *Okeechobee* must mean "immensely big wate," or does it? Driving over the soggiest trails requiring all his concentration, we were rousting long-beaked ibis-like birds of all sorts, watching pelicans with some booty in their satchel-like bills and John shooting garfish for supper—what an afternoon! Renting a swamp buggy gave us at least an approximate idea of the size of the swamp. We never came across a buoy marking a hook underneath to show Paul how they catch alligators but watching bubbles rising to the surface John could tell where one was feeding. Plying past endless expanses of purple water hyacinths, so dense that they would block any johnboat, passing mangrove curtains against the open sea, and then slowly meandering through dark cypress swamps, we were aware of being treated to an *eldorado* few Europeans had ever seen. Surely, studying Paul's reactions to myriad encounters, episodes and egrets made me relive my own.

It was a heartbreaking farewell, not merely because Paul had had such a marvelous time and I with him, but because a week before he flew back to Vienna, the Cold War had become hotter by a few notches with the *First Workers´ and Farmers´ State* deciding to build a wall across Berlin to keep a few millions from escaping or, as the former Soviet occupation zone, officially the *German Democratic Republic,* had it "to keep the influx of capitalist and spies" out. What were we both going back to? The first thing Paul showed me when I came back two months later was his Greyhound bus ticket from New York to Portsmouth. He is still carrying it with him, over sixty years later.

"YOU CAN'T GO HOME AGAIN"—OR CAN I? MY LONGED-FOR BUT DIFFICULT RETURN. DEFENDING AMERICAN VIEWS AMONG SKEPTICAL VIENNESE. TRYING TO GET MY PROFESSIONAL FOOT IN THE DOOR.

"You Can´t Go Home Again" was a famous novel very much on my mind as I was setting my return with the *Holland-America Line* for early October, the particularly bright foliage that autumn making it extra hard. The chairman of the English Department, who had been so encouraging when he had replied to my timid inquiry about financial aid two years ago, told me a story I could not really comprehend as I was saying good-bye. "About ten years ago, we had a fellow here from Holland, your age, your alert mind, and I hated to see him leave, again like you. As far as I know, he finished his degree, got married, found the type of work he wanted. Then one day came a sad letter, spelling out his problem. No matter how hard he was trying, he could never really go back to his friends, his family, his country, never fully. Whatever he was thinking or doing, there were always the Dutchman and the American quarreling within him. I am telling you this because I want you, sensitive soul that you are, to be aware of such possible problems. Maybe what we call the *Viennese mentality* over here will save you from it."

The last night in the New World turned out to be beautiful and scary at the same time. Jed´s father had set up a farewell dinner for the four of us, with Karl, Norma and Diana.

Laughing and singing we got out of the car to be suddenly confronted with two men yelling from the balcony, their guns pointed at us in the dark. Confusion, screams, and shouts of *Stop it!* Life-saving normalcy returned when we realized we had parked our car where nobody was expecting us because the family name of the neighbors was almost identical with that of our hosts. For once, I came close to agreeing with my America-skeptical friends that these people are gun freaks, even this side of Texas. My farewell supper was not my last supper after all. The four of us went on a trip through the Black Forest and Austria the following year.

Though I was excited about everything aboard the *SS Maasdam,* I thought a letter to Diana should have priority. The second mate, with whom I had already had lunch and supper, told me about a new passenger service, whereby letters to or from Europe could reach their destinations much faster. He would gladly deposit my love letter shortly after midnight when the *SS Maasdam* would pass a floating station firmly anchored at a relatively shallow spot. The company´s sister ship coming from Europe would take it on board and drop it in the New World. Where else but in America! Amazed, I handed him the letter. I´ll leave it to your imagination to picture the fun he had with me the following morning.

With lots of time and lots of thoughts to spend it on, I began to leaf through some of my thoughts collected in bits and pieces. Among them, the briefest summary of the essential difference between Europe and America I had found yet by French novelist *Balzac* over a century ago. "Europe is Time, America is Energy." Aren´t there perhaps two grains of truth in the catchy quip "Live fast, die young, be a good-looking corpse"? Isn´t there much more planning, energy, and money invested in research and development in every single discipline here? Labor-saving devices, these quintessential American inventions, show a built-in paradox, for who works harder at relaxing and gaining glimpses of happiness than Americans? Don´t all civilizations, not just in Europe, take many more centuries to grow, reach maturity, and decline than America does? As an American returned from one year in Vienna asked me, "Why is it that life in your beautiful Vienna feels like swimming through honey?" Wasn´t it exactly this somewhat slower pace in rural New England that I enjoyed so much? Is it true that American kids stepping off the Ferris Wheel in Vienna were disappointed because the ride over the roofs took eight long minutes?

Although I had not planned my return to the Old World to go through such reflections on Time vs. Energy, the medieval town of Maastricht at the southernmost tip of Holland offered me just that. I had taken the train from busy Rotterdam to a town of walls winding along moats, several old churches with their bell towers intact, and a languid brook between huge elm trees, the whole scene like a Dutch painting, especially the people perambulating on sidewalks. Ridiculous though it may sound thinking about it half a century later, the dark resounding gongs of the grandfather clock in the living room of my old hosts never left me. I had arrived where Time was in full command in the form of leisure and contemplation.

It is always difficult to describe the concept of *Vorfreude,* something like "bubbling over with anticipation." The night train took some of it away but seeing the huge signs on the platform announcing KÖLN, the first placename spelled with an *umlaut* in four years, I knew we were deep in the heart of Deutschland. Going through valleys of golden vineyards and past medieval cities at dawn even intensified my exuberance, their castles and cathedrals slowly attuning me to home. A real *Löwenbräu* in Munich and then Salzburg, the last longer stop, its medieval fortress reaching into a bright Alpine morning.

The first heartfelt hugs and kisses with mother after four years, then the small party opening their arms for first embraces. By God, here she is, Marie! The ruddy cheeks still round and healthy, her smiles choked with tears, her hugs loosened by a special blend of Viennese pronounced in good old Czech. With all their curiosity about my years abroad, not one who didn´t at least imply, some gingerly and others more directly, that "after all, home is home." Ah, how would I translate mother´s *Sachertorte*, the chocolate cake with a layer of red currant? When Paul remarked that he had often saw *Sacher tarte* on menus, my explanation of what a *tarte* is in America had the table roaring. Slowly, the Old -World atmosphere of the high ceilings over the varnished door jambs around the paneling really brought me home again, as did the six-armed chandelier and the oil painting of our beloved Hardegg over the frayed old carpet. The upright still stood across the fold-down bed, where I had seen my father dying and where I would sleep again beginning tonight. Tomorrow I would place my FSC and UNH diplomas there, one bound in red and the other in blue.

Substantial changes are more easily visible after longer spans of absence. Vienna was still pockmarked by ruins, but many new apartment buildings had filled out empty spaces left by the war. What was new and obviously successful were the first supermarkets, so typically American in sheer size, the stunning variety of their goods, and the underlying philosophy of allowing customers to pick goods off the shelves themselves. Huge shopping centers in the outskirts were soon to follow, but their success would not yet be reflected in the decline of small shops and businesses for some time to come. A tell-tale indicator of the growing prosperity was the number of cars, mostly *VW* and *Fiat*, and the elegant Italian *Vespa* scooter. More and more, people spent their holidays in the country, the first ones venturing into neighboring Italy or Bavaria. Switzerland had always been expensive, and the rest were behind the Iron Curtain. I had left Vienna as a city still visibly wounded by the war and came back to a city rebuilding itself in an upbeat atmosphere. On a national level, three main factors had proven to make all the difference: the largest steel works and several other industrial plants, nationalized after the war, had been very successful so far; their success would not have been possible without the *European Recovery Program*, better known as the *Marshall Plan,* which had begun granting loans and transferring machinery and goods to Western Europe in 1948; last but not least, the currency remained pegged to the strong German *mark* for decades to come.—Peter had not been able to get off his job as a waiter to welcome me, and so he was making up for it by picking me up on a funny contraption I had never even seen—on his second-hand scooter! The first long live conversation.Typical for extrovert Peter, he loved his position at the reception desk of a downtown hotel and spent a lot of time talking about how loud the Germans and Americans were, but that the former tended to be demanding while the Americans were much easier to please. He also liked them because of their generous tipping, and I should tell him whether they were used to that from the States. Refreshing his memory about my life in dormitories, I told him I had no clue. Still the old Francophile, he told me how much he admired *An American in Paris,* all the great chanson singers, and *Brigitte Bardot* especially for her acting. Yes, my friend, names like *Maine* or *Montpelier, Vermont* were French. It was not easy to convince him like most of my compatriots that there was something like American *cuisine,* that *cooking* would be a simpler and therefore better word. He had never heard of clam chowder but was prepared to accept it as superb because the word now came from me. *Boston baked beans* didn´t count because they were originally English. Origins and names of dishes are always difficult, partly because they tend to declare one region or nation the winner. My favorite example was *pizza* , for Peter and most Europeans the typical Italian national dish. Used to twenty-odd types of pizza from the States, I had ordered one in Rome in the early sixties to be told that I was in *Roma*, not in *Napoli*, where they were from. At long last, we found the simple tomato plus cheese version, but there was an answer to this. Neapolitan emigrants had developed a whole subculture of new varieties that eventually came to Europe. Peter described his living situation as still very Viennese, for he was renting a small room from the ancient widow of a World War One (!) colonel. Teaching him how to make his bed in accordance with her notion of order, to use wood and coals as sparingly as possible, whom not to invite, and how often to use the shower, she pretty much ran his life. This story was of great help to me because I was hoping to deal with American exchange programs soon.

Finding suitable rooming situations for students would certainly be a recurring problem, what with their insistence on a daily shower or, if a phone was available, a fair bill for hours chatted away or spent unawares on a call to, say, Vienna, Virginia, not really a local call. A culturally fascinating job for me, feeling for the American culprit and at the same time obligated to the Viennese victim, with the roles occasionally reversed. An old survivor of the war had gone out of his way to accept American exchange students and came up with this moving anecdote. "My renter, a nice girl, was complaining that she fell on the staircase and hurt her knee because the light suddenly went out. When I explained that these *minute lights* were not defective but helped save electricity, that they were a leftover from the war and postwar years when the whole city was pitch dark, she forgot about her knee and promised to turn off lights even in the bathroom. I hope this little experience taught her as much as they were learning in class that morning." –

Another bone of contention I ran up against more than once was *David Brinkley,* who had been in Vienna to show the glorious remnants of the Habsburg Empire to his American TV audiences. In the time-honored Baroque National Library, high up on a special ladder, he had swept his forefinger over the top shelf presented the piled-up dust to tens of thousands of viewers, adding some sassy remark to his smirk. Having enjoyed the excellent *Huntley-Brinkley* reports on NBC, I was not surprised at all but did have a hard time convincing people that Brinkley had only been his usual self and not out to offend. Coming under the heading of "American lack of manners," it was just a more visible example than the "typical" American legs on the table.—Quite a different puzzle from this strange New World, not really alarming but still causing doubts, was religious. "Herb, who really were these two young fellows who knocked on my door dressed up in dark suits over white shirts and tie, saying something in American German about God sending them? A bit curious, I invited them in and learned they were Mormons and out to convince us of the teachings of Christ from their own Holy Book. They were so awfully nice that I just didn´t feel like defending myself. Is it really true that they spend two years of their own time trying to get people to see the truth?" Here we go. Smiling myself over the naïve view that the Book of Mormons could possibly improve on what centuries of Catholic and Protestant theologians had maintained, I told my puzzled neighbor that she had just experienced an aspect of America we did not hear much about, idealists and sometimes nuts working for what they believe.— An altogether different issue arose over the fact that no professor had nudged, let alone told, me to write my thesis on a particular subject or writer he wanted, but that I was free to choose my own and broach it to him for approval. A family friend with a doctorate in engineering argued that European professors were motivated to steer their students in a specific direction because, after all, they knew where the problems lay waiting. He did not care for my answer that, while it might of course also happen in the States that a professor used a student´s work for his own publication, this proceeding was pretty much the normal way of affairs on the Continent, usually a footnote generously acknowledging the student´s contribution. Endless discussions, some among professionals and others among folks of different persuasions, all boiling down to the one grand theme of "American civilization vs European culture." *Franklin* and *Edison* and *Ford* yes, but where are the American *Rembrandt*, *Shakespeare*, or *Mozart*? Whether he was just curious or intentionally provocative, an Austrian debater once made the point to Henry Kissinger that a mere two hundred years could not possibly suffice for Americans to identify with history as intensely as Austrians could with a thousand years behind theirs. Wondering whether the man with the long history could identify with two, three, or all the various governmental systems Austria had gone through, the Secretary of State said that he could identify with one single system from 1776 until today, adding that as a native Bavarian his identification was all the stronger for it. Bingo!

THE ROOSEVELTS AND THE KENNEDYS. TALKING US POLITICS WITH PROFESSIONALS LEARNING ENGLISH, TEACHING GERMAN FOR *COLORADO WOMAN'S COLLEGE,* AND TRYING TO SORT OUT MY FUTURE.

Every Austrian knew exactly where he or she had been when they first heard that Kennedy was killed. We had attended a medieval morality play, every bit of the Gothic church an ominous reflection of what was awaiting us outside. Strangers asking each other questions and staring at the headlines breaking the news of the unfathomable. "The South strikes again" was my immediate reaction, though as we have learned over the decades since O. St. was the only pundit who could see through the thicket of real and imagined plots and conspiracy theories. We adored JFK in Europe maybe more so than in America because at the Iron Curtain in divided Berlin he had revealed "Ich bin ein Berliner" and promised to "pay any price, bear any burden, meet any hardship, support any friend, oppose any foe to assure the survival and the success of liberty." How could we disagree with his Vietnam policy, if saving us from Communism was his declared goal? He had initiated the space race, which the vast majority here wanted him to win, and he had wanted America to repeat its successful battles on past frontiers by summing up his many new efforts as the *New Frontier*. All these aspects I remember from teaching one of my first eager beaver SPIDI students, who were as fascinated by the finer points that we English teachers relished as bits and pieces of American civilization. As down-hearted by JFK`s death and as proud of the various upbeat presidential mottos as any good American, I remember adding "You know the basics of Franklin Roosevelt's *Fair Deal* and you have at least heard of Lyndon Johnson´s *Great Society* in the making now, but throughout American history and especially in the Kennedy context frontier expresses something forward-looking and continuously on the move."They were fully behind JFK's all-out war on organized crime and taking on the American Medical Association and the steel industry in the interest of average citizens. "Their Democrats are like our Socialists, their Republicans like our Conservatives, right?" was a frequent question over the years, one impossible to do justice to for lack of time and of course lack of detailed knowledge on all sides. "Well, roughly, yes. But you should take into consideration that there are leftist, rightist, and mainstream factions to use our terminology of the similar splits we have."—"No, not all Republicans are against mandatory socialized medicine. Even before World War One, Republican President Teddy Roosevelt, a relative of Democrat Franklin Delano, predicted that without major changes in the system society would eventually be headed for tough times. If you feel like quizzing your parents about America, ask them or your grandparents how the Teddy bear got his name. Funny, and an easy way not to confuse outdoorsman Teddy and his intellectual Franklin Delano, probably the most famous polio victim among world leaders."—On a painful subject for me, I had to agree in many a debate "You are right, the Bay of Pigs should never have happened. No matter what the subject, there´s nothing worse in decision-making than going halfway instead of the whole hog. As you know, Kennedy let the exile Cubans try to reconquer their island but refused to supply American air support, let alone troops." Realizing that, in his mind, I was dodging the real issue by not openly condemning the rookie President's support of the invasion, our Castro enthusiast was shocked that "even a Democrat attacked the newly independent country led by a progressive socialist leader." We agreed that there was no point in trying to convince our *amigo* that Cuba had only slid from an American-tolerated rightist dictatorship into a much tougher Soviet-backed one almost within eyesight. What so many of us admired about the American governmental system was that, deprived of its charismatic leader within hours, it kept functioning. Similar discussions, whether in class or over a beer, were my daily soul food for many decades, frustrating though they often were, especially with the instances of American success stories slowly dwindling and my almost congenital pro-American enthusiasm subsiding. Framed in black, JFK's close-up was to hang above my bed for decades.

My own situation as a returnee from "The Land of Unlimited Opportunities" was complicated for two different reasons, the first responsible for the second. By now fully aware that my future was in English, I could not believe the degree of ignorance and animosity coming from the *Institute of English.* Deciding that my four years in the US as a student of English could not be accepted at all, I was supposed to start from scratch. Nor was I the only one to suffer from this parochial atmosphere, as I learned from Dr. R, the Fulbright professor that year. Trying to find out where his office was and when he should begin to teach, he was told that he did not need an office because in Austria professors were not used to talking with students and that he could begin any time, but not before the Head. The situation was so ridiculous that John Irving , a student in Vienna at the time, raked the whole nonsensicality over the coals in one of his novels. Continuously toying with the idea of returning to America anyway, I started teaching

English for several institutions, the Vienna School of Police among them. It was a beginner´s course, all right, but I thought there was a limit to outlandish questions, even from rookie cops. Suddenly this huge fellow gets up right in front of me, asking "Vhat is se English vord for *gangster*?" The sitcom effect of this assault was such that, intuitively bending down as if to pick up something to keep from cracking up, I surfaced seconds later to break the news to him that the *gangster* was as English as they come, American at that. Some of them never managed to pronounce *"th"* correctly, and to demonstrate how faulty pronunciation could even be a question of life and death, I ventured into a joke, popular among us English teachers. "About to go under in the Atlantic one day, an English ship was desperately signaling for help, 'We are sinking, help, we are sinking!' The nearest ship received the message, but because it was German, the answer was, 'Yes, ve can hear you, but vhat are you sinking about?"—

A welcome change was the unexpected invitation to teach German for the Vienna program of *Colorado Woman´s College*, eighteen sophomores and juniors and one male, me. I have remembered two of them for maybe very American reasons. Having won my first experiences of teaching German at UNH, the language Mark Twain had declared was too difficult to learn in one lifetime, I spent many a session helping them differentiate between the Austrian, at daredevil moments even the Viennese variant of German from what most of us believe to be the real thing. To what extent my mindset and my emotional responses had become American became clear to me when I tried to defend the cringeworthy behavior of a student who had yelled awake her elderly landlord over a forgotten key long past midnight. Their visiting President helped me break the impasse in my decision-making process by inviting me to think things over in Denver for a year. So wonderfully

American, he answered my question of what I would be expected to teach with “whatever you feel qualified to teach the most!”

THE ACADEMIC YEAR IN DENVER: TEACHING AMERICAN LIT, WITNESSING BITTER POLITICAL ARGUMENTS, LEARNING POKER, AND ADDING A UNIQUE PERSONALITY TO MY LIST OF FRIENDS. GOING "BACK HOME" EAST.

The morning after my arrival in Denver the dean approached me, asking why I had not attended the meeting yesterday. No, I had not forgotten about it, I had just been here for a few hours and thought that as a newcomer I couldn´t contribute anything worthwhile anyway. He came back with something so eminently American that for this reason alone I was now 100% sure I was not in Austria anymore. "You don´t understand. We don´t want to have you in meetings because we will follow your ideas, but because your observations or questions might open our eyes where we can´t see any more for the rut we are in." Teaching Hawthorne´s *The Scarlet Letter* for starters to lovely but clueless blondes and brunettes was as exhilarating as the thin air of mile-high Denver. Rereading it after five years, I had to agree with whoever coined that quip, "There are two kinds of literature, one that´s tightly packed and the one that rambles." This novel sure did not ramble, even led to a Q&A game about the red capital A on Hester Prynne´s forehead, the little we thought we knew about sex morals in old New England and, within carefully designated limits, present-day Colorado. One Friday lunchtime when half the campus was ready to go *TGIFing*, two students came up to me with the most enticing invitation in a long time. Like every so often, one of their dads flew them home to Texas over the weekend, whether I wouldn´t want to come along. "Only in America." I still don´t know why I turned them down.

The faculty was a mix of very interesting and funny people. Joe Tennys H, who had left the CIA to write a critical though funny book about his time with the agency and to teach American History. I still hear him quoting his favorite, Lord Tennyson's "Tis better to have loved and lost / Than never to have loved at all" in the lilt of his West Virginia accent. Prof S. had taught me the basics of stud poker back at UNH the summer I took his *Milton* course, but now Tennys taught me the thrills of high-low games. Out in the college-owned *Rancho Tranquilo* we met for memorable weekends, some of us showing up with a five or ten gallon-Stetson, one with Raybans we made him take off, and one with a Saturday night special we let him keep. It was only during a little tiff that he pulled it out to soothe our nerves, a toy gun. Then there was the young Rev. Spring, whose answer "Why should I?" to my casual comment around Easter "spring in the air" showed a remarkable sense of humor. His cameo appearance in the chapel came when he introduced sitar player *Ravi Shankar* with a few well-chosen quotations on possible spiritual meeting grounds between India and America.

One of the board members of the school had heard that this teacher from Vienna who had taught his daughter German was looking for a car, not expensive and *asap*. He invited me "over to my place," several somber yet sunlit rooms, their stark shadows exuding the strange aloofness of hardly ever more than one person around. "Good to meet you. Our name is German, as you know, that´s why she took German. You are going to like this car I have put it aside for you with the help of my buddy downtown, it´s a blue VW beetle, used, but in top shape. They are fabulous in the cold winters here, you'll see, must be the engine in the back that does it." Without announcing the short break, he walked over to something resembling an upright. Giving me a huge smile, he started pumping the pedals and playing the notes without touching the keys. I was flabbergasted. Was I perhaps really in the world of an Edward Hopper painting? "You've never seen this? It's a player piano." Having treaded through one piece he shut the keyboard and sat down with me again. "How about $700, you'll find it's a good deal." Knowing less than nothing about the price of a used VW beetle in good shape and needing it fast, we shook hands and he had it brought to his doorstep for me. It really did perform well as I found out driving to and from campus every day, often seeing American cars stalled in subzero weather. What made meeting this board member extra special was that, as I heard later, his nickname was "Dry Hole Charlie." He had been in prospecting down in Texas and eventually quit beause he had run out of luck.

An almost comical surprise was the night watchman on his beat. Feeling more comfortable in my small office on campus than in my even smaller room next to the old widow I had rented it from, I had the light on preparing my lectures, writing letters, or browsing through the *Denver Post.* There was only one other office lit until late and that was Tennys' across the aisle. As time went by, both of us began to enjoy the visits of two very likeable students, one each. Nothing beyond historical and literary tidbits, nice conversations, and tall tales, we thoroughly enjoyed these visits occasionally merging into a lively quartet. Enter the night watchman in uniform, keys dangling from his belt, a headlight to find his way, and a club just to be on the safe side. Every time he turned the door open, of course without knocking, he was surprised to find me either alone or chit-chatting with my visitor at an uncompromising distance. Annoying though this was at first, it became more hilarious by the week. First, because the fellow´s original excitement about maybe catching me red-handed had worn off and he just opened the door to wish me good night; secondly, the stunning blonde who wanted to talk to me so badly had caught on to the whodunit mood of it all and sat waiting in a room beyond the night watchman´s rounds. I never left my safe office den: *lily-livered,* a metaphor I remembered from *Macbeth.* "Worse than that, Herb, *chicken-livered"* my eloquent history-cum-poker partner was teasing me.

My plans for the two-week Christmas vacation were still a bit shaky, not because I did not want to fly east to be with my friends from UNH days but because I was putting money into my piggy bank to invite mother over for the summer. So marvelously American again, the President had heard about my plan and offered me the round-trip flight to New York if I tried my level best to find a Russian teacher at the annual Modern Language Association meeting. Here I was, all of twenty-seven years old, milling around among dozens of talent scouts with their name tags announcing what they were offering or looking for. Lucky again, I spotted an elderly man on the lookout, his Russian name written out in both alphabets. It took us all of twenty minutes to reach a rough agreement because all I could offer him was the President´s phone numbe, his flight to Denver, and details to be arranged on campus. It would be *Beginning Russian* for sure. Dr. S. actually came to CWC and stayed until long after I left, a man grateful to "talk America" with another European of sorts and refresh his German with me. Fantastic, more than a week of snow and ice, enough for a white Christmas between Karl´s home on the coast and UNH with Donald.

When my turn came to address the student body in the multi-purpose chapel, I chose the complicated political situation in Europe in general and Austria in specific. I vividly recall dismissing Henry Ford's famous quip that "All history is bunk" for George Santayana's warning that "Those who cannot remember history are doomed to repeat it."

I had thoroughly enjoyed "preaching" from the pulpit and so I didn't mind at all when the two history colleagues wanted me to sit down for more about Europe. Tennys H. and John L. quickly locked horns over the most topical subject at the time, the escalation of the war in Vietnam after the so-called Tonkin incident. Here I was watching two professional historians and glowing defenders of American ideals gouging their eyes out. Tennys the Southerner, veteran of the Pacific war and thoroughly familiar with southeastern Asian politics as a secret service specialist, defended President Johnson´s decision to teach the North Vietnamese a lesson by sinking the speedboats that had attacked two destroyers. Half his age, John, the typical liberal Democrat from Minnesota countered that everybody and his cousin knew the speedboats had been provoked by the Navy. Going beyond the issue of who had provoked whom, unsolvable here and now, John insisted that he had always been afraid the US would be drawn into this conflict between two camps in a civil war and that now, thanks to this incident, bombing on a big scale had begun. "We are not any better than the French were, killing civilians by the thousands," John argued. "Not so," Tennys replied, "all the froggies wanted was holding on to their old colony, while we are at least trying to teach them some form of democracy and to keep Communism from spreading further. Domino effect, you know. You are right, killing innocent civilians is always the unfortunate part of every war, though unavoidable. You have to break an egg to make an omelet, right?" Somewhat unnerved by now, John replied, "Correct, but might it not be wiser at times not to eat omelets at all?" and suddenly looking at me, "ask Herb here whether all the tens of thousands we bombed to hell were glowing Nazis!" What made it so painful for me was that either presented a palpable interpretation of what those interests and values at stake were that had begun to tear the country apart—and many of us Europeans with it. Having grown up next to the *Iron Curtain* and acquainted with hundreds of stories by and about refugees, most of myself sided with Tennys' view. In those days I was still far away from deeper insights that would be gnawing away at me later.

Piling my belongings including a ten-gallon Stetson and high-heel black boots with blue yarn trimmings into my VW beetle, I was leaving Colorado flirting with the idea of my trans-Atlantic love affair now including the American West or at least some of its myth. Right here in the middle of nowhere, scary signs like "Do not fall asleep. Some mistakes you make only once" kept me from dosing off. If I had not read that Nebraska means "flat waters," I would have sworn it meant "flat lands." The rain lashing against me didn't make driving any easier with my rear-view mirror broken and my window blocked by my big trunk. To think that I was alone in the vast prairies made me feel like a puny pioneer one minute and scared to death the next. Having experienced a fair share of monotonous land, I eventually succumbed to the concrete lure of expressways and found myself driving on the old Mohawk Trail during early morning. Enchanted by the play of shadows between the first sunlit trees, I did not even want to think about the paradise of their dazzling colors in early October. This young man did go West, but he was happy to be back home East.

INTRODUCING MOTHER TO MY AMERICA BETWEEN NYC, BOSTON, NEW HAMPSHIRE, MAINE, AND D.C. THE FASCINATING VOYAGE AND MIRACULOUS CONVERSION ON THE *BLACK TERN.*

My old roommate Bill had taken me down to meet mother at Idlewild. This had to be her, her unmistakable way of toting a suitcase! My God, I hadn't seen this light summer coat in years! Now she spotted us, waving and appearing to walk a bit faster. A dream come true! First photos, first impressions, one she would never forget, that of immigration taking three oranges away from an old Italian couple in tears. Mother already knew Bill from my letters and was now getting along famously with him, their Viennese and Irish senses of humor heading off too much crossing of signals. A couple of muggy days of sightseeing was enough for us, though she just adored the "snail house" Guggenheim and the more manageable Frick Collection, that unique Old World oasis in boisterous Manhattan. Looking down on the art deco Chrysler Building from the Empire State was of course breathtaking, even more so than being shot up its hundred plus floors within ninety seconds. Agreeing that the Flat Iron Building well deserved its name and already looking forward to a closer view of the new Verrazano Bridge on our voyage home, mother was eager to go straight to Durham. We would catch more of New York "on the rebound" anyway, my recent idiomatic acquisition from watching basketball.

There he was, our good old Donald S, welcoming his beaming host from Vienna days with all sorts of Austrian greetings. Of course, she was going to be his guest and of course she was more than welcome to weed out an old bachelor's kitchen, which she did with gusto while I was resigning myself to mowing the lawn and going shopping with her. Disappointed that she could not find breadcrumbs indispensable for her homemade *Wiener Schnitzel*, she already knew that *un*salted butter was unheard of here. In those weeks of mutilated morsels of English and half-forgotten tidbits of German filling the air between them, all these language gaffs were adding extra spice to our happy reunion. Courageous enough to venture into the local food store without me as a translator, mother put it in her head one morning to buy lady fingers for a fancy cake. "Wasn't so hard, after a few minutes the young fellow understood that I needed something for a dessert. I knew the word *sweet* anyway, so I pointed to my fingers, not one or two but all of them. A bit confused, he suddenly pulled me over to where I actually found the lady fingers." What a treat for her to meet my lute-playing Shakespeare professor of four years ago, whom I caught red handed doing a waltz with her right on campus. Moving to watch them, she, complimenting him on his waltzing to the left, and he, raving about her exuberance. A gourmet of the first order, mother took to New England chowder right away and protected by a red-claw paper bib literally celebrated her first lobster meal. Hard work, but well worth it! We even took her camping with the sugar maples turning the most amazing reds and russets earlier than usual. Racoons to listen to rummaging outdoors, moose to watch occasionally in the morning, and bear to stay away from. On the beach she fell in love with the sandpipers racing along the edges of the incoming waves without ever getting caught. Or with the old lighthouses, where we landlubbers were watching screeching sea gulls and the quaint movements of crabs. Telling her they were named sidewalk Sally, she couldn't stop laughing. What fun it was to explain some of America and explore a bit more with her! Time for a trip to picturesque Gloucester– no, you pronounce it *Gloster.* Remember the other day you asked for *Worchestershire* sauce, but it´s *Wustersha.* "O.K." she shot back without much of an accent. What impressed her most about Harvard were the lines at the Widener Library dedicated to the founder's son who had drowned on the *Titanic* maiden voyage to Europe. Amazing how suddenly all her elementary school classmates came alive in her memory, talking about the poor people on that *unsinkable* ship but wondering if it could really have been an iceberg. She could hardly tear herself away from the collection of hundreds of glass flowers which over a century ago immigrants had brought over from Dresden, the idea of a botany professor to have natural scale objects to study all year round. Enjoying the lively atmosphere of Quincy Market and *Faneuil Hall* before we were moving down to *Pier 4* for yet another lobster, by now easier to tackle for her than the first one. What she did not understand was why we simply could not find an outdoor place to eat, neither upscale nor average. Explaining that people here argued that there were too many flies and mosquitoes, I had to admit they brought up the same argument in Denver where bugs would suffocate in the thin air. "Something simple I wish we had in Austria. Have you noticed that wherever we ate, the waitress brought a pitcher of ice water before we could even sit down? No water at all In Vienna, you wait until you order a beverage with your food. Our hotel manager Peter says, and he ought to know, that this is because on the Continent the money is in the drinks, whereas many places here don´t have a liquor license."—For want of a cozy bench to relax on, we spent quite a while watching two quad sculls competing on the Charles River.

Our emotional highpoint in Washington was mother standing in front of the *Lincoln Memorial,* Martin Luther King's words *I have a Dream* chiseled into stone before her. No need to convince her of the solemn power radiating from Lincoln, martyred exactly a century ago to the day. Having known her for twenty-seven years, I could well read her facial expression in moments of feeling grandeur and tragedy. What was of course so fascinating about Washington was that a Frenchman had built in the tradition of the Enlightenment. Neo-classical buildings all of them, straight streets and avenues at right angles and designed on a draft board and not historically grown like the old sections of other old cities here. Moving down to the narrow end of The Mall to see that we were in the middle between the tall obelisk of the Washington Memorial and the columned Jefferson Memorial, Tennys explained that Jefferson was the main architect of the Declaration of Independence and an all-round genius. "Without his original idea and support, *Lewis* and *Clark* could not have opened up the West, and Herb and I could not have met in Colorado." During a short visit to the grave of "our" President Kennedy we included Tennys in our recapitulations of how we had lived through the day when Dallas hit Vienna. To move a bit closer to our own history, he pointed out that the document of Germany's unconditional surrender was housed in yet another neo-classical building, *The Archives.* Tongue in cheek, mother was wondering what that had to do with us Austrians. A snap decision to have a drink to the innocent Austrians. A few final days in New York, where one funny experience stood out. Probably having switched lanes too fast in our VW beetle with the Colorado license plate of snow-covered peaks, I suddenly heard a fellow yell "Damn hillbilly!"

Absolutely hilarious, especially when I translated the message into Alpine jargon.

Looking up what a *tern* was in German, as if that had made any difference, I had made the reservation for our voyage on the *Black Tern,* a Norwegian freighter. Shooting a few final black and white pictures from the Brooklyn pier over into Manhattan at nightfall, we suddenly felt tugboats pulling us away, the city drowned in dazzling lights by now and our ship approaching the lit-up strings of the new Verrazano Bridge. We were twelve passengers and well taken care of by the seasoned first mate who regretted that the huge pile of coals on deck left us only limited space for walks. "Look, four dolphins out there, riding the waves in unison and staying ahead of us seemingly at will!" So many all-time firsts for mother, who had thoroughly enjoyed this summer between Durham and D.C., the two points between which I once had to choose. By coincidence our seats were across those of a Dutch painter and his family. A few introductory words, then his life´s story and ours in few English sentences. The weather was on our side and lunching on deck was a pleasure, except that the idea of two meals a day in English would be a bit rough on mother. Would he please proceed in German, which being Dutch and cosmopolitan he certainly knew. "After the war I decided never to speak German ever again. Sorry. If you knew what Holland in general, and my family in specific, had to live through, you might understand." Translating for mother, who had caught the gist of the message beyond language barriers, I was asking her what to do. "My fault, I never taught you any English," I was joking to defuse the situation. Appealing to his sense of propriety the following day again, I was surprised that it worked. Holy mackerel, our seafaring Van Gogh spent the rest of the cruise talking about everything under the sun except the war in pretty good German. By the time we reached Antwerp, we were almost friends. “It is probably the Czech part in you that makes you so likeable,” he felt obliged to comment during our last meal. “Assuming I am as likeable as you just said, would you think it possible that it is the German portion of my genes?” Wherever I traveled, the war was never far away.—Addressing the man at the railroad station in English about trains to Geneva and, that showing no recognizable response, in German, he gave me a quizzical look and broke the news to me that “en Belgique nous parlons francais.” Half prepared for such nonsense, I was pulling out my French dictionary and, looking up word after word, was trying to formulate my question. Suddenly, and obviously bored by the long time it would take me to finish my request, he continued in English. Mother, we are back on the Continent!

PROLONGED INDECISIVENESS AND A WRONG CHOICE. MY FUNNY SEVEN MONTHS OF MILITARY SERVICE. TWO NASTY JOLTS TRYING TO GET MY INTELLECTUAL FOOT IN THE DOOR.

My God, am I ever thinking back of the words of the chairman at UNH, "May you never go through the nightmare of being caught between two worlds!" Endless discussions with an endless number of friends, most of them not even beginning to comprehend my inner schism, have led to nothing. Nor has well-meant advice from clueless acquaintances like "A degree in economics or law, that will get you places!"

Between teaching English and doing translations, I eventually talked myself into applying for admission to the Department of Comparative Literature at the University of Iowa. Psychologically speaking, this felt like a stopgap move whose positive answer I would have to wait for, an alibi step. Admission triggered yet another round of the battle between me and myself. Being bilingual and knowing some Spanish, certainly not enough to read any writer fluently—would that be enough to compete with those émigré East Europeans who grew up with their native tongue, German, probably even French, and obligatory Russian on top of it? Was there anything like the White Mountains, the Maine coast, Boston, the mentality? Here I was, trying to convince myself that I could start learning a difficult Slavic language. Czech, for instance, and old Marie's ruddy face appeared again laughing at me for mispronouncing words chock full of consonants.

Doubting my own seizure of optimism, I was going to bed a wreck more than once and more depressed by the week, I was beginning to be a mental case. But how to snap out of it?

One unhappy morning, having not the faintest idea where it would eventually lead me, I was taking the bus to Luxembourg from where *Icelandic* took off, the one airline we America buffs and self-styled adventurers could afford. A terrible indication of my condition, I began to explain my situation to the total stranger sitting next to me. No need to introduce myself, just get on with it, maybe he will have an idea! It would have been a miracle if he could have understood what I was aiming at. He knew little about our own universities and less about those in the US. Besides, as he repeated more than once, I was already on the airport bus and would certainly not be refunded the air fare with this explanation. "Last call, flight number to New York." Walking out to the plane in a semi-trance and letting several passengers, all evidently clear about their destination, get in front of me to gain "more time" for a decision, I was pulling myself up the gangway far enough to face the stewardess reaching for my boarding pass. And then, as if lightning had hit my whole being, I withdrew my hand-cum-boarding pass in a daze, staggered down the gangway past passengers headed for the Big Apple, and plumped myself down on whatever. A huge load off my chest, I was slowly becoming aware of the relief flooding through me. Having studied some Shakespeare long ago, I even dug up the theater term for it, *catharsis.*—Never had I boarded a train more at peace with myself than the one to Paris now. Working there as a waiter and eager to show his teenage friend around Paris in convincingly nasal French, Peter was listening to my woes like the perfect therapist he was. From now on "my own private America" would be a welcome destination for summer trips, maybe even a guest semester, but I was going to grow my roots where they had been planted generations ago.

I had been granted a deferment from military service for as long as I was abroad, but now that returning to the States to stay was out, I thought of how much shorter and easier service would be here and decided to get rid of that millstone around my neck. Seven weeks boot camp made me proud of easily keeping up with all my buddies ten years younger—our sissified youth! Then seven months of translating Pentagon booklets on *Track and Halftrack Vehicles,* honing my translation skills without increasing my technical understanding beyond the necessary minimum. The best part of my regular day was teatime with the colonel and his aide, quizzing me about everything from the role of natural sciences in US schools, the meaning of *affirmative action* since Kennedy and Johnson, the alleged or real infiltration of the government by Communists. Did I think the world would eventually know more about Robert Kennedy's death than that of his brother? Did I think that, considering the anti-Vietnam demonstrations like the one with Martin Luther King, the whole war effort might be in vain? Mohammed Ali was a phenomenon they disagreed on. While the Colonel sided with the Greatest that he had "no problem with them Vietcong," his colleague insisted that people who spend their lives preaching equality should serve just like everybody else. What did I think? Of course, I had no personal problem with our fictitious enemy here and now, but the majority of people fighting Hitler or Stalin or Attila the Hun or anybody else did not have a personal problem with the opposing head honcho either. This last subject had them going to the point of asking a young draftee to serve us three jiggers of cognac. I was almost sorry that my stint of seven months was over, two months earlier than the norm because the captain of my unit was so impressed that I was working on a little publication at my young age. "O Captain! My Captain! The fearful trip is done!" (Walt Whitman)

Trying to get back on track, I registered at the University of Salzburg, this time my mind firmly made up for *Contemporary History*. A particularly beautiful city, it offered the advantage of a faculty living up to its first-rate reputation, of a small enrolment, and of most classes taught in medieval cross vault rooms. Three specialists on the twentieth century, their courses a sheer pleasure. Prof F., a Socialist historian on the two World Wars, Prof. W, the woman who was his Catholic counterpart, and Prof M, a political scientist. Within two years I had finished all the course work and was ready to broach my idea for the dissertation to Prof. M., who sounded almost excited about the title tying up my two backgrounds. "The first diplomatic relations between the Austro-Hungarian Empire and the young United States of America under President Monroe." Urging me to get started over the summer so that we could have a first meeting in fall, this was right down my alley. Finally.

Disaster struck when Prof M and his wife perished in a plane crash on their way back from a tour around the world. The cofounder of the U.S.-financed radio station and alleged sympathizer with the fascist *Ustasha* regime in Croatia during the war, he had become the victim of the bomb planted under his seat by the Yugoslav secret service. This brilliant and evidently controversial man had been on a tour meeting Croatian exiles around the world, supposedly helping with plans for an independent Croatia. As opposed to the United States, where the death of a professor entrusted with doctoral dissertations would not entail many months or years of uncertainty for the students, I was back to square one. None of the interim successors knew how long they could stay, which meant that I might well land in legal limbo, quite apart from the fact that no successor was obligated to accept the subject his predecessor had agreed to. What next?

Having learned over the years that reflecting, weighing one thing against its supposed opposite for too long, hesitating, worrying, and listening to the sundry bits of well-meant advice only leads to a loss of time, I arranged for a first meeting with the new Head of the *Institute of English* in Salzburg. How many courses would I still have to do, maybe even talk about a dissertation. Just because the *Institute* in Vienna had been so uncompromisingly negative was not necessarily a bad omen, or was it? What happened then was so unbelievable that I honestly thought I was living through a nightmare. Instead of discussing what I had come for, the new demi-god dismissed me with "You want to know how long it would take you to complete your degree? All I can tell you is that Hitler stole four years of my life, and I don´t see why anybody should get done with it faster." Leaning back and obviously waiting for my reaction, he nwatched me slowly heading for the door, numb. Once I had recovered, I was debating whether to report this to the dean. He could have gotten into real trouble over this, though having no witness, I would probably not get very far. He too was a member of the intelligentsia of my country.

AFRICA. THE ADVENTURE, THE FASCINATION, AND THE POSSIBLE SOLUTION TO MY ACADEMIC FUTURE.

Recalling discussions with Herr H, our POW-priest friend of younger years, about how free we humans are to make decisions if God is both omniscient and omnipotent, I started attending mass celebrated by an enigmatic young priest, who quickly became known for his lively sermons. Following what I would later think of as "an inner voice of sorts," I hung around after mass to ask him simple questions like the above. "This question is too good to be destroyed by a single answer" was a reply I thoroughly enjoyed, though it kept me asking for more. "Why don´t you come to a little get-together next Saturday at the home of my dear friend, a leading member of the *Communist Workers´ Union.*"—"Communist and Jewish, no thanks, I have been through a fair share of ideological stalemates in my life."—"Listen, she is one of those Jewish intellectual idealists, who has nothing but problems with her party, as you can imagine. You won't regret it." I went and it pushed me into an altogether different direction. My driftwood course of life on yet another round on the roller coaster.

White-haired and bespectacled, her intellectual face radiating "Peace to all men of good will" rather than "You have nothing to lose but your chains," she left us to introduce each other. Talking politics for a while, they were wondering whether Edwin Aldrin´s first steps on the moon would be as big for mankind as those of Janis Joplin and Jimi Hendrix in Woodstock. An awful lot of money had been spent, but not necessarily wasted, I joined in. We agreed that ridiculing this

American success as "landing of some clown on the moon" was not only incorrect in view of the brains, discipline, and courage it took the astronauts, but also because not even our hostess appeared to support a Soviet solo in space. They were even less interested in the budding American youth culture of free love and free everything. Straight blue-collar, they were planning to cross the Sahara a second time. "This is Hans, a mechanic and garage owner, this is Werner, a lathe operator, and over here's tough old Fredl, who works at the slaughterhouses." A funny looking fellow, he was considerably older and looked a bit out of place. Wondering what exactly his job entailed, I learned that he was a "butcher, position front, left. Later that evening, these three showed color slides of their great adventure that had led them from Hans´ garage down through Italy, then Algeria, the Sahel zone of Niger and Upper Volta, then back through southern Mali, Algeria and Tunisia. I had seen a lot of slides, but never any quite as stunning. Of all the manifold descriptions, stories, legends, and tall tales I heard Hans relate and rave about, several imprinted themselves on my memory even before the show was over. "We are going again end of November, why don´t you come along? You just said a while ago you didn´t have a clue what to do next after these two whammies at the University of Salzburg. There might well..."—"Please stop it," was all I could utter, still overwhelmed by the slides. "I am not a mechanic, and I am not a physician either."—"Look, you know now who we are, what we do, no need for a fourth guy clever with his hands. Franz, our fourth adventurer, who will probably join, is a plumber. On a trip like this, you have all the medication with you for the people down there and enough for us. If something serious happens, all you can do his head for the closest white hospital or an airport."

"I admire you for your courage, your skills, your interest in a world we know too little about, but I could not contribute anything meaningful. Thanks for the thought, anyway."—"Not true, you said your French is nowhere near your English, but you could help with simple stuff like, 'How far is the closest place for gasoline?' or 'Are there any snakes here?' The one ability you've got to have is to get along, the five of us, under any circumstances. No one can make it alone." Not realizing to what extent this invitation had already affected me, I thanked the lady of the house and took the last tram home. A full hour to come down from whatever cloud I was on, time to unravel.

About five months later the phone rang and a voice I did not recognize right away informed me "You will need the following three vaccinations and five visas. We are leaving the last week of November." Not really known for snap decisions, it took me about half a minute to plunge myself into this new type of adventure, far away from academia for a change.

From Vienna to Ouagadougou, Upper Volta, a long drive. Fending off teenage hustlers in the narrow lanes of Napoli, wading through the ashes of Vesuvius to stare into the first crater of my life, then watching cargo personnel heaving our Landrover 88 and converted VW bus on deck. Fredl, its proud owner, has the red-white-red flag mounted above the windshield, "so that everybody down there knows where we're from." To be on the safe side, he has the modest inscription, *Österreichische Afrika Expedition*, painted on the door. The first survival training of my French is in Tunis, but luckily almost everything is printed or painted in Arabic anyway. The highpoint of the sightseeing is Carthage where Fredl, hearing that it was destroyed three times by the Romans, the Crusaders, and somebody else, takes out his binoculars and, surveying the ancient ruins, comes out with a definitive "At least three times." Driving behind each other, we are zig-zagging our way up barren hills and, it´s early December, get bogged down in snow in solid Berber country. It is dark and we are shoveling snow in mountains named Atlas but have only a vague idea where we are. Dangerous though they say it is, we park our cars in a wide wadi, hoping the notorious rains won't flood us. Moving away from the freezing African cold, we are preparing for our first real African night outside on the Moroccan border. Collecting enough wood for a fire that will last well into the night, not all that easy around here, we open the first packages and boxes that various companies gave us in return for a few good slides. Up on the Landrover gallery next to three big barrels of gasoline we have crates of local beer, but a few bottles of Algerian red wine are good enough for tonight's debut. Studying road maps, talking about previous tours, getting into the right mood for the first night in my mummy bag. Only Fredl decides to spend the night in his bus and when asked why, his cryptical answer is "You never know." The first long stretches on the *piste,* the French word designating the imagined road we must not stray from. The word reminds me of skiing, the only difference being that here the ground is sandy yellowish but also packed down to an inch or so like in the Alps. Adrar, a small oasis in the middle of nowhere is the last place to stock up on baguettes, cous-cous, and Algerian red. We have enough water, a few liters per day kept ice cold by the airstream against a jute bag dangling from our antenna. None of us has a tooth ache, but even if he did, he would gladly suffer on rather than have the rusty forceps, pincers, and drills laid out on a goat skin before us invade his mouth. Toward sunset we detect round objects at regular intervals, watering places for camels in days long gone by. A long string of them, one per camel, everyone in those distant days wanting to be on the safe side. Then comes one of the most indelible impressions so far, the rusty remnants of an airfield, the windblown markers of the landing strip leading into nowhere, the lopsided skeleton of a watchtower, a handful of big barrels anchored in the sand. *Bidon 5,* the name meaning *bottle,* probably alluding to the *water bottles* used by the French parachutists of the *Foreign Legion* stationed here during World War Two. In hindsight not a good idea, but I am climbing up the iron rungs of the monster to get a better view of infinity. Absolutely nothing but dunes, some higher, some lower, some flattening out toward our *piste.* Half a day south of this ghost town a weathered stone block—there is enough "weather" from the daily heat, the constant winds, the cold nights, and tiny amounts of morning dew—shows the nearest points between 1500 km and 3500 km away. Suddenly a problem on the bus, easy to fix for three full-blooded mechanics. Franz is already under the front axle, yelling "Where is the goddam tool kit? You say it´s sitting on the workbench in your garage?" Nobody can believe it. The three of them, each trying something or other with makeshift tools, are concerned but their voices tell me they are hopeful. Withdrawing into a bit of isolation, easy to find here, I am going through the years of my childhood, my years in America, and have lots of time now to debate the pros and cons of my next academic move. But I have come here to leave all that behind for a while! After about four hours, Fredl's butcher voice resounds, "Sitting still in this emptiness is getting boring." Fortunately, we soon do our eight hours every day at average cruising speed and reach Gao at the knee of the Niger River on the ninth day. Driving, that is, through the most perfect definition of feeling deserted with the biggest objects stones the size of pebbles.

What will the first border crossing be like? We agreed in Vienna that carrying weapons could only lead to dangerous situations: at the border they might confiscate them and in case of a holdup, our only chance would be talking our way out of an untimely death. Nothing serious, only incredibly funny: next to the border to Niger there is a bilingual notice in French and Arabic "Office closed between 12 am and 2 pm." The official in charge is having his well-deserved nap about twenty yards into his sands. Bureaucracy is a French word.—By far the most beautiful times of the day are early morning and late afternoon, the former usually morphing into dazzling heat before we uncoil ourselves out of our mummy bags. The sand dunes changing shades and hues by the hour, the higher casting shadows on the lower ones, make for a daily performance of sheer beauty and tranquility. *Gao*, an old trading post for gold, copper, salt, and slaves leaves us with first impressions of colorful African clothes, women balancing gourds and saucepans on their heads, donkeys and camels carrying huge salt slabs tied to their sides. The fully dressed men and women point to solidly Muslim country, as do the prayer calls in *Arabic*, the only language Allah listens to. The main ethnic group and language here is *Hausa,* which, though partly written in our alphabet, is just as unintelligible as the beautiful Arabic calligraphy. It´s the first time that our bus gets stuck in sand. Discussing our mishap, a few *Fulani*, the majority ethnic group here, are offering advice in a language we don´t understand. Neither low gear nor reverse helps, and we are stuck with the tedious and strenuous job of placing our sand ladders in front of both front wheels. Place the ladders over three meters of sand, drive over them for three meters, and keep this rhythm up for the afternoon, all of it for two cars. An hour's worth of beautifully dressed schoolgirls, their baton swinging leader reminding me of high school parades in Florida, and military contingents are welcoming us on the country's national holiday. Most exciting, a whole battalion of men dressed in heavy medieval mail that suits the designs of the blankets thrown over their horses. A bit bewildered at first, we remember that our own medieval tournaments nowadays put on for tourists, the jousting, the heavy mail, and the weapons all originated in the Arab world. The parade takes its course past the only supermarket in the country and on the only asphalt road about 40 km into the desert on either end. Pleasantly decadent, we can´t resist some superfluous shopping in airconditioned relief to experience the clash of civilizations. Trying to fall asleep in the unbearable heat of the night, we hear and feel something-or-other dropping from the trees. All the same size, probably harmless bugs, but we are bugged enough waiting for the next drops at predictable intervals to look for a quieter place. The next surprise is meant for me only. Striking up a conversation with one of the very few foreigners, an American working for the Peace Corps, makes my day. Telling me about his wonderful English lessons with the Head of State—three cheers for the American pioneer spirit!—he suggests I treat his well-traveled pupil to a German lesson and promises to bring the idea up with him. Meeting by the burial place of a Sufi scholar the following day, the exuberant volunteer signals success, wishes me good luck, and describes the short walk to the residence. Surprisingly easy, all it takes to get past the guard is to flash my Austrian student card. Welcoming me with a few German words, the amiable man briefly mentions his trips to Europe and makes us both laugh reminiscing about an interview in his favorite Viennese café. A graduate in economics, he explains that it is not easy to walk the tightrope between independence and aid from France as well as playing just the right role in the *Communauté Francaise*, something like the British Commonwealth. Regretting that our lesson will be the only one but looking forward to more English with his Peace Corps teacher, he sees me to the door to meet my four cronies. *Viel Glück* and *bonne chance!* Four years later, somebody else would flash an ID card in the guard´s face and assume military power.

The camel race is not quite like the *Kentucky Derby*, but we are amused enough to watch these desert ships racing along and Fredl betting on the one he thinks has the biggest hump—and losing. Watching *Touaregs* watering their camels at dozens of round wells, we agree that their four-legged friends do look haughty because, as we are told more than once, they alone know Allah's hundredth name. Wearing indigo *lithams* with miniature copies of the Quran, the men pull this headgear over nose and mouth against dust and the heat, but not over their eyes. They are easy to recognize, especially when they say something in *Tamasheq* or write it out in *Tifinaq*, both completely different from Arabic, even to us. Crossing the wide Niger River is a spectacle all by itself. Shape and size of a somewhat elongated tennis court, the ferry unloads its only passenger, a camel, and takes us on with our cars. Pointing to where we are going, the captain shows his nautical skills by adjusting the Yugoslav outboard motor every other minute or so. Heaving it out of the water and putting it back at another angle, he stays the course against the current. We understand him well enough to learn that occasionally the motor stalls and passengers end up many miles down the river. —

At Christmas we are driving into a village with a beautiful modern church of a very African exterior, reminding us of the many simple sunbaked clay dwellings we have passed. Attending mass amid the colorfully dressed congregation singing hymns in their language *Gurunsi*, we learn that a Swiss architect built it, enthusiastically including the pictorial elements of their culture. Foremost on our list is trying to find the small community we have heard about, a tough challenge indeed because it is nowhere near any village and of course on no map. There the cult of the caiman, representing a deity, or being the deity, is still practiced. To solve this crucial anthropological question would make my day, but not with my French! Fredl lets us know that, as far as that goes, he does not care one way or the other. Realizing that we have been driving around in circles, we are spotting this huge baobab tree and full of anticipation are about to commit a serious blunder. Parking our cars under the fetish tree turns out to be a disaster. Whatever the language growling at us may be saying, it sounds threatening enough for us to profusely apologize with a few devout gestures, offering some rice and salt. Of course, we should have asked first, not acted like clods or, worse, a bunch of white neo-Colonialists. After a while we get the spiritual head, the fellow with the maroon beret, to agree to at least show us the lizard. Calling the animal by name, *zamba,* which means *come here,* its only function in the local universe, even the chief keeps a safe distance dangling a bloody chicken in front of himself. Here it comes, the emanation of the divine, at first slowly, then faster, jumps up to grab the sacrifice, and disappears *dans le marigot,* into the swamp. We are all fascinated and, expressing our *merci beaucoups* to the chief hear Fredl trying to test his rapport with the scaled creature by yelling *zamba.* Without a bloody bait and evidently with the wrong timbre or foreign accent—awesome silence. It must have struck the chief as utterly ridiculous and therefore not at all offensive, for he raised no objection. Instead, it takes us a while to find out what he is trying to tell us until, mostly by sign language laced with a few French words. He is warning us not to go down into the gorge behind their compound where the souls of their dead reside. Long before his time—the five of us are helping him to get his point across bit by bit—a group of French ignored the warning and had a fatal accident. Just a thought, but could it be that, self-conscious about transgressing a taboo, they were careless driving down the unknown terrain? Mind food for us enlightened Europeans.

It has happened before, but this time we will fight back. No border, no flag, no sign, just a chain strung across the road. The fellow asking a few technical questions does not seem to want to squeeze money out of us. "How long your bus, how wide your bus, how kilo?" Hans gives him the correct measurements but decides to say *400 kilos.* Tempted to laugh, we are checking ourselves when the follow-up question is "400 kilos mean empty or full, with you?" Without batting an eyelash, Hans answers *full.* In a way this is a lot sadder, we agree, than being held up for money. It demonstrates hundreds of years of zero comprehension of simple modern terminology and technology. Wrangling about aid to the third world we are pushing on.

On the way to the capital, a long caravan, close enough for us to see bundles of kindling wood tied to each camel's sides. Curious about a whitewashed building next to a local watering hole in downtown Ouagadougou, I suddenly find myself in fairyland. All by myself and inhaling the intense scent of wood never smelled before, I am wandering along rows of masks, some staring at me from walls, others piled up to be sorted out, still others as if ready for the taking. Embroidered clothing, javelins, daggers, ankle bracelets, and necklaces galore. Where am I? On my way out a boy tells me in a medley of the regional *Mossi* and French that these objects have been brought in from all over country to be the basis of the future National Museum. Gesturing more than explaining, he assures me that he alone is guarding all these treasures.

He seems very alert and certainly proud of his job. Thanking him, or spoiling him, I give him more than his due and leave resisting the temptation to sneak at least one of these little gems into my pocket.

Some of us want to go down all the way to Accra across *Ashanti* country. We don´t have a visa for Ghana, and they may not let us in. 2:3 against Hans and me, and so we are heading for the border. Different from all borders so far, this one consists of a sizable stone building, the Ghanaian flag on the pole next to *Republic of Ghana* in clearly visible letters. Within minutes, the officer in charge lets us know us that there are no visas in our passports. Maintaining that we are aware of that, but that we decided to include Ghana only six hours ago and that he could surely issue visas right here, we add that we would of course pay whatever it takes. His tone sharpening while we are standing around mumbling, he says that we should have made that decision in Vienna. Our last attempt turns out to be the straw that breaks the camel´s back, this time ours. "Sir, we have been across four borders in Africa, and they barely looked at our passports." By now his colleague has joined him, "Gentlemen, you should be aware that you are dealing here with officials of a former British colony, not a French one. Have a good trip!" Recriminations lead nowhere, and we backtrack to where we turned south, toward a lake on the Mali border.

Hans suddenly honks at a blue VW bus coming our way. "For God´s sake, this is our car of three years ago, the red-white-red painted band is still there." The owner proudly tells us he found it not far from here, towed it home, and somehow got it going again. They had an awful time on their previous tour, Hans explains, even tried to cast ball bearings before leaving it on the roadside and catching a ride to safety. Wishing each other well, we celebrate the proverbial cannibalizing skills of these natives. We are already in the greenest part we have been through yet, really a treat for our eyes. It is New Year´s Eve and we are celebrating accordingly, even more so discovering a Swedish couple pitching tent by the lake. They are in the middle of their two-year honeymoon and won´t mind joining us at all. Great, finally somebody to talk to outside our quintet. On New Year's morning, the lone fisherman out on the lake motions us to get into the other scow. His second or third brother, or fourth or fifth cousin—the African extended family may include up to forty closer relatives—is going to take us out to watch hippos diving and surfacing close range. Together with only two others, I am scared even more when our skipper tells us that we are going right over a hippo at this instant. Laughing, he assures us in well-practiced French that so no hippo has ever surfaced at the wrong time.—

Sangha in eastern Mali is the center of the culturally most prominent ethnic group, the *Dogon.* Two drummers and eight masked dancers on tall stilts are performing a ritual for us, the hourglass-like symbol of their culture, a stylized figure painted in white, bobbing on every head. Judging by the precision of their movements, they must have done this often, and the perfect French of their leader proves it. We are accepting his offer to take us on a hike along the *Bandiagara* geological fault and its cliff dwellings. Similar to *Mesa Verde* but without savvy guides explaining every detail. The huge baobab trees along the steep steps hewn into solid rock are a bizarre sight, the natives leading incredibly frugal lives with their goats, gourds, and chickens around them in this arid climate. Unbelievable, but true: trying to say a few words to an old man leaning on his cane, I am puzzled when he talks to me first. Hearing *Autriche,* he tells me in *dog-on* German that he served with the French in Innsbruck. Yes, it was an interesting time, but no, he does not want to go back. Early the next morning our far-traveled *Dogon* takes us on a two-hour hike with nothing but flies, thorns, and heat. Yet one discovery makes our day. A grey hose-like something, about two inches wide, lies motionless but in a zig-zag pattern to our left. "A python footprint of about fifteen minutes ago, hard to say how far it has slithered away." Shock, curiosity. Not a good idea to follow it, besides, we are running late. The heat is unbearable at 11 am, and so we pay him the fair price he asks and share a huge gourd of millet beer he has tugged along. With straw and flies removed, the rest of the refreshment goes down faster than it should have. Powerful stuff in this heat.—*Mopti* on the Niger River is famous for the second biggest mosque in West Africa. No problem climbing up to enjoy a fantastic view over this big city nor with spending a few barefoot minutes on the mosque's cool clay floor. Vivacious bare-breasted women, unusual in a Muslim society, are doing their laundry in the river with their children splashing around them. As everywhere south of the desert, the colors and the bustling life are fascinating, long barges loading and unloading along a surprisingly busy riverbank. Following the knee of the Niger, we stop under a giant tree to escape the blistering heat and are watching women making huge baskets from the chaff of sorghum and placing the fresh fish from the incoming boats into little stoves.

Obviously understanding enough of what we are telling him about Europe and the distances we have covered, a bearded old man wonders why people risk their health and willingly leave their families. Asking whether it isn´t nice where we are from, he is not convinced when we tell him that life is wonderful in Austria but that we are happy to have come this far. Adventure does not mean much to him. On the way back to *Gao*, we are welcomed by a group of girls dancing and beating the drums in broad daylight. No chance to communicate, they are really putting their souls into this. None of us has ever been welcomed like that at home. Some of the older girls, those watching the scene and us, are wearing huge earrings of pure gold. No classless society here.

Our way back means more brush but soon raw desert again. And more time to plan, ponder and philosophize in this stark emptiness. Nothing to distract me from toying with possible new approaches to my doctorate. Mulling it over in my mind, not for the first time but more consistently than before, I am wondering whether there isn´t something like an *Afrikanistik Institut* at home. Don´t discard this idea, there might be a way of somehow combining my past experiences! Is it blasphemy to think that many great men have had great ideas in the stillness of the desert?

The importance of kindling wood and slabs of salt is evident and so is water. A frequent sight is full buckets being heaved up by oxen doing their turns around wells. On our long way to Tamanrasset, the old hub of *Touareg* culture, sand dunes become our chief enemies with the extra task of helping out the Swedish lovebirds. We have no extra sand ladders to lend them but leaving somebody behind is a no-no in the desert. The procedure takes us a lot longer, but that won't keep us from a brotherly bonfire under yet another starry sky. Entering the town on a high plateau surrounded by treeless mountains is a revelation all its own. The most artistic mosques, old walls, office buildings, and homes—all in sunbaked clay. Rows of date palms around several small oases, the roads lined by tamarisks. A visit to the museum of arts and crafts, all turquois and maroon like the dagger and satchel I just traded for salt and menthol cigarettes a few days ago. There is no doubt a certain mystique about this dying culture that the Arabs call "Those forsaken by God."

Their black bodies set off against the haze, a bevy of vultures are circling over something dying or already dead. Like on the way south, dried bodies of goats or camels thrown overboard from trans-desert trucks tell us we are on the right track. Careless drivers have perished here veering off course on the uniform *piste*. Looking for rock engravings on the bizarre-shaped granite towers, we find some proving that the desert was indeed inhabited thousands of years ago. Hunting scenes reduced to basic geometric shapes, precisely where painters like Picasso have come full circle with humanity's beginnings. By the time we reach the oasis of *Ain-shalah*, its name meaning "God willing," we fully understand this implied prayer. We have been scouting around for them for some time and here they are, a whole "flower bed" of sand roses of different sizes and designs, sand compressed into floral shapes by wind and morning dew. Perfect souvenirs, maybe not even illegal. Remembering this oasis is easy, for I have never waded into an indoor post office counter in ankle-deep sand. Eager to remain by themselves, the *Mozabites* fled from another Muslim sect a thousand years ago but will be gratefully remembered by our eyes for their blue, green, and turquois homes after the perennial browns and yellows of the desert. Gradually leaving "the real thing" behind between touristy *Chott el-Jerid* and Tunis, we are debating how best to survive the short but notoriously stormy passage to Palermo. 'Don't eat anything' or 'Eat anything you want' have the same result on the five adventurers leaning against, holding on to, or bending over the rails, port or starboard fully occupied Something unexpected but understandable in hindsight happens in Palermo. Though I have never been here and would normally love to visit the cemetery and bone house with its famous painted skulls, our minds and souls are too busy digesting literally hundreds of impressions and experiences from a different world.

Here we come, the *Glorious Five.* Yes, good luck was on our side indeed. Two flat tires and one scary breakdown without the tool kit and maybe many a close shave we will never know about. Weeks and months of showing our slides to family and friends, even to my old history teacher. Questions galore: "You sound as if you had always been received as friends, is this really true?" —"99% correct, 1% for the Ghana adventure I'll tell you about."-"Without weapons, weren't you afraid of holdups?"—"There's always a certain risk, but weapons would probably have only hurt us in a showdown."—"What we call racism, did you experience any the other way around, so to speak?"—"None. I don't think that's possible where you have 99.9% blacks. There is this problem in South Africa with a large white population, or in American cities, where the ratio is usually fairly even or whites predominating. Mostly we were ignored, stared at by many like curiosities, and celebrated by a few."—"Did Fredl's flag and inscription help?"—"No idea, maybe some thought we were the Red Cross."—"Sleeping outdoors most of the time, were you afraid of wild animals?"—"What you need to do is check your shoes for scorpions in the morning and keep your eyes peeled on your trail because of snakes. No wild cats."—"Would you do it again?" "For three of us it was the third time already, the first time for Fredl and me. "I guess I would, but only with such a savvy team of mechanics."—"Any personal exchange you will never forget?"—This question brought back the encounter with a white-bearded African watching us with some curiosity. "Maybe because of this or maybe because of his long pipe" so my surfacing memory, "we sat down with him, describing our trials and tribulations crossing all this desert and bush country. Listening intently, he just shook his head. Assuring the sage that we just wanted to explore a bit of the world, we also let him feel our envy that he was obviously living at peace with himself in his community. Coming full circle with similar sentiments in only slightly different variations, much of this also boiling down to "The white man has a watch, the African has time."

Paying our *thank you visits* armed with a few choice slides to the companies that had provided us with canned food, rolls of film, and lots of cigarettes, the classical little bribe to get things done faster or done at all, we enjoyed reliving our adventure before it would soon lose its immediacy. Faces, accents, and above all the exuberant colors were still lingering as was the penetrating silence of the desert. For the first time ever, I felt I could differentiate between what in life was important, what less so, and what of no importance at all. Most important now, though, was to organize the myriad impressions that had blown into my mind while crossing the great stillness for a specific purpose.

DELVING INTO AFRICAN LANGUAGES AND LITERATURE FOR THE DOCTORATE.—TEACHING BUSINESSPEOPLE AND ENGINEERS WITH A BRILLIANT TEAM OF ENGLISH BUFFS, ALL OF US IN LOVE WITH THE LANGUAGE.

Yes, there was an *Afrikanistik Institut* in Vienna, and I lost no time to arrange an interview with Professor M. Surprised that somebody should want to tackle this at my age of thirty-three, he explained that he had first studied literature himself but then changed to something "more tangible," which to him was linguistics as applied to African languages. "Prof. M, if you are suggesting I bury myself in studying transformational grammar and similar schools, I can´t do it. I failed math in high school and barely lasted through one single course of statistics. Why not let me learn a few African languages as spoken today?" I noticed that he had begun to listen to me, obviously impressed I was still willing to tackle both course work and the dissertation. After an obviously helpful exchange about many aspects of "the dark continent," he quite unexpectedly spoke the decisive sentence, "As far as the dissertation goes, come back the minute you have a clear concept of a working title that I can accept." Realizing that he was not at all disinterested in literature but wanted me to delve into its function of nation-building, I suggested dealing with five West Africans writing in English. Learning, or trying to learn, two African languages was a challenge I would enjoy. *Swahili,* the most widely spoken African language, was highly structured and its vocabulary fascinating. Simplifying only a little, everything dealing with religion, nature, and everyday life is of Bantu origin, everything mathematical or abstract Arabic, and most modern concepts and products English, occasionally German. My favorite example is *mbenzi /wabenzi,* meaning capitalist /-s, from Mercedes-Benz. *Ewe,* however, a tonal language spoken in southern Togo, remained undefeated by me. It was hopeless to try to pronounce a one-syllable word in eight different tonal variations to get eight totally different meanings. "Wisdom is like the baobab tree, not even two men with their arms stretched out can encompass it" is still on my pin-board in *Ewe.*

Collecting material for the dissertation was not easy in those days, especially trying to reserve books on loan by someone else, often far away. The concept of *African Studies* had not yet reached Vienna and *Afrikanistik* meant above all the study of the development of languages over the centuries. The *African Writers Series* recently published in London proved to be my treasure trove of inexpensive pocketbook novels with Achebe's *Things Fall Apart* the first one, though a few days at *Boston University* during my summers "at home" also helped.

By now I had been teaching at SPIDI for several years, the *Language Institute of Industry,* which was always looking for freelance teachers with years of experience in an English-speaking country. Everything from grammar to technical or business vocabulary to conversation including the culturally challenging *Do's and Don'ts.* "Unless you are already well acquainted with someone, you don´t ask *How is Jennifer?* but *How is Mrs. McKane"?* Or answering the question why while dining Americans usually keep their left hand on their knee. "No, it's not to hide a gun." Trying to translate titles is always challenging, occasionally hilarious. "Why can't I translate *Kommerzialrat,* my title for various successful business projects into English? When I tried *commercial rat* recently, this English fellow broke out laughing and then advised me not to use it. I certainly won't now that understand. But there must be some equivalent!"—"Not necessarily. We are much more title-conscious than the English-speaking world."

Five-day seminars, no German allowed, a totally new experience with mutual respect building between us language experts and our pupils, most of them engineers or business wizards participating in international meetings or working on site abroad. A pool of about four or five *top-drawer* teachers—how I loved that word my New England roommate once taught me!—we thoroughly enjoyed our work and the dough that kept rolling in. "But *dough* is something important in cookbooks," as one attentive pupil objected. To argue whether something was slang, already colloquial, or perhaps even standard "turned us on," as we used to put it. There was nothing more exciting than to exchange different pronunciations heard in different countries or to prove to a *limey* colleague that in so many aspects Scottish was closer to American standard than to Oxbridge; that maybe Africans have a right to develop their own English and that this is a main reason why it has become the world language. And even more exciting, to coopt the intellectually most curious seminar participants into these discussions. What we thoroughly enjoyed was going way beyond grammar issues into language in general and, therefore, into cultural aspects. More than once, I left some of our pupils unconvinced that psychological-sociological-linguistic-cultural interaction would in the long run alter a person's behavior. "You weren't half as grouchy when you returned from the States years ago" was what I often heard, "which is not a value judgment, just a fact."

Some of my colleagues became close friends over the years, like Maria V. As a teenager, she had to scour pavements in Vienna, then made it to England from where she, reunited with her mother in time to board the last ship leaving burning Liverpool, escaped to the States. An idealist Communist, she always had a hard time between being grateful to America and attacking it. Equally correct, she suffered even more from the vast discrepancies between the paradise promised by Karl Marx and the reality of Communism in the here and now. A simultaneous interpreter like Maria, Silvia S has certainly been one of the strongest links in my wonderful chain of close friends. Eugene F., a convinced English Laborite and devout Sufi, who had lived in several Muslim countries before he tried to explain English tenses and the absence of logic in English spelling to our students. Also joining us was Gerda B., a half German music teacher from Pennsylvania, the specialist for idioms such as "put your shoulders to the wheel," forever engraved in my memory after a student was wondering whether she could also use that without a car. We had John M as a frequent guest speaker, possibly the only all-round genius I ever met. Stationed in Japan for five years, he was the author of the allegedly best book ever on Kyoto. Wherever John lived, he became something like a superb connoisseur of the country and its culture, the antidote of all the clichés about the typically superficial American. Another unique character was Jack K, prize-winning poet at the Edinburgh Festival and Olympic participant in bantam weight boxing. It was neither his poetry nor his *ad lib* teaching that made Jack a sure winner, but simply his Irish "gift of the gab." Unforgettable the day when I invited him and my old boxer friend Peter to a little shindig without telling either in advance. Let them find out, round by round, that they had both participated in Tokyo.

TEACHING *AUSTRIAN HISTORY* TO AMERICAN STUDENTS. LEARNING BY TRAVELING THROUGH THE BALKANS.

Much of my teaching was for American junior-year abroad programs at the downtown premises of the *Austro-American Institute of Education.* One course was German for *St. Lawrence University,* which nearly did me in on the serious side of life. Surely, there was nothing wrong with teaching history by climbing up to the ruins where *Richard the Lionhearted* had spent time in prison centuries ago. History was also another reason to return to Hardegg with this half German girl from Long Island. Doing the picturesque circular route along the river separating us from barbed-wire Czechoslovak fences, we were beginning to wonder where it might all lead to. Back to upstate New York for her, and back to toiling for my degree, both of us already planning the next summer.

An intellectually much more challenging course was teaching *Balkan Studies* for Beaver College, its name later changed for *P.C.* reasons. Though an overview of history of the countries that once made up the Austro-Hungarian Monarchy was central to the syllabus, the director surprised me one morning, "Would you like to take thirty-five students, about half of them women, on an excursion through the Balkans as far as *Istanbul* for three weeks? If you do, we need a woman along for obvious reasons." My good friend Renate, the type to go stealing horses with. was more than willing to join. -The first border into Slovenia took us an hour to cross, a first whiff of what to expect! If all Communist countries were notorious for their lengthy border procedures, it was still important to remember the many differences between *Tito´s* home-grown form of Communism and the Soviet-oriented versions further down the roads in Bulgaria and Romania. Nonstop to *Ljubljana,* the capital, where we had a lecture at the university on "The overall situation of Yugoslavia" by Prof. B, son of one of President *Tito´s* inner circle. A hardliner, he denied that a major reason the Yugoslav economy did rather well was *Tito's* permission to let millions of Yugoslavs work in Central Europe and transfer their hard currency earnings home. Most of our students had met, or at least seen, so-called Yugoslav guest workers in Vienna and were wondering why the professor denied their positive role. In perfect English and a rather presumptuous tone, he insisted that the country's good economic performance was the result of the *Alliance of Socialist Workers* determining the quotas of their planned economy without any political interference. Patience with debating in incomprehensible English was running low on both sides of the ideological fence when the Communist economist, just having won another verbal battle against us Austro-American capitalists, gingerly approached me about what he called "the stipend." A bit surprised by his sudden mellow tone, I replied that I had it ready for him. "I hope that it´s in dollars and not in dinars" the Marxist, well shielded from his young folks, wondered as I handed him the envelope, The first of many seminal experiences proving that no amount of book learning can match *Learning by Traveling.*

Taking Renate and me aside to confront us with a little problem, the Slovenian guide warned us of a few students smoking hash which she could tell by their eyes. The suspects she pointed out did not even deny the obvious, and we made it clear to them that the stuff would have to be left behind or they would be sent home on the spot. At breakfast four of the culprits casually reported that they had smoked it all off in a nearby forest.—A tour through the old town of Zagreb, capital of Croatia. Reminders of the many centuries in the Habsburg Empire, the downtown area showed the same yellow houses and Baroque churches that we saw in *Ljubljana* and which the students knew from Vienna. Though focusing on history and politics, we tried to give the trip something like an inter-humanities touch. Nobody should return to America without being able to tell Gothic from Baroque. One by one, gingerly at first and then with more and more appreciation, some of them even began to like what they saw of the Easter resurrection ceremony. Great music and a sermon none of us could understand, not a problem in officially atheist but solidly Catholic Croatia. Driving through unspoiled landscape with trees in full blossom on Easter Sunday was truly beautiful until suddenly we had to stop in a little village because of a flat tire. Lots of books have been written about the easy-going, food and drink-loving natives of the Balkans. The more sober and disciplined northerners versus the more easygoing and chaotic southerners? Eager to experience something *live* off the bus, we joined the locals in an almost communal experience. Some of ours dancing with these country folk celebrating a traditional wedding, others tasting the local firewater *slivovice* and clapping to the rhythms of an accordion, a fiddle, and enthusiastic vocal cords. Mary Anne and other anti-teetotalers were having the time of their lives but somehow managed to keep it to bearable quantities. Despite their embryonic English and our non-existing Croatian, it was not hard to sense that with the checkered Croatian flag all over they were definitely Croatian first and Yugoslav second. "Hey, this is the way we ought to study history! Now we even understand it!" Built for summer tourists, the hotel in Split was a bit rough for us without heating in the rooms, but the old town built inside the walls of the palace of Roman Emperor Diocletian helped us survive. So did the island town of *Trogir* with its stunning stone buildings from the fourth century, Venetian Romanesque and Gothic elements all over. "Yes, John, good you are interested in architecture more than in history, work that into your oral presentation!" Awed by the arched stone bridge in *Mostar*, we must have appeared like drunk or stoned to the waterpipe-inhaling males. Which photos to click first, the breath-taking view or the backgammon-playing men? If we had stayed longer and, more importantly, had understood the language, we might well have sensed the religious-ethnic-political tensions between *Serbs*, *Croats*, and *Bosniaks* (*Muslims*). About half a century ago, this bridge had been the bottleneck over which a hundred thousand of Tito's *partisans* had escaped the Nazis. In *Sarajevo* we had an altogether different experience, triggered by Nancy's tonsils. A doctor whose practice happened to be next to us offered to look at her and decided that, except for painful spells, she would have no problems on the trip. Declining payment with a smile ranging between that of a good Samaritan and that of a representative of a superior political system, he explained that unlike in America medical treatment was free in Yugoslavia and wished us well. This was the type of experience we needed to trigger a discussion about present-day politics. With this experience of the more humane side of Communism in mind, our evening ended with lots of fun and some of her classmates treating Nancy with toasts "to your tonsils."—All of us knew the historic importance of the capital of Bosnia-Hercegovina, which seemed to surprise our tour guide. Hurrah to our history students! We started the tour at the spot where Archduke Francis Ferdinand and his wife had been assassinated by the secret Serbian *Black Hand.* The contrast between this literally earth-shaking killing and the modern surroundings could not have been greater, especially when we stepped single file into the assassins' footprints, the imitation of their original eleven bullet holes visible in the wall. On the way to Belgrade our driver Karl had stopped by a filling station but pulled back out right away, skillfully turning the bus around on the road to head for the station across. "Why not try across the road?" Good for us, the second gas station operator was in the mood to sell. A tell-tale example of Communist inefficiency or just laziness hard to beat. That Belgrade, "the white city" by the Danube, was both the capital of Serbia and the capital of Yugoslavia as all our budding historians knew. Some of them even remembered that the name Danube changes five times on its way into the Black Sea. Those proud of a better rote memory eventually came up with all the names, a neat way of demonstrating the many languages we were exposed to. During World War II the town was badly destroyed by the *Luftwaffe*, sentiments about that still lingering among older people. "Doing" a modern art museum, picnicking on the bus, the boys playing soccer as if it was an American pastime. Solidly Serbian, Beograd represented the major ethnic conflict in *Tito´s* Yugoslavia. A *Croat* by birth, he had to weather many a storm because his socialist (communist) multinational Federal Government was often at odds with the solidly *Serbian* government of its largest republic *Serbia*. "Isn't this similar to our arguing about *states' rights* vis-à-vis Washington?"—"Maybe roughly similar, but certainly a lot deadlier."

Sofia, capital of Bulgaria. This time the fault for the long wait at the border was ours because we had a student on board whose name must have made the authorities suspicious for some reason. Dave *Zadnoff* from New York City, with whom I had had several discussions on authoritarian and totalitarian systems in Central Europe, where he was studying now, and southern Europe, where we were now learning by traveling. Applying *Hannah Arendt's* famous distinction which they had all read, we agreed that while Yugoslavia was merely authoritarian, Hitler´s Germany including Austria had been totalitarian. Failing to convince Dave that in these Soviet satellite states absolute power was administered top down, I must have rattled him even more by telling him that only a few decades ago several "nationalist Communist" leaders had been executed for pursuing the classless society without Moscow. Well-read Dave even knew that *Georgi Dimitrov* had drawn up a Stalin-style Bulgarian constitution, but "somehow everything bad in Communism is blown out of proportion by our Western news media," as he put it. A liberal Jew, he also had a hard time believing that despite a vociferous rightist party in Austria today, the overall situation in the country he had come to had absolutely nothing to do with Hitlerism. Checking our documents, the border guard kept turning the pages of Dave´s passport, stepped off the bus to talk to his superior, then came back and motioned Dave, only Dave, to follow him. Some of us were upset, but Dave was in a shock. „Herb, what are they gonna do, I didn´t do anything wrong! Can´t you talk to them?" All I could do was advise him not to lie, whatever their questions, and that even in the U.S. a foreigner could easily be singled out and questioned. Returning with a wan smile, he suggested that they were probably looking for somebody with a similar name, an illegal emigrant? Great relief, various hidden bottles suddenly making the round.—Our tour guide was not exactly in love with her job but did tell us that the city had been conquered by Attila the Hun and bombed by the Nazis. Noticing that most of us wanted to see the inside of the spectacular *Nevsky Cathedral,* she was a bit put off because "this waste of time" would not allow her to show us more interesting sights. She eventually agreed to accompany us into the church "strictly for security reasons" as if pickpockets were a threat in the church of a police state. Not surprising at all, several students began to long for outgoing, friendly

Yugoslavia. We returned to the cathedral for the magnificent midnight Easter ceremony to find most of our normally indifferent nonbelievers quite moved by the Orthodox choir singing.—Watching a crew mounting giant photos of Bulgarian Communist heroes dwarfed by the even bigger ones of Marx, Engels, and Lenin for the May Day celebrations, some of us were cracking jokes about how much funnier Labor Day would be at home. Descending the *Dimitrov Mausoleum* to the glass coffin with the embalmed body of Bulgaria′s Communist saint, we single-filed past four soldiers clad in colorful pre-Communist uniforms, sabers dangling from their hips and guns slung around their shoulders. Psychologically very clever, only one soldier at a time visible below a flickering torch building up an eerie atmosphere that wiped the smiles off our faces. *Dimitrov* himself had passed away in *Uncle Joe (Stalin's)* Moscow and was cremated six days later, the six days it took to build this whole mausoleum. Efficiency where the system demanded it. On the surface again, many of ours bought *Baby Lenins* and Baby *Dimitrovs* now that they were just little cute souvenirs.

Dinner at midnight after half a day on the bus, but the day was not over yet! The hotel in Edirne in the European part of Turkey turned out to be a mild disaster because it was full of big black bugs. Next morning Mary Anne let me read what she had written in her diary. "You took a slice of bread from the basket, and a bug or two used the opportunity to escape. Since there were many bread baskets, there were many scurrying across the table like mad. Guess the girls were too tired to start screaming. The ugly critters were in the rooms and bathrooms too. Renate and Herb said they were completely harmless, just the Turkish relatives of our cockroaches, but yikes." Joking John chimed in with "I expected a bugged hotel in Commie countries, o.k., but here?" Yet another problem tonight. Right after checking in, some of the personnel started chasing our girls, some trying to get into their rooms, others pretending they were room service. What none of ours understood was that girls in shorts and sleeveless shirts were almost naked women to these fellows. Renate's attempts to stop the nonsense helped some but not enough, and so I had to step in. Man talking to man would help. Confronting the manager, I found out with the help of the girls that even he had been among the chasers! At first playing it all down, he must have understood we were dead serious, for not only did the chasing end, but he later took us all to the *bazaar* as a sign of peace, personally watching that we wouldn't get gypped.

Sporting an almost prototypical Turkish black moustache, the new guide began to give us a few basic facts in pretty good English. "Literally meaning *City of Constantine*, Constantinople became the capital of the Roman Empire until split into West Rome, comprising numerous lands of Europe, and East Rome, which held on to it under the name of the Byzantine Empire until the Ottomans conquered it in 1453." With a little smile looking like an apology, he continued, "As students of history you will of course know, but if you are religious, you will know even better that Christianity split into Catholic and Orthodox. The Ottomans made it their capital until 1923 when it was called Istanbul. Deciding at the time that the capital's location close to European borders was too vulnerable, *Kemal AtaTürk,* the founder of modern Turkey, made Ankara the new capital. "His is the only really important name you should remember" and trying his level best to pronounce the name correctly, *moustacheman,* his nickname by now, added "Maybe like George Washington." Before visiting the famous *Blue Mosque,* we spent some time marveling at the surrounding six sleek minarets. "Just be sure you remember where you put your shoes," our guide reminded the students, "and if you must take pictures, be sure to ask whoever is near you. You know that Muslim culture and pictures are not really good friends." Wondering whether we were correctly interpreting the Turkish mottos laid out in Allah's green calligraphy, *moustacheman* explained that there was a movement underway to turn the *Hagia Sophia*, now a secular museum, into a mosque again. Most of us liked him, not just for his accent and his bushy upper lip, but also because he had hit the right tone with us who were maybe more interesting than the average visitor. "A mosque is a mosque is a mosque" and a clear majority opted for tasty food and maybe a beer, which might raise eyebrows in some places. We thought we could sense the push toward Islamization just discussed, but it had not fully set in yet and we had no problem quenching our thirst.

The *Topkapi*, the sultan´s palace with the *harem*, the word aptly meaning *closed-in*, made a couple of our guys very curious, though all we saw was a stunning treasury. How were we supposed to understand the sultan's reign over his women? "First was the sultan's mother," the guide explained, "next his seven legal wives followed by five of his favorite wives, and then the *odalisques,* an unlimited number of women" he ended vacillating between straitlaced comments and barely suppressed smiles. The days of official polygamy ended only in 1926 as part of the strict separation of state and religion to be replaced by monogamy, he explained, which made Rick wisecrack whether that had been at all successful. Some of our male participants were finishing the day in a Turkish bath, "very relaxing" and "so un-American!"

Imploring the students to stay together during their free afternoon, if not necessarily in huge groups, then close enough to keep an eye on each other we reminded them that we were in Asia Minor. They had been pretty good so far, and Mary Anne's problem would hopefully have no other chance to surface.—My godchild via the *Save the Children Fund* and his brother were already waiting for us in "their Sunday best." Not yet teenagers, they were very shy, kissed their donor´s hands (mine) and didn´t quite know where to put Renate. Accompanied by a translator for a little adventure, they were certainly enjoying their first ever boat trip to one of the islands. Making them promise to work hard at school so that they could someday visit us in faraway Austria or even America, we let them return into their own world which we would never have found by ourselves.—Catching some more of Bulgaria on the rebound, we were accompanied by a tour guide whose order may well have been „Teach them about our history without getting too close to them!" *Shipka* Pass on the edge of the *Balkan* Mountains was well worth visiting. A memorial dedicated to the soldiers who died in the Russian-Turkish war of 1876 was surrounded by dozens of names written in Cyrillic on whitewashed stones. Trying to decipher the names was a fun game, four of us figuring out five letters each. Probably because of this historical help by their Orthodox Slav brothers, Russians are supposedly still more welcome in Bulgaria than in other Communist countries.

Stopping by an outdoor museum with buildings typical of previous centuries, we are in for another adventure. Realizing full well that we are visiting a museum and that the crystal-clear creek running through it is of off limits, Rick, usually a boon for his great sense of humor, is probably already plotting his own refreshment. Near the official cashier he suddenly takes a plunge into the brook owned by the people of Bulgaria and, since it is neither wide nor deep, he cannot do any swimming and comes crawling back out with a big smirk. Acting cool like *Charlie Brown*, the cartoon hero of those years, he thinks we are making too big a deal about it. Aware that this behavior would not be tolerated in Austria or the States either, I am going back to the fellow at the gate to apologize for Rick´s behavior. Then the official says something I have used in numerous courses since as proof of how Americans are often seen abroad, not just by Commies. „You are from Austria. Don't worry about it, they are just Americans." His condescending grin is tough to bear. Is he a convinced party member or just a Bulgarian offended by rowdy behavior? Almost a lifetime later, as I am retelling this episode, the man´s remark is still entrenched in the American half of my psyche. Yet there is a sequel to the story, as unexpected as Rick´s prank. A woman obviously watching the scene tries to console me and smiling at Rick says, „Boy wrong, yes. But he feel very hot and, important, he from a free country." Unforgettable. Learning by traveling.

Having already spent an hour on the bus trying to get into Romania, Renate is trying to get the fellow guarding us to allow our puffing fiend off the bus. The scene is good enough for a movie. A young man in khaki uniform with a gun slung around his shoulder is exchanging a few words in broken English with a pretty coed. Great, this might even lead to time off the bus for us all in this awful heat. Far from it! Snatching the cigarette that she is about to light from her lips without batting an eyelash, he acts surprised that she is scared but fortunately too dumbstruck to provoke him. Defiance at this point could easily lengthen our wait. Motioning her to keep calm, we are explaining later that there is also another aspect to this act of sheer rudeness. While an awful lot of East Europeans smoke, American cigarettes carry enormous prestige here. Available only on the black market at ferocious prices, smoking them raises you to the status of a real dude almost as much as wearing American levies.

Like so many places in the Balkans, the old city of *Cluj* is a perfect example for us to learn the complex network of different ethnicities. *Cluj* is Romanian, *Koloszvár* is Hungarian, *Klausenburg* is German, its ancient Roman name *Napoca* revived in history-conscious modern Romania. *Sighisoara*, a beautiful town radiating the medieval atmosphere of Gothic architecture, stands out for the tall tales around *Vlad Tepes*, aka *Dracula,* the historic count given to impaling his enemies. Many of our kids are having a great time scaring each other, index and middle fingers protruding from their teeth. Funny, how they are all familiar with this monster, reminding me that I first heard about Dracula while selling sandwiches in Florida at night. "Recognizing that studying history is always a constant battle for a credible percentage of objectivity—was the count really insane, slandered, or slandered because he was insane? We'll never know and not even having been here in person can help us." Probably to be expected, most opt for real insanity, for where is the fascination with one more slandered ruler?

Budapest, everything so much closer to Austria again! Just to get them used to approaching home again, I am putting on the tape that I had them listen to before we left Vienna. After all, there will be a final exam soon and hearing a few things more than once won't hurt. *"After centuries of war, stability had been achieved under King Stephen, who in the easy-to-remember year 1,000 turned Hungary into a Christian nation. In the 16th century the Habsburg emperor brought Hungary into his empire by marrying the Hungarian queen. A result of the Habsburg defeat by the Prussians in 1866, Emperor Franz Joseph had to give in to old Hungarian demands for equality. The monarchy was renamed Austro-Hungary in the so-called Dual Compromise of 1867 and from then on, one and the same Habsburg ruler was both Emperor of Austria and King of Hungary, k.& k., which stands for imperial and royal on coat-*

of-arms, flags, stamps, or banknotes. Hungary became a Republic in 1920 and like all successor states of Austro-Hungary gradually turned authoritarian and eventually became a Hitler ally under Admiral Horthy. Too independent-minded, he was arrested in 1944 and a no-nonsense successor brought in who allowed Adolf Eichmann, the mastermind behind the extinction of Jews, to have many hundreds of thousands carted off to concentration camps. With the help of the victorious Soviet army, the Communists took over shortly after the war, but the revolution of 1956 swept away the Communist regime, reinstalled a few months later by the Moscow-led Warsaw Pact invasion. 400,000 Hungarians escaped to Austria, many moved on to other countries like the US, where I met my friend Béla S. at UNH. Every time I need an x-ray, I still see him for a chat about "the good ole days."

Looking down on the neo-Gothic Parliament across the Danube from Fisherman´s Bastion drowned in white lilac in full bloom makes for a leisurely afternoon. A few of our more alert students have noticed that written Hungarian not only looks longer, but also sounds completely different from the Slavic languages. Sitting at *Vörösmarty*, the famous pastry-shop since imperial days, many of the girls decide to forget about calories while a history-minded minority are marveling at a dozen Hungarian leaders sculptured in stone. Converting into the fifth currency within a month is obviously confronting some of us with a last obstacle. Hoping on the last lap to Vienna that Dave Zadnoff has noticed the little differences between the *fascist Österreich* he came to and the *progressive Socialist (i.e., Communist) societies* he has just experienced, we are almost shocked by what's happening in front of us. Barely off the bus in Vienna, he kneels down for a few seconds to kiss Austrian soil. Passing around a few half-empty bottles, we are celebrating

Dave's conversion by singing in German.—History class on Monday. The same students, but full of new insights.

MY NOSTALGIA FOR FARAWAY PLACES WINNING OUT AGAIN. NIGERIA AND TWO IRISH SUMMERS IN A ROW.

I had become used to the dangerous lifestyle of interrupting work on the dissertation by going on trips that had nothing much to do with getting closer to the degree, but this interruption would certainly broaden my views of this most populous and complex *Federal Republic of Nigeria.* Günter, a wildlife zoologist at the university, suggested flying to Nigeria to find the right native in the right region with the right knowhow of how to go about a little crocodile hunting. Of course, Günter was a bit crazy. My main reason for agreeing to the trip, though not to his hunting phantasies, was to interview one of the African writers I was dealing with. Having successfully invited ourselves to the Austrian ambassador as advanced students of aspects of Africa, we landed in *Ikoye*, the *Beverly Hills* of Nigeria. Dr. G was extremely hospitable and treated us to several bits of advice of how to survive here. Of his unusual experiences, this one lingered. "An angry crowd was chasing a thief, who disappeared around a corner. No way he could have run that fast, the pursuers argued until somebody suggested the culprit must have, by an act of witchcraft, assumed the shape of the goat in front of him. The crowd chasing him ended up arguing, the more educated half protesting that Nigerians were not in the days of their forefathers anymore, that 'such irrational nonsense was an insult to our people'. With the thief vanished and the goat brought to safety, the arguing had escalated until police was called in. Rather than tracking down the supposed thief, they eventually succeeded in calming down the overwrought imaginations to have a vote. 'After all, we are a democracy! Remember, you might kill an innocent goat! If you killed it, what or whom do you expect to find?' The goat survived."

It was not easy to see or do anything in this megacity of the *Go-Slow,* an appropriate term for the worst uninterrupted traffic jam anywhere. The only attraction of a rare kind was the public execution of criminals on the beach every Friday night and getting a rough idea of what a *ship jam* might be. For weeks on end, ships trying to come into the harbor and others trying to get out had been so hopelessly entangled that bombing the entire mess was considered an option. We never made it to the beach but did see the hopeless standstill in the harbor. When we moved to the slums in *Suru Lere* to stay with a Yoruba living off hauling used cars across the Sahara from Vienna, we were back in the real Africa. Leaving luxury behind to live in a room with neon lights on all night for safety reasons was not easy. The nice part came every morning with a lovely girl balancing a tray of fresh fish on her head, never forgetting a smiling "You like?" Our Viennese Yoruba car dealer was worth a fortune because he was a sunny boy well connected in the neighborhood and eager to help or warn us at the right time. Yoruba being a tonal language, I did not even try to learn more than a few words. Whenever I said my "hello" the answer from everybody was "hello" often said with a grin. Funny, isn't "hello" more American? We had a lot of fun when our troubleshooter solved the riddle, "They're not greetin' you at all but simply surprised to see you here. *Oybó,* sounds a bit like your *"hello."* And cracking up, "they're saying *a whitie!"*— Breaking away from those lovely fish food breakfasts to catch the bus to Ibadan, the second largest city and home of the University of Nigeria, we were in for a shock. A bus turned over smack in the middle of the road, teeming with people like scavenging vultures disemboweling a carcass. A cluster of ultramodern white buildings with occasional trees brightening the scorched landscape was the unreal scene of a tall academic in a dark suit and tie kicking up the dust behind him to get into his white Mercedes. Preoccupied with another aspect of Nigeria altogether, Günter had bought a few lizards that he was keeping in a cage, carefully stowed away under his seat during our bus rides. In the evenings he would tell me details he had worked out for our hunting expedition. A strange couple indeed, neither of us only remotely understanding what the other was after. At the *University of Ile-Ife* I had the unexpected pleasure of running into a professor of German. When it turned out that he taught Kafka, I honestly felt I was in a surrealist movie. The whole country of about ninety million at the time, subdivided into three major ethnic and language groups and dozens of minor ones, each obligated to teach their children English and at least one major native language, and here I was talking with a Yoruba egghead teaching one of the world's most difficult novelists, and bits and pieces in German at that! Involving him in a chat about why Kafka should be taught here at all and how *The Metamorphosis* might be interpreted differently in Nigeria than in Austria, I thanked him for his ideas about African literature he had shared with me. The Federal capital of Abuja in the middle of nowhere was being built along the idea of Washington, D.C. and therefore outside any of the thirteen individual states. The few glimpses we could catch of the nation-wide census underway on the sparsely populated northeastern Jos plateau made our day regarding domestic politics. Here and there and now and then somebody would step out of a car or pop up out of nowhere and ask people to show their fingers. If they could not show a finger already dipped into indigo ink, they would have to undergo the procedure on the spot. This was precisely the region where many years later *Boko Haram* began abducting and killing people accused of spreading western thinking. On the long bus ride south, part of it involuntarily in second gear, Günter was responsible for a show that was funny to some but a nuisance to others. One of his lizards had bitten itself to freedom and vanished under the seats. Pitch dark and the passengers asleep, Günter went on a careful hunt, apologizing for bothering sleepers and trying to explain his funny search as a zoologist's typical problem.

To us the Biafra War that had ended four years ago meant creeping along between potholes, passing destroyed buildings, and crossing others that would hopefully hold up. The civil war between the Christian *Ibo*, trying to break away from the Federal government dominated by the *Hausa* and other northern Muslim ethnic groups, had cost over a million lives. Predominantly Christian Biafra along the coast in the southeast was the result of Europeans landing there over the centuries, whereas the northern Muslim regions were the result of Islam pushing south across the Sahara. Two *Ibo* explained this to us in pretty good English, one of them also mentioning that the U.S. had supplied arms, though not enough and too late. Here it was again, the everlasting subject of the US supporting a breakaway nation for a good reason and earning criticism even from parts of the population backed. Asking the two whether a bigger American engagement could have kept Biafra from joining or being joined to Nigeria again, we got a rather non-committal "maybe not."

This being Christmas, the writer I had hoped to meet was not at the *University of Nsukka* but I was fortunate to meet his colleague. Some of the time we spent talking about Achebe, the famous *Ibo* novelist now in exile and teaching in the U.S. While on campus I learned that the university had been founded five years before Nigeria's independence in 1960 by the later first president *N. Azikiwe*, the first university to be patterned after the US system and run entirely by Africans. Amazed how things could come full circle after decades, I suddenly remembered that this president's son had been my student in *Freshman English* at UNH. Improving his English together with his New Hampshire classmates, he had been puzzled by the daily loads of snow more than by anything else.—The closer we came to the Niger delta, the more Günter started wrecking his brain about his forthcoming hunt. In a tiny village known as the habitat of the pointed-muzzle crocs he was after rather than the flat-mouth species, he was introduced to a supposedly seasoned hunter. Squatting by the water in a blue ankle-length native costume, his English was good enough to proclaim *"easy job"* and to set up a tight fence across the little bay. "Pointed-croc like place." Shortly after sundown, watching and listening to him luring his prey by imitating their scary bellowing, we were wondering why a croc would not just dive under the fence, chew it open, or bite it to pieces. Several pairs of glowing lizard eyes were slowly approaching, but his repeated alluring calls were in vain. Asking enough *nairas* for his efforts, he revealed to Günter, a "man studied in animals," that the behavior of crocs depended on many factors, especially their proverbial sensitivity to danger. Günter had just learned this first-hand but was still disappointed, I had a few laughs, and the old hunter went home with more *naira* than he had expected for not catching anything. Finding two samples of the pointed-muzzle crocs on a marketplace, my hunter buddy now had the new problem of getting his cuties through Security on the way out. Gutsy as always and sometimes also successful, he ended up feeding them a strong sleeping pill, one each, a few hours before we boarded the plane, squeezed them under his belt, and pulled his oversized blue *djellaba* over the restful scene. Getting in line in front of me, he countered the officer's "Anything to declare?"

by handing the officer two boxes of local food. "Maybe these presents?"—"No, but what have you got under your *djellaba*?"—"Oh that. Two crocodiles." Right behind him I literally froze. Holy crocodile! The fellow waved him through, but if he had caught him, it would have meant the loss of the plane ticket and a major delay, perhaps even in jail. Günter supposedly really needed his crocs for research, but I never learned whether he clued his colleagues in on how he caught them. Months later his neighbor had to bandage his mangled arm ripped open by the elder of the critters he had monitored growing in his bathtub. Apart from this somewhat zany return to West Africa, I had enough new African viewpoints and impressions now to boost my understanding of native texts. I never saw croc man again.

DISCOVERING THE MANIFOLD SPELLS OF THE EMERALD ISLE

My well-read friend Rudi was responsible for awakening my interest in Irish literature by *George Bertrand Shaw* and *Oscar Finghal O'Flahertie Wills Wilde* among them, all known as "English literature." He and his wife Gloria had been to Ireland "when it was still the real thing" but after meeting the director of *Aer Lingus* explaining the origin of its three-leaf clover logo and reciting Irish poetry over Tullamore whiskey in a business meeting they were motivated to go again. "He told us that St. Patrick once explained to puzzled believers how easy it was to understand Holy Trinity by drawing the *shamrock, a* clover leaf, three in one" Rudi remembered and turning to me, "and you told us about the Boston Irish, even about Irish pols playing a certain role in American politics, Irish fiddle music, let alone the many Irish words in American English, so let's just go!"

By the time I met them in Clifden in Connemara, I had already had a scary encounter with the political upheavals in the Republic. Eager to cut across the island from Dublin, I had taken the bus into a western suburb, taken out my Austrian flag and positioned myself on the wrong side of the highway going west. Not that anybody would recognize the flag, but they might well be curious to find out where I was from. Known for being kind to hitchhikers, a car pulled up within minutes. Police! *"Sláinte*, where is the crack?" Not hard to figure out what they wanted, I told them that I was trying to go to Connemara to meet friends. Not unfriendly, but definite in their gestures which I would have understood even in pure

Celtic, "You're not going to Connemara anytime soon. The most dangerous IRA killer jumped *Portlaoise Prison* last night, the whole region is looking for him, and with your red beard you look just like him!"

Our reunion was Irish, sautéed salmon with three *Murphys* to brag that we knew more than just *Guinness*, and the unforgettable dancing act of the only guest. Suddenly mustering enough energy to jump up, he worked himself into a veritable sweat, his faded red muffler swirling around him and his feet doing the steps to the jig blaring from above. About twice our age, he excused himself for not being able to carry on anymore, introduced himself as—surprise—Pattie, and showered us with blessings in Gaelic. He was phenomenal, the caliber they don't make anymore.—Settling in the annex to the Benedictine *Kylemore Abbey*, built by an English industrialist for his wife, the three of us were on the verge of exploring old Ireland, literature and ghosts included. Three candles flickering under a vaulted ceiling made for great dinners as did reciting Irish poems to each other or just trying to remember and pronounce Gaelic blessings and curses without anybody around to tell us which was which. The clincher of all our toying with Celtic was a T-shirt I had bought for the fancy Celtic writing around its neck. Correctly pronounced, it meant *I don't know because I can't speak Gaelic.*—Not even "Cast a Cold Eye on Life, on Death, Horseman Pass by, "the prudent advice on W. B. Yeats' stone grave in County Sligo, kept us from reading his *The Lake Isle of Innisfree,* reflecting the remoteness of barren hills between lochs mirroring blue skies. On the way back that night we passed the lake where the English language was enriched by a man who never knew about his feat. *Captain Boycott*, whose tenants boycotted him for excessive rents during the disastrous potato famine a century and half ago. Proud to have made it up *Croagh Patrick*, the holiest mountain of Ireland, with our shoes pierced by sharp stones or slipping on rolling scree, we were rewarded with the divine view of sea and clouds blending into one hazy blue. The three of us somberly folding our arms in prayer on the way up should make for great slides! Licking our wounds in more ways than one we were welcomed by Father Joseph, our hermit neighbor, with a hearty "Tá tù an ceann fear," meaning "You are the best." Surprised that coming from the Alps we should have such a rough time on the 2,100-foot holy hill, he consoled us that "in the ol' days, pilgrims went up barrefoot on stones getting sharrper everry time." Long evenings with Father about the expansion of the oldest western religious order and the teachings of its founder Benedict all over the continent as far as here. Ghost stories and legends galore being much of the soul of the Emerald Isle, we heard one by the famous *Cliffs of Moher.* "An old hag, in love with *Cú Chulainn*, the ultimate mythical Irish hero, kept chasing him until he saw no way out but to have her crash against the cliffs, the bloody water forever proof of what had happened." None of us detected a reddish tinge in the waves but would not have been surprised if one of the cows absent-mindedly grazing right up to the edges had stepped out of bounds, adding some color to both the sea and the myth. In a mood much better than the proverbial good mood and unaware that an elderly couple nearby would overhear my declaration, let alone take it seriously, I stepped up on a ledge, declaring "I hereby claim this land in honor of Elizabeth, our Queen under God Almighty." Hard work to convince Paddie and Sheela, popular nicknames going back to Saint Patrick and his wife, that it was only a prank of mine brought on by the exhilarating beauty of the cliffs and one delicious dram too many! -Franciscan *Ross Abbey*, among the best preserved medieval holy sites, was yet another example of Ireland as a vast retreat of Catholicism away from Rome. Nobody to make us pay entrance, in some of the older ruins even cattle grazing on yellow gorse around ancient walls. Galway, palm trees telling of the Gulf Stream and living up to its reputation as medieval and bohemian lured us back more than once, its pubs painted in bright colors and Irish politics always present, here as *26+6*=32 in white paint across walls. The twenty-six counties of the Republic plus the six of Ulster, calling for a united Ireland, the slogan of the IRA. A gem all its own, *Clonfert Abbey*, still radiating the glory of 3,000 monks praying and teaching in this thriving center of learning. The weathered rough-hewn stones outside and the stark holy figures inside the cathedral, Romanesque at its best and a magnificent excuse for not attending mass! The sixth century ruins of the monastic site of *Clonmacnoise* with its typical Celtic crosses and pre-Romanesque cathedral right by the Shannon, yielding ample food for pondering transience and eternity, the stuff that Ireland is made of. Unforgettable the shepherd driving his flock across the street, some with red and others with blue marks on their shaggy backs but all of them kept together by Lassie incarnate, as we knew him as kids from the movie. Driving home on a dark country road, we decided to stop for an old woman trudging along. "Could we give you a ride?"—"Holy Jesus, quare nice of you 'cause I feel wretched." Forgetting that a few minutes ago we were debating the notion of the banshee really existing, the female ghost from the world of the dead appearing to those about to die, I risked a shy, "You don't believe in banshees, do you?" A bit shaken but summoning her courage, "No I don't" and after a few seconds, "but they arrre out therrre!"—Preparing for a visit to Limerick and not aware there were offers of "How to write a limerick poem-poetry course", the three of us had memorized a few. So as not to forget the intricate rhyme scheme, let me practice one of my favorites for your benefit. Nothing unbecoming, let alone randy, just a finely chiseled work of words. For full impact, it needs to be recited out loud. "Once there was a girl from Chichester / With breasts like statues in niches, Sir. / One morning at matin´s / Her breasts in white satins / Made the Bishop of Chichester's breeches stir." Though not "a long way to Tipperary" at all, we did not mind a pit stop refreshing our memory of the popular tune over a round of pints. "Ah, if you're from Vienna, you must remember that the Irish tenor *John McCormack* made this song popular here early in World War I so much so that British troops sang it marching against the enemy." And toasting us to the tune, he joined for a wee taste of Tipperary whiskey. Irish pub culture, the gift of the gab, and the steady back and forth between fact and fiction, present and distant past. "Once spat out by the devil, but now a tourist magnet," the *Rock of Cashel*, a monster turned museum set off against the sky. Rather than tackling the myriad relics of a thousand years of regional history, we were talking to a fellow squatting on a contraption resembling a chair, his jaded cap hiding his balding head and listening to his deliberations on Ireland and the world. "The only place in the Republic"—now snickering, he pronounced it Repooblic—"with seats for both of them, the Roman-Catholic archbishop and the Anglican bishop. *Cashel* means stonewalled fortification, so that ought to be good enough for them to keep the peace. *26+6* is our real problem. Not just the Catholic green, but together with the Protestant orange into a united Emerald Isle." Making light of our recent experience—afraid that it might be the hideout of a gunman feeling threatened, Rudi had kept me from taking closeups of a remote thatched-roof cottage—he just shook his head. "Not an Irish ghost of a chance in hell, for nobody would want to kill an innocent tourist. Besides, the killers are up in Ulster." Exhausted from catching only bits and pieces about his young years as an honor guard at Buckingham Palace, we understood that for all his Irish soul he was proud to have served the King. "Is the Blarney Stone another Irish figment of the imagination, or does it really exist?" Showering us with details of his own excursion to kiss the magic stone for the gift of the gab, he let us go with a hearty "Bless your little German hearts and all your other German parts!" At *Mellifont*, the oldest Cistercian abbey in the country, we learned that the troops of William of Orange were quartered here during the famous *Battle of the Boyne* in 1690. A long subject for tonight's supper, an uphill battle of retrieving names and dates of English and Irish history! Hard to believe, the three High Crosses among the ruins of nearby *Monasterboice,* the Tall Cross rising 5,5 m, left us overwhelmed by its spiritual power. Telling the story of the Bible, these awe-inspiring crosses had withstood almost a thousand years amidst graveyards still in operation. Fleeting glimpses of the transience of things, our daily Irish diet of conversation. "Be sure to have a few good ones at *The Brazen Head* in Dublin*!*" a pubkeeper encouraged us. "You like history," you said, "so here it is from a native. Yeah, that´s what it must have taken that *strumpet*—look it up!—to stick her neck out of that whore house into the streets when Cromwell's troops were shootin´ up the area. Fact is, she got her darn head blown off." Taking his hint, we were pleasantly surprised to hear a professional folklore group recording their latest at this pub without a strumpet, harlot, slut, or woman of ill repute within eyesight. Not having enough time for a *midnight pub crawl*, we instead opted for a census bureau focusing on Irish trivialities like that last year in all of California only five babies were baptized *Dublin!* For all its literary fame, the *Martello Tower* from *Ulysses* was a sad sight in low tide. Wandering through quaint but shabby lanes confirmed our suspicion about a general Irish aversion toward too much cleanliness. Equally obvious, in both Joyce's Dublin and our own, the nonchalant manner of dealing with time. Asking a stranger for directions, we ended up driving half across us across *Bhaila Átha Cliath.* "This," he proudly practiced its pronunciation with us, "is Irish for *Dublin.*" Whether he was on leave today, a Tuesday? "No, not at all, it's just such a lovely situation at our school. Whenever one of us can't come for whatever reason, another takes over. Mutual trust, it works fine." Paying tribute to the statues of *Connolly* and *Pearse,* the martyred freedom fighters of the 1916 Easter Uprising, we also stopped at *Eamon de Valera's,* founder of the Irish Free State, who escaped execution for his role in the Easter Uprising only because of his U.S. citizenship. He had kept the country out of World War Two and even condemned the death sentences against top Nazis at the Nuremberg Trial. After all, it was the English who had starved millions of Irish a century ago, and whatever Hitler's dubious activities might have been, he was fighting the Brits to the finish. Lots of mind food for yet another facet of World War Two for me and my American students! Browsing through a bookshop that really deserved its name, I paid a few Irish pounds for literary gems and sheepishly filched a jaded booklet with photos of Irish sheep, the chapters neatly broken down into sheep husbandry, sheep shearing, regional breeds. After all, Ireland was also a land of jokes and pranks played by the mischievous mythical leprechauns, mostly. Reading the Celtic half of announcements at the airport on our way out was as hopeless as finding two clocks showing the same time.

Still under the spell of Ireland a year ago, I had no problem contemplating a return with Anne, my eager German student with the St. Lawrence Vienna program. Hiking across the island's highest range but staying away from climbing its 3,000-foot peak, we spent quite some time absorbing the magic vistas of the sea without mosquitoes or black flies and thanks to St. Patrick a millennium and a half ago no more snakes on Christian soil. Thyme soup, canned salmon, assorted regional cheeses. We knew that a little wine making existed here thanks to the expertise brought back from France by Irish monks ages ago but let it go at a total of two bottles before resorting to imported Spanish reds. Oh yes, there *is* some accounting for taste. Perched on the hem of the Atlantic, Dingle peninsula offered vistas each too enchanting to leave for the next one. Located within the *Gaeltacht*, where Irish was never extinct, the town of Dingle presented itself chock full of pubs shrouded in wafts of whiskeys and stouts and echoing with the sounds of folksingers and fiddlers. Unaware that we had stopped for a beer at the pub where David Lean had filmed *Ryan's Daughter* only a few years ago, we were browsing through an essay on Anglicized Irish losing its punch and the Irish their identity "I went fishing for a lost word / and found myself. // The word was Gaelic lost in English." What a precious quote to take with me! Bales of hay on meadows slanted toward the sea, the contours of a sailboat glinting—what on earth could possibly match, let alone beat that? Realizing that "beauty is in the eye of the beholder," we had a little quasi-philosophical debate about whether the scene would be just as beautiful to anyone else, or whether it was "objectively, innately" beautiful without anybody at all looking at it.

Wasn't it here somewhere, supposedly a true story, that a band of revolutionaries during the Civil War had missed the only turnoff and plunged into the Atlantic? Returning to *The Brogue Inn* with the lyrics of the popular "Rose of Tralee" painted on a wooden board above a pair of oversized boots, we kept hearing the catchy tune until long after the cows came home. It was here in Tralee last year that the girl at the reception ran after us, giving the money back that we had overpaid her. Wishing her to "always stay the way you are," we certainly remembered her smiling "Of course, this is Ireland!" At Bantry on the southern coast, the modern wooden sculpture of *St. Brendan the Navigator* pointing out into the Atlantic, suggesting that he had reached America from here, a saga believed by a handful of die-hards. The small town of Skibbereen, meaning "little boat harbor," had become synonymous with starvation when three quarters of its population died during the Potato Famine in the 1840s. A tiny portion of the two million fleeing the "shipwreck of an island" had crossed the Atlantic within a decade. Boats were leaving for *Michael Skellig* from here, the rock island dedicated to St. Michael, but the three-mile voyage had to be canceled because of stormy weather. Watching the ocean in turmoil and reading up on the *skellig,* we were getting ready for the unique experience the following day. Slowly approaching the two pyramid-shaped islands in winds bouncing our nutshell quite a bit, even blowing a roll of toilet paper out of Anne's backpack, felt like the utmost seafaring adventure. Steering the boat into the narrow landing slot without crashing against the rocks was no mean accomplishment, as was ascending over sheer rock and slippery steps for us. About two thirds up, we reached level ground with ancient beehive-like structures, the monks' stone dwellings. In the tenth century a community of about a dozen had spent their lives up here, cultivating vegetables, probably only the fittest up and down the rocks to catch fish. Unimaginable the hardships that must have gone with their motto *Closer my God to Thee.* Fascinating in retrospect, how similar experiences sometimes intersect and blend into a whole. Distinctly remembering a tent meeting in Florida eighteen years ago, when a religious soul had screamed the same basic message from the top of a pole, I certainly preferred wandering between the relics built by these hermits, their theology shrouded by the mists of the ocean and those of a millennium. Absolutely divine the views, one side offering a closeup of the neighboring smaller *skellig* full of screeching gulls and puffins, the wind blowing the biting scent of bird shit over toward us. Adjusting our cameras to the changing afternoon light in the days when we still worked hard to get a few prize shots out of a 36-exposure film, we finally tore ourselves away. As on so many memorable trips, I felt like wrapping up this surfeit of beauty and saving it for bit-by-bit release on some miserable day. To this day, a black and white woodcut of a fellow rowing toward the triangle of *Michael Skellig* adorns my room. Anne did not know these lines by Emily D but did not call me a silly romantic for quoting them here and now. "Beauty crowds me till I die / Beauty, mercy have on me. / But if I should expire today / Let it be in sight of thee."

Saturated with weather, wind, and wine for the day, we drove out into the wilds to park our compact in the middle of nowhere and went to sleep, she a few inches shorter squeezing in between the steering wheel on the "wrong" side and the front door, and I in the back, legs alternately pulled up and diagonally stretched out toward the roof. Two tired travelers, but not tired enough to ignore the slow rhythmic swaying of the car. Good grief, it's pitch dark outside! Less noticeable now, did we perhaps just imagine it? Again, now a little stronger and releasing enough adrenalin in me to roll down the window and, a bit scared, asking some silly question into the night. Then the great relief of the cow running away after scratching her side against our car a last time. Miles and miles of red fuchsia, their intensity heightened by a slight film of morning dew, took us past several graveyards, one warning visitors *Be careful* and another with *Dead End* on the access route. Still under the spell of *the skelligs,* we asked the skipper busy loading his boat whether he would give us a ride to that little island he was obviously headed for. "*Clare Island.* Glad to, but just for the ride 'cause I won't stay long." To be on the safe side, we sat down on a rough wooden crate between all sorts of boxes and sacks and had a few unexpected words with the fellow. "No, I don't live out there, but Johnny did." Looking at him and at each other a bit confused, he went on "Ah, Johnny, you didn't get to know him, but you are closer to him than you think. What I mean is, you are sitting on his casket." Upset, we jumped up, but he quickly put us at ease, "I'm taking him home. He would love the idea of two young folks from far away with him. He was on his way out over the last few weeks and last night he left us for good." Opening a few beers, we lifted the dark reddish *Kilkennys* with loud *sláinte* to Johnny and thanked his buddy with *mo chara, my friend,* he had just taught us.—The remains of *Jerpoint Abbey*, its Romanesque cloister and short columns with only rudimentary capitals matching the Cistercian simplicity that once prevailed, led to yet another discussion. Anne, skeptical about any religious tenets invented by fallible old men, and I trying to discard outdated strictures while holding on to our basic faith. "Credo *ut* intelligam" or "Credo *quia* absurdum est."—"I believe *so that I may* see" and "I believe *because* it (the world) is absurd."—"I understand, I have had some Latin" she quipped. "Impressive, but studying medicine, will I ever need to dwell on all this?" The last hours with Anne before she boarded the plane for the Big Apple were not spent on such heavy stuff but in a hootenanny by the Liffey. Are you really returning to America to begin your medical studies there?

JULY 4, 1976. ENJOYING TWO VERY DIFFERENT FREEDOM CELEBRATIONS. ANOTHER SAILING TURN OFF MAINE.—THE SHOCK OF MY LIFE AND ITS BITTER-SWEET AFTERMATHS.

All these years I had not really been able to fully enjoy anything with that "Sword of Damocles" dangling above me, the orals and the approval of the dissertation. Over the last year or so, I had put some oomph behind it so that mother could still be proud of her son after commiserating with me over these years of see-saw decisions. Here we finally were, mother among the festive guests at the graduation ceremony. Receiving my diploma in a maroon roll from the *Rektor* of the university as did twenty-odd students of different fields, I saw her smiling but somehow not fully concentrating. Inviting her for a more personal celebration afterwards, she did of course say many times over how happy she was for both of us, but it was not mother the way we had known her for over thirty years anymore.—Three days after celebrating my freedom, America was celebrating its own. Surrounded by my closest friends, I had to watch the Bicentennial on TV, black and white at that, though the festive mood did come across with the old bark *Eagle* leading sixteen tall sailboats past the Statue of Liberty up the Hudson River. "Maybe just as well," they tried to console me, "right there in New York you could never see half of what we are watching from right here."—The same summer took me back to my beloved *alma mater*, but more importantly to go sailing again in this anniversary season of ships of all sizes and shapes casting anchor. On this special occasion, Chancellor *Bruno Kreisky* donated two Chairs to the U.S. university system, one at Stanford and the other at the University of Minnesota, where students would do *Austrian Studies.* Great idea to write out a gift to someone on condition he promises to study you inside out, body and soul.

Three of us from fifteen years ago at UNH and Anne. Karl had chartered the sloop we were sailing up into the pristine beauty of the Maine coast again. He at the helm, Norma and I doing what the captain told us because two captains in one boat is a no-no. "A tall ship and a star to steer her by," John Masefield's famous poem "Sea Fever" could have been his guideline, though his life was physics and sailing, not English and poetry. Refreshing my memory of a similar turn a few summers ago, I learned again not to confuse port and starboard, jibing and tacking, yawls and ketches. Great to learn this maritime jargon again, even more of a challenge, though, to land the German equivalents for vocab contests with my friends back home. Yelling "watch out" Karl saved my head more than once from the big boom swinging from port to starboard or the other way around. Tightening the sail by using the winch kept my physical exercising to a minimum, and when the wind was right the white-crested waves batting our hull were enough excitement to keep us alert. Most beautiful the late afternoons, finding our way to a free anchoring spot by carefully steering between buoys and nuns. Making sure there was enough leeway for the sloop to turn full circle without crashing into a neighboring boat was the last precautionary step before casting anchor, a job even a landlubber like me could handle. A round of stiff Tanqueray gin tonics then often set the mood for another one, though we always managed to stop short of being "two sheets into the wind" or, occasionally, "three sheets."

Spending time below deck to work out tomorrow's course and check the weather forecast was one of Karl's fortes.

"This is the quaintest tiny village we have seen yet, let's have a closer look at these weather-worn wooden shacks on stilts against the high tide and the orange buoys and lobster traps stored all over. No better picture on any Maine calendar!" Curious about a red wooden building with two wide open stories exposing fish dangling on long rods, obviously to be dried, I ventured up to the fellow busy with his fishing gear. "Excuse me, but what kind of fish is this up there?"—"Them's not fish, them's herring" his terse reply taught me a lesson. Island hopping was probably the neatest part, so much more exciting than sailing way out in the Atlantic with nothing to see other than seagulls and occasional trawlers. Amazing, Karl over the depth finder slowly steering us between rocks toward a landing site deep enough. On most of these islands we were alone, sometimes digging clams on mudflats and steaming them for supper and sometimes just turning in after too many hours of exposure to salt, sea, sun and storms. Casting anchor a little further out to dodge any shallows, we sometimes lowered the dinghy and rowed ashore. The view of our own sloop in the distance between stone slabs and pinewood forests never failed to egg us on to take more slides. Different shades of pink, red, maroon, and purple with the angle of the sunlight changing, what a treat! Watching the seagulls picking up shells, rising to a genetically prescribed altitude, and dropping them on rocks to swoop down for the bare flesh was great fun, no bird brains there!

We had seen them on previous turns, but here they were again on offshore islands, square cement towers with embrasures on all sides to defend the country against our German *U-Boote.* It was not until a few years ago that I had the unexpected opportunity to talk to a witness of the landing of six

German saboteurs at *Amagansett* on *Long Island* in 1942.—On the way back, we stopped at that quintessentially American haven for style-conscious outdoor freaks, *L.L. Beans.* Might just as well go the whole hog, turn in after a late supper and go browsing and shopping way after midnight. After all, *Open twenty-four a Day.* I found the atmosphere of woodsy novelties, trailblazing color combinations, self-adjusting mummy bags, and state-of-the-art gear intriguing enough to keep looking for more beyond the chammy shirts I settled for. Astounding, because entering a clothing store anywhere else never even entered my mind.

In July of that eventful year, the deadly blow I had been afraid of for years came within seconds. Asking mother one morning whether she wanted coffee yet, I immediately saw that her answer was *No, never again.* Impossible to describe the shock, the death of the woman who had said NO to her husband threatening to jump out of the window unless...—Is there not a whole school of thought doing research on prenatal influences? "Eternal love between man and woman really exists. It's the love between mother and her son." It was Sigmund Freud who said this.

Realizing I could not possibly stay in the apartment, I rented it to a young mother with her son. Studying at the *Institute* where I was now going to teach, she had come from Edinburgh to spend a semester in a German-speaking country. I under the shock of my life and Ingrid living in an impossible marriage full of violence—what a perfect situation to try a new beginning. Vivacious and trilingual, Ingrid was the storm that might help me mitigate my misery, in the process rekindling embers this forty-year-old did not know he still had. After painful months of trying to solve a snafu situation—no way her husband was going to agree to a divorce, and if she had just left him anyway, she could not have kept her two children—we agreed that she should return and try to mend the broken relationship. In the meantime, her husband had visited Vienna long enough to make it extremely difficult nine months later to decide whether the healthy boy born in Edinburgh was pure Scotch.

Many years later the phone call from Scotland one December afternoon was unexpected. "Is this Herb? Hi, this is Chris. They're tellin' me up here that you're probably my dad." All these years since that Scottish *femme fatale* and I had tried to bring some lasting peace into our derailed lives, I had toyed with the possibility of *live* circumstantial evidence of her extended visit. I never really believed it existed, but here it was, audibly so with a rrrolling Scottish accent! "This is a real possibility, and all I can say is come on down to Vienna as soon as you can. We'll figure it all out, and I want you to know that whatever the outcome, my wife and I are really looking forward to getting to know you!" Catching my breath between fits of remorse and subtle stirrings of joy, I returned to the living room where Marianne, used to English phone calls in our home, wanted to know why I had withdrawn next door. "That was Chris, my son, from Edinburgh" I was nervously scratching my head, as she later described the situation.

"You are joking!"—"No, it's not a joke, would I lie to you about such an important matter?" The next years were spent wondering how it would all play out. Curiosity, anticipation, joy?

All of these for a while, but evidently no amount of trying to integrate him into my family tree and into our lives could make up for the traumas he had been through in Scotland, violence and alcoholism ruining their family life. Having passed the Hilton Hotel School with flying colors, he eventually discovered his made-to-measure profession, that of setting up exhibitions and Formula-I races, all the derigging included.

Eventually married in Queensland and the father of two children, he went from doing well to roughing it until COVID-19 wiped out all his options. A daredevil decision at his age of forty-one, plunging himself into the Officers' Training Programme of the Australian Defence Forces might well have saved his family life and given him the steadfast anchor he needed.

The four years with Roslyn, a beautiful violinist, were wonderful in a novel way, her daily practicing sessions a boon, barring the double stops. Watching and listening to her in concert was unique, as was her love for Schubert and Emily D. Coopting her into our freelance English teaching team was a hit because students did respond to a charming teacher with a pronounced New England accent. Teaching extra history lessons by taking the boat up the Danube and hiking up to the castle where *Richard the Lionhearted* had been jailed seven hundred years ago was part of my syllabus before, but this specific autumn day between dazzling yellow vineyards beat all previous ascents.—It still hurts after all these years to bring this up because it was probably the first shattering instance that left me uncertain whether my innermost self was indeed made up of a European and an American half. An unforgettable quarrel that had to do with her being uncompromisingly American, something I usually appreciated and often admired. After a recital by *Manitas de Plata,* the great flamenco guitarist, Roslyn was as overwhelmed by his music as I was and asked me whether I would mind if she went backstage to express her enthusiasm. "Of course not, just be careful" I said, but when she did not come back after twenty minutes or so, I went home. Horrifying minutes, no, two full hours of waiting! When she finally came, half in tears but visibly relieved, she told me the story. He had invited her to a dinner with his whole troupe, and while they were waiting for dessert, he had already made it clear to her that she was going to stay the night with him. In her desperation she had signaled the waiter to help, who then asked her out to a fake phone call. Skipping the dessert, she managed to escape.—This alone would have been reason enough to argue with her, but worse was her insistence. "This man had no right to act like he did. It's time men learned how to behave like civilized beings." All my normally pro-American attitudes vanished, I spent a long time telling her that she was dead wrong to expect a gypsy from southern France, a highly celebrated musician at that, to behave as she had learned it in New England. "Ideally correct though you may be, dear, some of the world just doesn't see it like that. Not even to accept this invitation for dinner would have been the best option." What I had underestimated as we were drifting apart was the age difference of twenty-one years and her plans to continue with her career at home. The wife of a New York musician and the mother of two baby boys, Roslyn died at forty-seven of the lymphoma she had been afraid of all her life.

LISTENING TO SOME BUT INFURIATED BY MOST ANTI-VIETNAM CRITICS. FLYING THE WINDSOCK IN TIMES OF SPREADING ANTI-AMERICANISM. AMENITIES OF AMERICAN LIFE CREEPING IN.—THE QUINTESSENTIAL VIENNESE *NEW HAMPSHIRITE.*

In many a discussion about the complex relationship between the U.S. and Europe, whether NATO or the rough road toward a better EU, it seemed to me that anti-American sentiments from conservative circles had become more frequent. That Socialists of all stripes had a hard time looking at America as something other than the haven of unmitigated capitalism was neither new nor surprising, always conceding that most mainstream socialists admired American values. But now it seemed that the trans-Atlantic partnership, firmly welded together and backed by official politics and public sentiment on both sides since 1945, was more and more exposed to attacks from the right. "You must admit that since the collapse of the Soviet system Europe should consider its own history again and not blindly follow American interests" was an argument heard more often, and it would not have upset me so much if the rationale behind it made more sense. In my book, these attacks came from ultra-conservative circles with their age-old contempt for democracy and the decadent egalitarianism it allegedly leads to. "With their short history, Americans simply cannot understand the essence of organically grown cultures that have made up Europe for two thousand years" was the recurring argument heard more often. An old friend and connoisseur of American pop culture kept knocking "our superficial Americanized fun society," an intellectually dispensable argument if it had not been for the fascinating detail that it came from a sterling egghead. "It is hard to be an American" many a sensitive mind has proclaimed in the past," alluding to the battle between its high ideals and the failure to live up to them! I for one have never heard of anybody complaining "It's hard to be a Finn!"

The rage during those years in the States but still unseen over here were windsocks, and I had brought one with me, the Star-Spangled Banner fastened around a metal rim with both ends open. What a joy to watch it dancing in the wind or shooting up straight in a storm! The fifty stars fluttering and my mood taking off with them felt like one joint maneuver. Marianne thought it was childish, a return to my days of flying kites; and my old friend Peter suggested I put up our Austrian colors as well. No way, this was neither the *Austro-American Institute* nor our National Holiday. My windsock flag meant something more serious to me over here, and when we first watched it going up Paul put on Glenn Miller's *American Patrol,* music we used to dig as teenagers. In the nineties, one could still count on a basically pro-American atmosphere, die-hard political views limited to self-styled leftist intellectuals, a dwindling number of Communist fellow travelers, and the constant number of Nazi sympathizers with Islamist attacks still only rumbling in the distance. Quite apart from the attractive color combination, our fluttering banner turned out to trigger many a discussion. "If you are such an avid America fan, tell us why so many Americans think that baseball is fascinating" one would ask, but a more serious question was why so many Americans think that the medical R&D conducted at US universities should mean their medical system was superior. Most upset at seeing my flying colors many years later was good old Otto L, a fanatic member of the Communist party, who during his exile in the U.S. had succeeded in convincing American Communists and exiled Jews to help endangered people emigrate from Vienna. Tipped off just in time, he had left the US to escape McCarthy's *Un-American Activities Committee.* Even that first memorable meeting with believer Otto ended with a human touch when he was wondering whether he could return to the US to see his old comrades a last time. Having advised my young Communist colleague Alfred years ago to apply for a visa, I calmed down Otto. "Just do it! In this age of mass tourism things are different, and your warrant for arrest must have been subject to the statute of limitations long ago. No, Otto, they couldn't arrest you off the street if they tried. The very question tells me you are still comparing Washington with Moscow." A soft-spoken man, so stubborn that he refused to renounce Stalinism when the party was struggling to reinvent itself, he was permitted to live his dream. It was not only the first frayed ends of my windsock that made me wonder whether what was so exhilarating thirty years ago was still so harmless now. The time to defend my rooftop pride had arrived, the time to take it down time not yet.

By the time the Vietnam War had ended officially in 1975 with lives and dollars spent far beyond all calculations and respect for American foreign policy at an all-time low, even I thought that signing the peace treaty was painful but unavoidable. What still infuriated me, though, were arguments claiming that it was a typical imperialist war with America trying to cash in on resources, that the only reason behind it was the "military-industrial complex" selling arms on a hitherto unparalleled level, or that the ideal of introducing democracy was but a cynical excuse. No, it was precisely American idealism, coupled with the fear of communism, that were the driving forces behind the catastrophe. Looking at China, Indochina, and North Korea, certainly made this fear understandable, but was it not perhaps also true that these totalitarian Asian regimes stood a better chance of feeding their millions than the nominal democracies America had put in place? Subtly uttered caveats and barely noticeable shifts of insight of convinced democrats had begun to gnaw away at my political beliefs, but not the leftist and expatriate "American idealists" quoting *Mao* and *Ho Chi Minh,* some strumming their guitars to the lyrics of *Woodie Guthrie* and *Pete Seeger.*

There was Alfred, a brilliant young Communist party member, who had sweated over Swahili texts with me a couple of years ago and loved to talk world revolution over too many beers. Well-read and convincing in his arguments, he freely admitted his continuous quarrels with his comrades. The most farsighted evaluation of the political situation in the Soviet Union I had ever heard came from him. "You know, one of these years, and it may not be that far away, both you (smiling) imperialists and we are going to have one huge common enemy, Islam. The rumblings in the Soviet Union have become more audible, but here we don't hear much about it. Remember my words."—Maria V. was a totally different case. "The party is my life," she had put down in her memoirs, her view consistent with an ideology that saw democracy as a precursor of, or at best naïve collaborator with, Nazism. But it was more complicated than that. "Assuming for the sake of discussion that Stalin, despite his millions of victims at home, had to be supported by FDR to defeat Hitler, why did you continue to support a regime that went on killing millions after Hitler was gone?" Shocked by the murderous excesses among East European comrades, Maria was not a party member anymore.

Yet the concept known as the *equidistance* between Moscow and Washington, a position taken by too many Europeans still prevailed. Allowing for all the American failures and faults, and there were many, how could these mental jugglers even mention the two systems in the same draw of breath?

Notwithstanding all these manifold criticisms, suspicions, and antagonisms, it must have been in the seventies and eighties that certain amenities of American life gradually became popular or in due time were even seen as *Austrian as applestrudel.* Notorious for looking down on the British and American custom of queuing or standing in line, Viennese banks and post offices began to clamp down on pushing and shoving in front of windows and counters by painting a clearly visible line to keep customers from ogling over each other's shoulders. To be on the safe side, "Distance, please" was sometimes added. Why it had taken this simple practical innovation many decades to appear in front of our checkrooms in theaters or concert halls remained a riddle. Wasn't it here that audiences, still lingering in seventh heaven over what they had just heard, were most upset having to fight for their coats? Caught in one such enervating battle to reconquer mine, I heard a Viennese yelling from the tail end of the pushing crowd that this lack of discipline showed an embarrassing absence of culture. Wow! Quite a few approving nods and comments.— That cheating at school was seen as a mere peccadillo in much of Europe but as an indicator of incipient moral degradation in the U.S. was well known. What was not so widely known, simply because fewer people were concerned, was that recently doctoral dissertations were rejected and degrees revoked for plagiarizing even here.

Fortunate enough to compare notes on these topics with a few Americans acquainted with our customs, I was often tempted to see one of them as more Viennese than I was. He had become a close friend since the distant day he welcomed me on campus by playing *The Blue Danube Waltz.* Donald S, the quintessential renegade from what we generally call the Puritan lifestyle, had studied piano in Vienna years before we met. The highpoint of his visits to Vienna was a recital in a little palace, more than one visitor commenting that his approach to Schubert was remarkable. His sense of humor was proverbial, and so were his experiences abroad. "I was on this Viennese bus with tourists interested in classical music. In a good mood we were listening to the young guide´s explanations. He knew quite a lot, threw in a few anecdotes that fit, but had the habit of using the wrong tense. *This is where Schubert is playing all night` or 'over there Mozart coming from Salzburg works hard' and so on. No problem, nothing could spoil our gorgeous experience, but then a short loudmouth character got up and blasted our poor guide in his Brooklyn accent, 'Christ, here we're tryin' to make sense of what you're sayin' and you keep talkin' about these guys in the goddam present tense!' If some of us were less than happy with our guide's grammar, at this point the whole bus shouted, 'Just stop it, everybody knows Schubert and Mozart are dead!"*—When my Catalonian friend Ramón, whom I had urged to improve his English in Durham over the summer, called from there, he left me little time to catch my breath. "An hour ago, waiting for a haircut at the Greek barber shop you probably remember, I overheard a fellow talking about how Don Steele had dropped dead in England. Having just finished his recital on the first night in Portsmouth, he got up to receive standing ovations and collapsed."

THE TRIALS AND ERRORS OF TEACHING ENGLISH AND DISCUSSING ASSORTED *AMERICANA*. TO MY SECOND HOME AGAIN, BUT THIS TIME WITH THE MOST SERIOUS CANDIDATE. LOSING KARL THE SKIPPER TO KARL THE GYPPER. THE UNIQUE *FULBRIGHTER*.

The hundreds of five-day SPIDI seminars were not only the welcome source of small cash before I was eventually tenured at the university, but they never lost the appeal of supplying us with fascinating minds or out-of-the-ordinary personalities. What they had in common was that they needed English on the highest level possible. The times had changed since the fifties and sixties when British English, no matter how substandard, was considered superior to American English, even if spoken by a Nobel Prize winner. No, it is not uneducated to spell *color, honor,* or *labor* without *"u"* because these were the original Latin roots which then changed under the influence of Norman French. Not even our English colleague can explain how an *f*-sound gets into *lieutenant,* no "f" anywhere near it! Often anecdotes or jokes help because in context we all tend to remember things more easily. A London scene: calling an Australian to order because he crossed an intersection on red in heavy traffic, a bobby yells, "Hey you, did you come here to *die*?"—"No, yester*day*!"—"Why is it that I have trouble understanding English in the U.S. but not in Britain?" The answer, my friend, is not blowing in the wind, it depends on what you are used to. Always be sure to compare equals, never compare big city with countryside, never compare highly educated with grade school level. Congratulations, by the way, if you can understand half of what a Yorkshire bus driver tells you, let alone a London Cockney. "But that ugly American -*r*-sound, like in pa*r*k you*r* ca*r,* they don't have that in the "real English!"—"Please listen to someone from New England, where they drop the "*r*" to the point of being the butt of jokes throughout the country. It's 'pa*h*k youa ca*h in* Ha*h*vard ya*h*d.' Besides, have you had a chance to listen to Irish, full of your ugly American—*r*-sounds? Yes, English is easy at the beginning, but after two decades we are beginning to find out how difficult it really is, especially its huge vocabulary, larger than that of any other Indo-European language." Many of our pupils were stationed in developing countries or traveling to sites where customers knew English but admixed with their native tongues. One fascinating participant, a lawyer, became a good friend after we discovered that we were jazz fans. Hans-Jörg K. had been present when classical pianist *F Gulda* was playing jazz in a way his friend, self-taught genius Joe Zawinul, did not relish. "Got to play it black, man" Joe admonished his friend who, intellectual that he was, transposed the piece to include more black keys. "Not black keys, you jerk, the *soul* is what I mean!"—The son of Nazi killer Ernst K., sentenced to death at Nürnberg, Hans-Jörg had to go through terrible times as a boy and later as a law student. An enthusiastic chess player, he told us about his meeting with *Bobby Fischer*. For obvious reasons interested in Hans-Jörg's family history, the American champ had announced his arrival. Nothing more exciting for my friend than to have a celebrated chess champion as a guest, maybe even for a game. If he wanted any insider information about his father, he wouldn't give any, chess champion or not. Not surprising, Fischer won the two games they played. This chess adventure is important to understand another encounter went through shortly afterwards. Opening his door to an American student about to explain why he had tracked him down, my friend asked him in, still unsure many years later why he had done so. The longer they were talking about the only subject the stranger was interested in, the more my friend felt he had done the right thing. "I can't explain it. There was something about him I liked, and he was obviously not in this for money. I gave Mr. Schwarz, obviously Jewish, material substantial enough to include in his dissertation on my father, freely accessible at a famous American university. And this after I had turned away many dozens of journalists, editors, film people, and such like."

Practicing *small talk* with guest speakers after supper was more difficult to acquire and more important than perfectly applied grammar rules. As a rule, we featured speakers whose topic then often led to grammatically wrong but interesting questions or ended in lively quarrels with or without "reaching across the aisle," an idiom we insisted they remember. Dealing with American politics was a double-edged sword because it tended to develop into verbal battles.

Not easy for them to understand that so many laws differ from state to state, that taking a minor across a state line may get you a charge of *statutory rape*, that somebody clumsy enough to spill a cup of scorching coffee over her knee may win a law suit against a big-name company because it had not explicitly warned of such a possibility; that an eighteen-year old may join the army but is not allowed to drink alcohol until three years later; that a society as free as the US is so amazingly litigious with the number of lawyers *per capita* much higher than anywhere else. "Is it really true that the American business code is as informal as we believe it is? Why is it not a good idea to tell a harmless Jewish joke, even if nobody present is Jewish?

What is your view on the typical smiling American salesclerk vis-á-vis the Austrian grouch feeling annoyed by your mere appearance?" The secretive Austrian employee vs the naïve American, the former jealously hiding how much he makes and the latter freely telling you. Material enough for our students to formulate correct questions and for us to strike a sensible balance between correcting their language and meeting their views with appropriate *cool.* Playing *charades* proved to be an excellent way of differentiating between the word order in questions and that in statements as well as stimulating their dormant acting skills. A giant *Scrabble* board with four groups trying to fit letters into gaps, no matter whether an existing word resulted or not, was fun until the novices realized that a combination had to make sense vertically and horizontally.

Teaching at the Austrian equivalent of the American EXIM Bank was not all that different from our SPIDI seminars. What was new, though, was that I first did not see her as somebody who might eventually penetrate the defensive shell of my midlife crisis. Introduced as bright and busy as a bee, Marianne looked a bit upset when I told her she should join my English *Group B,* the second best. When she let me know with a certain "I'll teach you" smile that she had joined an English course taught by a native Londoner, I decided to read this as a sign that her huff might have let up. Weeks led to weeks, concerts to concerts, months to months, dinners to dinners, trips to my childhood cradle *Hardegg.* It was a question of time until she would join me to discover my overseas home.

Our crossing to New York was something like the opening pages of my American saga for her, the realization that perhaps most of us have two homes, the one of our childhood and early teens to grow up in emotionally and one somewhere else for our intellectual development. After the initial strain of craning her neck to trace the canyons of Manhattan, she admitted that the streets were not at all narrower but even wider than in Vienna! Ghastly, these ambulances and police cars with their sirens blaring, but haven't we heard and seen them often enough "for real" on TV? Endowed with a dry sense of humor, Marianne's comment on being pulled up the Empire State in all of ninety seconds was that it would take her *lift* in Vienna longer to return from the fifth floor. Haze and smog dipping the downtown island into impressionist ambiguity, we nevertheless managed to spot the *Chrysler Building* with its *art deco* personality, the recent *Twin Towers*, the appropriately named *Flat Iron*. "This oblong green space is *Central Park*, and if we are lucky, we'll get to see one of their well-reviewed Shakespeare productions."—Knowing full well how to get me riled up about English, she answered that "whatever the play, it would obviously not be in English worthy of Shakespeare," and I assured her that none of the roles would be delivered in a broad New York accent. My friend Karl S, head of the German translation department at the UN, took us through the Security Council but first, barely suppressing a tell-tale smile, showed us a bed of Waldheim roses. The security check was negligible compared to that of the dress code I did not meet. "Here you are, sir, a fitting jacket" the usher and I agreed on "and any tie to go with it, of course free of charge." Luckily, Marianne was dressed in accordance with UN standards, and Karl could take us to the wall where ex-Secretary General Waldheim's portrait had not yet been removed from the row of his worthier predecessors. For us the high point was watching Foucault's famous pendulum swinging in the foyer, demonstrating that the earth does, indeed, move. Hilarious but quite to the point, a brochure about the pendulum gave the number of believers in a flat earth as approaching half a million. Marianne's fascination with the *Guggenheim Museum* came with looking at paintings while imperceptibly winding our way up and down the giant snail. Remembering that the best deals were often free, we went on that most memorable ferry boat round-trip to Staten Island. The spectacular view of the southern tip of Manhattan, slowly receding and slowly approaching again on the return. Past Ellis Island and the Statue of Liberty, both rallying points for reflecting and discussing reality and myth of many a "rags to riches" biography. All of this for 50 cents, and if we had had the time, we would gladly have stayed on board—no second fare. The other special treat cost nothing at all—walking across Brooklyn Bridge, each spectacular view changing place with the following one within minutes and the impact of each enriched by giant cables and trusses pulled across it. "You see *The Watchtower* on the riverbank? Right behind it, the twin skyscrapers? Up on the twenty-fifth or so floor, we will pitch tent tonight. We are fortunate, the mother of one of my students invited us to stay for a few days while she is away." Walking past the liveried doorman who announced our arrival, the two of us felt a bit like out of a movie. A psychiatrist by profession, warm-hearted Alice kept telling Marianne how close I had brought her and her daughter to Vienna, how happy she was to have somebody reliable to feed her two cats the right food at the right time and wishing us unforgettable impressions from this unusual angle of her balcony sticking out toward Manhattan. Luckily, our generous hostess never learned about our feline disaster until after she came back, and then she took it laughing out loud. One evening we found the kitchen floor covered with cat food, two bags torn to pieces by the two culprits lying half bloated on the couch. Impressed though Marianne certainly was, she later admitted that she had been afraid. Of what? "Just looking down vertically took me a while but walking through subway tunnels at night to come home to our own watchtower was even spookier."

Trailways to Portsmouth through so many picturesque little towns with their clapboard houses and a couple of white church spires in between. "Yes, so many of these names are English, of course, just put yourself in the situation of founding a new life in the wilderness. Couldn't they have baptized your first village *Bärnkopf*, Bears' Head, for the same reason? Not easy to coopt Marianne into all my previous adventures. Could she at least understand what I kept raving about? Off to the beach one day, up the coast to feast on lobster, wandering around campus, each nook and cranny of some, even if infinitesimal, importance in my memory. "Homecoming" like to Hardegg, where after many years the old cellar still smelled of wet stones that brought back childhood. "That's what you have never gone through, dear, life in the world of a campus," my words whenever we disagreed on something that had to do with living almost exclusively among students. Like so many visitors from Europe, the poor girl seemed more upset by students munching burghers off plastic plates and running around in more or less uniform T-shirts and sneakers, by fraternity guys playing frisbee across the street, or by the apparent complete absence of taste, style, good manners. To her university had meant grad school in economics, saving money enough to pay tuition, her youth spent among relatives in a rural straitlaced world with Catholicism playing pretty much the social role several of Protestant denominations here. Her first job, whose ladder of success she had been climbing catapulted her into the cosmopolitan world of her workmates. A little more each year I was now being subtly steered by a successful and highly respected woman, but fortunately not a *women's libber*.

The days in Boston went quickly between visiting the green-domed Christian Science mother church, browsing through the *Monitor* to check on Old World news and to see whether Mary Baker Eddy's column was also printed in Spanish today. Sipping first-rate Italian coffee on Quincy Market, a distant dream forty years ago, and comparing the fashion stores on Tremont Street with those in Vienna—that's what I call the Europeanization of America. Rummaging in Filene's basement with its incredible variety of perfectly undamaged rejects was still fun, but we didn't find what I had been raving about decades ago—the thickest, fuzziest terrycloth towels anywhere. Let's have lunch at *The Black Rose*! Solidly Irish, any number of smokers around to please Marianne, who hated what she thought amounted to the dictatorship of a minority now. No need to hang around outdoors to light one up, how about a few good drinks at the bar? "Boston was always Irish, so the hell with these laws, have all the smokes and drinks you want!" Black and white photos of the Easter Uprising of 1916, portraits of all the heroes against the British. With the observation that Vienna had always been a musical center and Boston an intellectual one, I used to surprise many of my foreign students in Vienna. It is of course a generalization but does have its historical justifications, one of them being New England`s heavily Protestant background with its early emphasis on reading, learning, and freedom from church or imperial regimentation. "Anyway, this here is *John Harvard*, credited with having founded a theological seminary, which eventually developed into one of the thirteen so-called Ivy League schools." Why this name? "Look around, and you'll see many of the redbrick buildings green with ivy."—Karl and Norma had to leave for a few days and let us have the house across the state line in Maine to ourselves, not a big deal among good friends over here with whom I had spent many summer months and who had borrowed the money for their lot and the house on it. In other words, both English and German, a *handshake quality* friendship. "Don't worry" Karl calmed us down. "This is a safe area, never mind there are no curtains." To hear noises outside at night was still spooky until I realized it was racoons rummaging through the garbage cans, but at breakfast, oh my God, a big moose was staring at us! In retrospect, this first American experience for Marianne proved to be a milestone in our growing relationship. She had begun to be a part of my American home, gingerly at first but more so with each little discovery that "Americans aren't really what we think they are at home."—Hard to believe, but the friendship with Karl became increasingly problematic and eventually soured completely when he surprised me with the argument that he could not repay the money I had lent them. Too shocked to grasp that this was neither a figurative way of expressing himself nor a silly prank but dead earnest, I soon realized that trying to convince him of his debt was in vain. From the lawyer I later learned that I would have had a fair chance of recouping the twenty thousand plus interest, if I had sued within a year. Sue Karl? It had never even entered my mind. I had been their best man! His last excuse made me wonder how I could be that wrong for so long about a man's character. "You don´t have children, but I have two daughters who will go to college." Poor Norma, totally dependent on Karl, just looked at me, "I know you are right, but what can I do?" After many fabulous summers, I never saw them again. Learning by sailing can be costly and emotionally disastrous.

At just that time the Fulbright Commission asked me whether I would consider renting a room for the academic year. Whomever the Commission suggested would certainly be trustworthy, maybe even interesting. Opening the door, I was looking into the face of a somewhat reluctant, bespectacled dark-haired fellow, who obviously in response to my own surprise smilingly introduced himself, "Sam Albert my name." Granting me less than half a minute to ponder his background, he, now less reluctant but with a bigger smile, added "Well, actually our name used to be *Albertinovic*, but when my grandmother arrived on Ellis Island from Austrian Galicia, they told her *Albert* was good enough." I complimented him on his brilliant introduction, which quickly turned out to be just an opener for batting punchlines back and forth. Nobody could tell Jewish jokes the way Sam could, his Yiddish betraying thorough familiarity with his German. Particularly interesting was his decision to come to Vienna in the year when on both sides of the Atlantic the Waldheim affair was causing animosities. "My grandmother was so much against Vienna, but my parents backed me, arguing that I was old enough to make my own decision and that while I would certainly run up against *meshugge* characters, I would meet the *kosher* majority." To that we both raised our glasses, appreciating our respect for each other by cracking up over many more punchlines. A memorable dinner with his parents in New York told me how glad they were to have predicted an excellent year for their son. How talented Sam was became even clearer when he told us that he would write his thesis on turn-of-the-century art in Budapest in Hungarian, the most daunting language on the continent. He did.

TEACHING AUSTRIAN HISTORY FOR *HOPE COLLEGE* AND *THE INSTITUTE OF EUROPEAN STUDIES.* THE END OF THE SOVIET EMPIRE AND EXPLAINING AUSTRIAN POLITICS. TAKING STUDENTS TO THE IRON CURTAIN AND PRAGUE

Looking for someone qualified to teach *Austrian Literature* in English and familiar with the American system, Professor S. H., director of the *Vienna Summer School* of Hope College, hired me the minute he realized I knew what a *midterm* was, that students were not used to oral exams because they were supposedly less objective, and that the times were long gone when *B* was a good grade and *D* meant at least passing. Beyond this, immediate rapport on the joys and tribulations of intercultural exchange.

Going to school by Lake Michigan, *Hope* students begin their European venture by a much smaller lake, yet Austria´s biggest at the Hungarian border with "orientation." How to use the Viennese public transport system, to leave a maximum of 10% tips, to memorize a few important German words beyond *ja bitte* and *nein danke*, to keep the noise level below that of Italian tourists, and to trust taxi drivers but to stay away from a few areas at night, etc. "If you have a medical problem, consult *Doc* because he knows the system here. You will meet your host parents the day after tomorrow—at least one person in the family speaks English. Be sure to work out the dinner plan with them because while many want you to eat with them, others will give you all the leeway you want. The *Austro-American Institute* right by the State Opera, where your classes will be held, has known these families for years, so just be yourselves and you'll make good friends." Depending on their eventual majors at home, the students choose between *Music History*, *Art History*, *Austrian Literature*, and sometimes German if there is enough interest. During the opening boat trip comes my first chance to use the term *Dual Monarchy* and to point out a tower manned by two Communist border guards with submachineguns. Most of the students don't know each other yet, many are overwhelmed by the many new impressions, some perhaps missing their boyfriends. Nothing that wine, but definitely not more than a glass, and accordion gypsy music won' t cure.

Hurrah, teaching material far away from pounding grammar rules and correcting unfortunate accents at my *Institute of Translation*! There, my requests to search the rich domain of the English language for ever new mistakes rather than committing the same ones over again tend to be lost on the average learners. Evidently, talent scout Hemingway feels the way I do, namely that teaching literature does not change with an author's language but that analyzing and discussing structure, language, and content remain the same. Absolutely free to choose the Austrian authors, I have begun to read short stories and poems I never read before plus rereading familiar ones in English. Amazing how reading texts in your own language grabs you on the rebound in a foreign tongue! Meeting their host families is a big step into another culture, our first classes the next one. Putting myself into their situation, comparing it with mine thirty years ago in America, makes sense only considering the vast changes in both worlds. Not only have decades gone by in which Europe has become ever more Americanized but America has also undergone changes toward being, if not more distinctly European, then certainly less American. On average, twenty-year old Michiganders, no matter how small-town their background, are also partly products of mass media and modern communication that no Europeans were exposed to at their age. They have come to a different language and culture, but one where just about every shop sign or public notice is in both languages and where most people, including recent immigrants, know some English. Hurrah for the *lingua franca* of our age, *Broken English*! It cannot be avoided that students′ parents in the U.S. know every detail of the Vienna program within days thanks to mobile phones, the seamy side of the coin being that our students sometimes hear bad news from home or are more interested in how the local football team made out rather than venturing into a soccer game here. To be honest, would I at their age really have preferred to wait for a hand-written letter every ten days if I could have grabbed the phone any time of the day to chitchat?

"I have heard of several German writers, but never of an Austrian one, so I am curious about the course."— "We don't have all that much time, so we'll focus on a play by Schnitzler, a few poems by Rilke, several Kafka stories, and maybe somebody contemporary."—"I have never heard the first name, but surely Rilke and Kafka are German."—"Now one at a time. If you don't know Schnitzler, no problem, but maybe you have seen *Wide Eyes Shut* with Nicole Kidman? You have, well, it is based on a Schnitzler story and in class we'll get into why it is eminently non-German. Rilke and Kafka were Austrian writers in German. Both were born and lived in the Austro-Hungarian Monarchy, which comprised fourteen different ethnic groups and languages. The major one was German, but they were not born in, nor citizens of, the neighboring German Empire. This may sound like historical-political bickering, but it's more than that because the way they wrote in German and the gist of what they had to say were different from anything written in Germany. Let me put it like this, Kafka was not any more German than Faulkner was English. He wrote in English, but none of his novels took place outside the South with all its racial issues. You follow me? The reason why you think these writers are German is that German Departments throughout the US categorize all literature written in German under *German Literature* rather than *German-language Literature."* My favorite student comment on a poem we spent some time discussing was so basic that I couldn't really quarrel with it. "Why don't poets ever say what they really mean?" just made the class roar with laughter. Having attended a stage performance of Kafka's *The Metamorphosis* and having coffee where many of these writers used to be regulars they would certainly remember.

The one jackpot I could rescue from my twelve wonderful years of teaching a similar full-year course at the *Institute of European Studies* was Kent C., a psychologist, whom my poker partners affectionately nicknamed *Italian Hellion* because he certainly added some flavor to our penthouse. Hailing from Chicago, Kent showed his poker routine by insisting on a new deck of cards, demonstrated what honest shuffling looked like, and occasionally even inspected our footwear for reflecting mirrors on the big toe. Another native American, Allan J., author of the trailblazing *Wittgenstein's Vienna*, widened our range of games by introducing a high-low variant he had dreamed up with a friend once upon a decade. An extra benefit for the Austrian gamblers, the working language was English, the amounts lost or won on site were not chips but real money. Even our more advanced speakers of English learned that it was *three of a kind* and not the dangerous-sounding German *Drilling*, and that one may have a *flash* of insight but that five cards of one *suit* were a *flush*, and that calling a player a *four-flusher* was risky.

Watching dynamic General Secretary *Mikhail Gorbachev* congratulate die-hard Communist leader *Honecker* on the fortieth anniversary of his fenced-in *German Democratic Republic*, warning his host that "he who comes too late will be forgotten by history" was a positive shock. Russian-style bear hugs apart, *glasnost* (opening) and *perestroika* (restructuring) were the new buzzwords, ushering in the collapse of the Soviet world much sooner than even specialists had anticipated. With the chaotic mass escape of East Germans into the West German embassies in Budapest and Prague and from there into the West, we were witnessing the first steps of the reunification of Germany without realizing it yet. A tourist in Berlin to experience the unexpected sea change, I was the only human forcing my way into East Berlin with thousands pushing against me. Visibly confused, the Communist border guard stamped a visa into my passport "just for historical reasons." Lots of first-hand material within a few weeks to discuss with my American students, an important one being the unequivocal support of German unification by *President George H W Bush* two years after *Ronald Reagan's* memorable words "Tear down this wall, *Mr. Gorbachev*!" Consistent though this viewpoint was with American principles and as such no surprise to me, *Gorbachev's* political realism and his understanding of history were amazing. While my history students understood and welcomed most of this, there was a lot to be explained about Austrian neutrality and *Chancellor Kreisky*. A Socialist leader as a confirmed democrat, a believer in a mix of free enterprise and nationalized industry? A grateful, if often critical friend of the US, and yet a brilliant statesman walking the tight rope between the two power blocs? "John, I realize that for many Americans Socialist is a dirty word, but as a student of history we should aim for more precision in terminology and help wipe out semantic confusion. Those we call Socialists in Europe are not any more radical than your Democrats, each party of course with factions ranging across the board from left to right."—"Hard to understand. Don't the Soviets call themselves Socialist, although they claim to be moving toward a classless Communist world?"—"You are close, they call their way Socialist and the end product Communist when, as Marx claimed, 'the state will wither away' because all class warfare will have disappeared."—"Okay, but where does Socialist Chancellor and his party stand, considering the country is obligated to maintain neutrality between the free West and the Soviet camp behind barbed wire?"—"Just as you said, the government is obligated to pursue political neutrality as laid down in the State Treaty of 1955. Neither the Chancellor nor Socialist party members are compelled to view America and the Soviet Union as six of one and half a dozen of the other. Be careful with generalizations and judgments like 'the Free West versus the Unfree East.' We had half the class laughing the other day when I used the German expression 'the devil often sits in the details,' meaning that solutions that appear crystal clear in theory often become muddled when applied to reality."—"That may well be, but isn´t it obvious both in theory and practice that people living this side of the Iron Curtain are by definition happier than those locked up behind it?" Eager to coopt the class into participating, I thought of having them vote on John´s 'free happy Western citizens versus their unhappy counterparts.' Not surprising, more agreed with John´s equation, though gradually more began to admit that maintaining freedom means continued hard work whereas being deprived of political choices may even have certain advantages. Such as? "Well, forget about traveling abroad, read the books and papers available, spend less money on keeping up with the Jones' and maybe more time with your family" John's challengers argued. Dispersing any possible doubts what was really worth fighting for, we went on an excursion to my childhood paradise on the barbed wire border against escapees from the *C*zecho-*S*lovak *S*ocialist *R*epublic. No class I ever took up there left without hearing me tell the stories of what really happened, how we children saw it, and above it all, *why* it had happened. Learning by traveling beyond textbook and atlas.

By the time we boarded the train to Prague, most students knew enough about Vienna and had absorbed enough of its architecture and general atmosphere to see similarities between the two former Habsburg hubs. True, Saint Vitus Cathedral, the first Gothic church outside of France, has no equivalent in Vienna nor do the old bridges across the Vltava River in downtown Prague, but the Baroque palaces and churches certainly do. The recurring question, why whole sections seemed to have retained their original structure more so than in Vienna quickly led to recent history. "I think I know. Unlike Vienna and Budapest, Prague was not destroyed by anybody during the war. I learned this on our trip to Budapest last year, where much of the city had been rebuilt after the war until partly destroyed again during the anti-Soviet uprising in 1956." So many age-old cultural gems to see here, and so many relics of sheer barbarity! Strange though it may sound, many of our group saw it as a blessing in disguise that throngs of visitors milling around them were blocking their view of the appalling drawings of Jewish children before they were gassed. During earlier student trips behind the Iron Curtain there was none of the pushing and shoving of tourists in the original Golden Lane past Kafka's little blue birthplace, though it used to be difficult then to hear anything meaningful about him from Communist guides, one even asking us why we were interested in this bourgeois decadent writer. On this trip now we almost suffered from the opposite—endless posters, ads, T-shirts, and memorabilia, all celebrating the author of the absurd. Now students had a great time distinguishing between the Lennon Wall set up and decorated with all sorts of street art by music fans, and the same wall earlier named Lenin Wall by the regime in honor of an altogether different hero. "Very political and maybe hard for you to grasp, but the Beatles stood for freedom in a system that officially relegated them to junk music." Impossible to explain the enormous changes between flourishing *Golden Prague* throughout history, its grim face under Nazi occupation and their Communist successors, and its gradual opening toward freedom into our millennium during the *Velvet Revolution* three decades ago.

THIS IS THE WAY: BY CONTAINER SHIP TO AMERICA. LOOKING AT AMERICA WITH MY ARMENIAN-RUSSIAN ARTIST FRIEND.

I was surprised when my Armenian-Russian friend Artak decided to go to America with me by boat because he was not all that much of an America freak, let alone fond of the sea. It is already our third day aboard the GIOVANNA, with over fifteen hundred full containers on two levels on deck and four below. Giant stabilizers are maintaining their balance. Asking the first officer about the content, we get "chocolate" for an answer with a grin and the soothing info that not even the captain knows. "No need to worry because the codes lie buried in a safe." The crew consists of twelve Croatians, Italian kitchen personnel, and five mates from Samoa, a German colony until World War I. One of them fondly remembers the German marine academy and his time on a German ship, contrasts it to the poor condition of our ship, which doesn't mean much to us yet until one at a time, our officers, mates, and machinists show up on the bridge to study the black smoke rising from the funnel. "Is this the right mix of oil and oxygen?" *Giovanna* is so big that even huge waves can't sway her, which makes us feel good regarding our containers. What is this pronounced smell of vanilla between two of them, very strong, almost inviting? Their content or the freshly applied anti-corrosive paint? Suddenly two loud blasts! At lunch the machinist calms us down, saying it was just the one boiler that always causes trouble. With all these quieting bits of news, we are playing mid-Atlantic

Battleship, taking turns sinking subs or damaging cruisers. Overwhelmed by the turquois splashing of the waves, I am trying to write letters in a mood where one tends to see things much more clearly and suddenly imagines grasping what's important in life and what is not. The last time I had this feeling was crossing the Sahara over eight days of absolute emptiness. The small point on the horizon, off to starboard, a freighter that will pass us in two hours the way we are going at twenty knots per hour, the Samoan explains. Almost a full program all day long, three quarters of an hour of walking from stern to prow, up and down staircases and stepping over safety thresholds between segments of the hull. There! Twelve dolphins shooting out of the waves, four of them in perfect parallel formation. The heavy haze changing into different hues and tints makes for yet another fabulous sundown, which we celebrate with two stiff *sundowners* for semantic reasons. A bit of a mystery, a red banner on a white buoy next to something like a lobster trap? No, we are going across shallows, where tied to a big post thick ropes with dozens of hooks are waiting for bites. The surface is like a mirror, the concentric circles set in motion by the wingtips of gulls. Memories of my dear Prof. Howard S. reciting Shakespeare, sonnet LX. "Like as the waves make towards the pebbled shore / so do our minutes hasten to their end; / Each changing place with that which goes before / In sequent toil all forwards do contend." In this quiet sea south of Newfoundland, we should be able to spot whales. There! Waiting too long, Artak misses it, arguing that he wanted to catch all of the whale in midair. Some are so big that the head appears separate from the tail, he explains, up to twenty meters long these bodies, just lounging around slurping plankton until they dive, their huge three-pronged tailfins the most visible spectacle. Still invisible behind the haze, *Beantown.* Off to starboard must be Maine with its cliffs, bays, and beacons and somewhere to the south my thirteen miles of NH coastline. The closer we get to America, the better our mood, Artak quoting his all-purpose English sentence, "Just beginning to go grey" even if this is of no immediate concern. The old Fortress of the Colonial War, there the monument to the *Battle of Bunker Hill.* This gradual coming closer, this overwhelming gut feeling of time in suspension, that's what I call traveling! In front of us, their white triangular sails dark against backlighting, sloops jibing and tacking and trawlers hauling in their catch. Over there, Cape Cod, *God and Cod,* a concept too complex to explain to Artak excited about too much visible reality. The green roofed Customs House, where *Nathaniel Hawthorne* worked as a customs officer. Zooming in on some of these sights, Artak laments "too bad one knows them all from TV already." Emotionally too involved with them, I have not "seen them on TV already."

Artak wants me to accompany him to the immigration booth, very different and civilized compared to an airport. Before I can join him, I hear the officer say *deutsch* and then admit my friend to the USA. Thirty years ago, nobody would have known a German word, other than what they still remembered from Hitler movies. But now the place is full of Europeans, especially Germans. Is it true that money can talk? A first lesson in current politics after twenty yards on the pier, a poster of Ireland. To the left, a long list of Irish names, on the right a dagger saying "Britain" and stabbing into a green heart. The list is for voluntary contributions to the I.R.A. from all these Boston Irish dockworkers. Modern interpretations of what a nation should be aside, the ethnic element wins out.

All excited, Artak asks me where this little island of Manhattan is—a joke, he assures me. Unbelievable that the oldest representation of this original Dutch village was found only two years ago in our *Austrian National Library.* A Greek cabbie takes us to Alice´s unusual home on the twenty-fifth floor right behind *The Watchtower Building.* A first for Artak, the breathtaking view right across the *Twin Towers* to *Ellis Island* with its famous inscription "Give me your millions," who nowadays arrive by plane or swim the Rio Grande as *wetbacks.* A first walk in *Brooklyn Heights,* old brownstones with wooden houses between them. "Yes, Artak, this is a mailbox and this a garbage can," I remember my first major blunder in New Hampshire when I mailed a letter home that never arrived. Walking along the East River, we are suddenly confronted by a black man talking so someone nobody else can see. When this happens again, Alice explains, it is the result of the Civil Rights movement demanding that mental patients be reintegrated into society on condition that the community look after them. The latter doesn't seem to work too well.

Like so many Europeans, Artak wants to go to *Harlem* right away, the music and the myth! Easy does it, I don't really know my way around there, and it's certainly not like it was in Lakeland thirty years ago when my roommate and I attended the black church "across the railroad tracks" where we were warmly welcomed. Maybe later. Our minds still on jazz, we are humming "Take the A-Train" while boarding one. Fascinated by the mix of different shades of black and tan, Artak comments that we are the only whites. My friend, this really shows that you are just "off the pickle boat," I tease him, explaining the idiom occasionally targeted at me long ago. Suddenly he yanks around his camera, zooming in on a woman dressed in shock colors, a white paper crown and antennae swinging on her head like out of a space suit. Even more unusual, her perfectly normal looking husband with two children right behind her. Here we are in one of the greatest experiments in history, the discovery, exploration, and ongoing tight rope act of inventing a new society—and my actor friend is most interested in the way some folks look, move, act, run, or communicate! Blade runners everywhere, some circling around an old white-haired man with a countertenor voice and a sign around his neck, "I am a singer and I want your contribution." This new *Trump Tower* is beautiful, but doesn't it suggest raw power more than anything else? Glass façades, more like cascades higher up with real trees on several levels. A feast outdoors, but awful *kitsch* inside with waterfalls plunging over gold-guilt facades. The man's name is *Trump,* and we are told he is of German descent. Sense and nonsense of skyscrapers is with us again, but we do like our "Lipstick," oval and in reddish stone. The uniformity of merchandise and the sameness of its presentation strike Artak, high priest of individualism, but he hasn't noticed the no-name brands, packaged in white, placed separately, and always less expensive. How many little grocery stores can survive here is another very European question, especially considering the usual opening times around the clock. "This long white stretch limo is probably Mafia," he comments, but talking to the driver for a minute my friend is almost disillusioned that we could rent it for seven hundred bucks an hour.—Time and again, these contradictory views, experiences, and reactions. The pace is awfully fast here, no doubt. "If you live in New York, you need a shrink," I translate this famous quip for Artak, and we agree that this it might even make sense. Maybe people are inconsiderate and impolite, but I cannot find the other fifty percent in Vienna. Nowhere have I heard more *excuse me's* for a shoulder hardly touched, a foot barely stepped on, or someone's path inadvertently cut off. Money talks, no doubt, but how quiet is it in Europe? To argue that there is corruption everywhere is a platitude that one should qualify by comparing, say, American and Austrian taxpayers' morality.

A black cleaning woman, like out of an anthropological documentary, surprises us in our swank residence. Interested in her unusual attire and her turbanlike headgear, I am getting curious. "That's the Original Hebrews," she explains, but before I can ask more questions, we are told in her now merciless tone of voice that "all the others, every one of them betrayed the Lord." Meeting my boxer-poet friend Jack K is wonderful but strenuous because it involves interpreting into English for Jack and into German for Artak. "Still no upscale area now, the *Bouwerie* meant rock bottom for many until a few decades ago," Jack explains. "Yes, it's a Dutch name meaning *farm* and was Peter Stuyvesant's place, the governor of New Netherlands beginning in 1664. *Brooklyn, Bronx, Harlem,* they are all Dutch names, you know that." Stopping by the old Brooklyn fire brigade with us, Jack points to the high shiny brass columns on which they have come sliding down for the last 130 years in case of need. Yelling up to chase them away from their card games, as he puts it, he is glad two of them respond by actually dropping down before our eyes.

Karl and Evelyn are taking us through the Security Council, where years ago he showed me the five empty spots after the paintings of the Secretary Generals were removed. It was less of a problem to take all of them down rather than just that of *Kurt Waldheim.* We are about to do the best free walk the city offers across the *Brooklyn Bridge,* its constantly shifting views between steel girders and giant cables a visual symphony of hanging and counter-hanging. Down in the subway tunnel I take a closeup of the *"BB"* emblem on the old *art deco* tiles, remnants of a bygone century. A student with a Russian T-shirt looks amazed when Artak tells her the message she is wearing, reads "Shakespeare or Tolstoy—that is the question."

Finally, to the Baptist Church in Harlem, where I called ahead to make sure we would be welcome. "If you feel you want to come, then come." There is still time, and we are hanging around, eagerly absorbing this world within a world. We are hiding our cameras, police are standing around trying to quench a fire, arson? Crossing *Malcolm X Blvd* and then *Frederick Douglass Blvd*, I am initiating Artak to these black movers and shakers. Ordering the strongest coffee "so that I can really wake up," I am getting a rhetorical question for an answer: "If your dream was nice, why would you want to wake up?" Entranced by this reply, Artak keeps talking about it for days, stuff for debates on being black in America but maybe just as valid in our own lives? Black middle class, the *ebony* counterpart to *ivory*. Ushers guiding newcomers to their seats, the music traditional church hymns rather than *soul*. The guest speaker from Virginia, building up his points like a Roman orator in a Shakespeare play while delivering jabs at fictitious enemies in the air, drops back exhausted to gather energy for yet another message. "Amen" calls are picking up as he urges the congregation to pray for Michael Jackson, guilty or not. Talking about a one-armed baseball player who made it from Saul to Paul, he chides today's kids who have no idea what it meant to be black in his youth. Striking up a few words with a black CNN reporter, we are surprised to hear him tell us how naïve he was about Harlem after the old elegant Harlem he had known was destroyed by drugs in the fifties. Sizing us up, he invites us to follow him a few steps into a circle we would not possibly have found, let alone joined ourselves. Half a dozen blacks, all between thirty and forty and probably professional friend. Modern art on the paneled walls, soft jazz from the record player. A few brief introductions, then the unexpected inquiry, why we have come all the way up to Harlem. Admitting that we have come to find more of the earlier Harlem including black church music, we find our own feelings confirmed. "Too gentrified, too middle class, too removed from their roots." Referring to my years in the South, they agree that visiting black services there must indeed have been a worthwhile experience. Laughter among best wishes for us and the warning to be careful without our well-versed guide. Aware of leaving an upscale area, we are soon reminded that customs and behavioral codes tend to change within a couple of blocks in American cities. About to take a picture of a vintage house, I am stopped by a voice, "Watch your camera, mister, just watch it." And a few minutes later, trying to take a picture of Duke Ellington's *Apollo Theater* being rebuilt, another soft warning, "Some of de brothers wouldn´t like dat." On the way home, we are focusing our attention on the advertising culture in subways. "Attend the worship of your choice." Doubting my positive interpretation, Artak thinks that the vast majority probably couldn't care less anyway and if they did, they wouldn't need this reminder. A funnier ad, "Torn ear lobe? Also nose and breast surgery. Call our 800-number!"

Spending a long afternoon in Williamsburg takes my friend back to the Russia of his childhood. Any number of young mothers with head scarves, chatting or pushing their baby carriages, an even larger number of men clad in black, gesturing and discussing religious issues, Artak is certain. Neither of us has ever seen more Hebrew writing. Suspicious eyes on us, I am trying to take pictures of children in black uniforms getting off their yellow school bus. Ordering bagels, I am surprised my friend has never heard the word but when he sees them, goes "*Ah, bubliki!*" *Kike* is sprayed on a wall, telling us that not everyone is of the same opinion here.

After a moving farewell from Alice and her cozy little skyscraper den we are off to Boston, leaving from the impressive art deco Penn Station. Here they are, Mark and Lois D with whom Artak can speak German! Tasty *Sam Adams* beer of a small regional brewery, another example of America becoming more European. Playing Prokofiev for us on the piano, Mark is so bewildered by Artak's Russian pronunciation of the name that he doesn't even recognize it as the composer´s. Having converted to Judaism for his wife's sake on condition she let him savor pork *Schnitzels* during his annual jaunts to Vienna, he teaches at *Tufts University*, where a sizable segment of the faculty and students are Jewish. My other friend Tom S, a specialist on the Near East, just left the same university for this very reason. I`ve got to keep out of these heated debates during the few days we are enjoying with them. A ritual between us by now, Artak and I are clashing right hands to "Gimme five!"

To be on the safe side for her guests, Lois warns us not to strip in the sauna, a cultural novelty for Artak. Remembering how years ago I was almost arrested by *Tufts* campus police for sweating naked by myself when a coed entered and started screaming, we are promising to behave. The sign on the fake flickering flames, "These coals are for decorative purposes. Do not put water on them." In the campus cafeteria we are in for yet another little intercultural treat when a lady psychologist, an immigrant from Novosibirsk, bitterly complains to Artak about American customs. "But you doon't goo to a restaurant to eeat just a saandvich!" Oh, yes, we do! While her boss is explaining the recent financial crunch on campus to me, Artak relaxes—does he?—talking Russian to her. "There is no research without money and so even the dean greets me first. As the head of the psychology department, I can get sizable amounts from Washington, which my colleagues cannot, and your theater friend couldn't either."

The Red Line to Harvard, where I want Artak to see and breathe the air of these hallowed halls. "Please shoot a few closeups of me in front of *John Harvard!"* Proudly showing him around the premises, I am giving in to a bit of a sentimental journey imagining how wonderful another student life might be. Pondering other imaginary choices with my friend, I am reminded of Hemingway's verdict, "The wisdom of life consists of believing that whatever IS is the optimal." Artak doubtful, "If so, why did he shoot himself?" Around the corner from Harvard Square, the club where I heard *Joan Baez* years before she made it big. Joining Jed and Perry again, we are walking past the monument dedicated to the only black regiment fighting for the Union in the Civil War. Then over real cobblestones—"Herb, you have those in Vienna too?—Now we are on *Beacon Hill*, where "the Lowells talk only to the Cabots, and the Cabots talk only to God."—"Yes, Artak, we have also had our aristocracy, even here in the cradle of American democracy."

Spotting the huge *Gateway Arch* of St. Louis from the plane, we are intoning the St. Louis Blues over two stiff G&Ts. This is the point, I tell Artak, from where Lewis and Clark began the first crossing of the continent in 1803, which does not seem to arouse his curiosity as much as the—sociologically more interesting discovery of the clever all-American men's toilets. Not reaching all the way to the floor, the doors tell you instantly where to turn in times of need because you either spot two feet per stall or you do not. For many years we have had these funny debates with our students in Vienna because they knock at the locked door, as if to tell you to hurry up. Their usual explanation is that the door may not be locked, but only closed. Looking at this domestic traffic problem from their viewpoint, they are used to leaving the door open so that the next customer knows.

The reunion with Anne is full of compliments and questions like whether I am married yet. "You haven't changed much, have I?" Working hard at med school, she does not appear to regret having returned from Vienna, where finishing her M.D. would not have been accepted in the States. The last day of the Chicago Jazz Festival means great music, especially from a group of playing jazz from *Kid Ory* times. The giant tuba going from deep to deeper is the anchor of the combo, their *joie-de-vivre* contagious. "The difference between the best of old Vienna and old New Orleans is only that between a 3/4 and a 4/4 beat." Anne thinks America and Europe were more alike when she was in my class thirty years ago, whereas I think they have become much more similar, except that the U.S. is much less of a white society now. It turns out she means that in the wake of the feminist revolution, the US has pulled ahead of the Old World. Smiles and agreement and yet another farewell. *Emily D* fans both of us makes us quote that haunting line at the same split second, "Parting is all we know of heaven, and all we need of hell."

Right by Lake Michigan the spectacular cloverleaf of *Mies van der Rohe.* Getting to know Chicago by boat, the birthplace of the idea of scraping the skies, we are cruising through the condensed dynamics of skyscrapers, locks, and bridges. Historically first, the sugar icing *Wrigley Building and* the *Marina Towers* nicknamed corn cobs for their nibbled-at shape. For a change, everything here is as new to me as to my friend. Poet *Carl Sandburg* talked about "The Giant Shoulders of Chicago" and "Prayer of Steel," a eulogy bursting with energy and celebrating America's glorious future as a foregone conclusion at a time when people could still believe in endless technical progress. *"Lay me on an anvil, O God. Beat me and hammer me into a steel pike. Drive me into the girders that hold a skyscraper together. Take red-hot rivets and fasten me into the central girders. Let me be the great nail holding a skyscraper through blue nights into white stars."* Tough though it is to convey the power of his poetry in translation, I notice Artak wincing under its punch. The *Sears Tower,* the highest in the world at 438 m, its structure resembling cigarette boxes of vertical parallel tubes lifted to level-above-level in a tapered arrangement. From the top, the white dots of dozens of sailboats behind the magic towers and the clincher, the roof of a prison with inmates playing ball under a net, a precaution since a helicopter heaved a few ball-playing gangsters to freedom. A smile of satisfaction on his face, Artak returns from a spot that gave him the unique chance to—four-letter word—on the world.

On the plane to Paris, I am reminded how fascinated I once was reading *de Tocqueville's* "Democracy in America" and am making sure my friend will tackle it in Russian or German. Full of incredibly far-sighted impressions collected while traveling across the continent a century and a half ago, the perceptive count came up with amazing parallels between America and—Russia. Exchanging *gimme fives,* we are celebrating the unique trip. My fourteenth to the U. S. of A. but my first by boat, my first to Chicago, and my first with a wide awake artist friend.

RETURN TO NEW ENGLAND WITH MARIANNE. OUR FIRST AND ONLY WEDDING IN HER NECK OF THE WOODS. OUR PRIVATE VIENNESE THANKSGIVING.

I had never quite given up on the idea of going through two absolute contrasts within the shortest time possible, and this time my mood and the weather would combine to tackle the first leg of this experiment. Hiking along the meandering Thaya in four hours of absolute tranquility except for the occasional yelling of hawks, the rushing of water over little weirs, and my own breathing and slipping, I am trying against my better senses to catch, store, and pile up this pristine green paradise fully aware that in less than twenty-four hours I might want to release a fraction of this precious peace to combat the shrillness of Manhattan. I am not telling Marianne until we are on the plane *en route* to sealing her liaison with the New World. It has been heart-warming to watch my American students digging into the country-style dumplings embedded in venison from Marianne's neck of the woods, while those with a sweet tooth preferred to wait for her frugal walnut and poppyseed chocolate cake. What fun for us all to listen to her explain the recipes in English, cooking terms constituting a science all by itself.

Revisiting some of the sights in Manhattan will be a bit of a homecoming to her, though walking across *Brooklyn Bridge* is just as exciting as seven years ago, as is riding the *Staten Island Ferry* with the red sun smudged by haze going down behind the skyscrapers. Insisting that we stop in Amherst, where Emily Dickinson was born and is buried, I am not quite sure whether

her poetry could mean quite that much to her. "*Apparently with no surprise / To any happy Flower / The Frost beheads it at it's play—In accidental power—The blond Assassin passes on—The Sun proceeds unmoved / To measure off another Day / For an Approving God.*"—Accepting the invitation of a couple from UNH days, we find them the personifications of the proverbial American spirit of helping within the community. Dividing his spare time between driving an ambulance and waiting for a call from the fire brigade, he enjoys volunteering as does Sharon giving first-aid courses and swimming lessons. An all-time first for us, they are showing us their outdoor pool equipped with a countercurrent arrangement for doing the crawl stroke on the spot. Only in America! Exchanging endless anecdotes about brilliant minds and borderline cases on campus in our days, we agree that we are perhaps not quite so positive as we once were that "the other side across the fence is always greener." What has brought on this gradual and possibly more realistic view of our America?

Not all that long ago and far from New England, one of the unrests triggered by black traffic violations and white cops overreacting had escalated to the point of laying waste to an entire section of Los Angeles. It was neither the first riot nor will it be the last one that made the nation shudder at pictures resembling outright war. While most students in this casual gathering now agree that the real reason for these recurring tragedies are lack of education leading to unemployment and eventually poverty, a woman in the group is asking me how I see this national cancer as someone "from Germany of all places, who spent two years in the South." When a few in the group are suggesting that America might also be headed toward concentration camps, if not by an increasingly reactionary governmental system, then certainly by putting off overdue indispensable legislation, my reply is that these fears are understandable but vastly exaggerated. "The murder of millions in Germany had been brought about by centuries of anti-Semitism in a population without any successful democratic background. The biggest difference, it was engineered by Hitler and his consorts, the *d'evil* himself, literally meaning *he of evil* for anyone here turned on by the origin of words." It is seemingly hard for this group to understand that while all these problems were just as topical during my student years in the late fifties, they just did not play the same overriding role before the murderous mid-sixties and Vietnam, fire accelerants both. The session dissolves with the majority acknowledging that a lot of progress has been made on many fronts but also that, not strangely but logically enough, this very progress is making present-day demands even more urgent and their supporters more aggressive. Small wonder that my African American music professor friend—yes, there are half a dozen blacks teaching at UNH by now!—keeps pleading with his son not to destroy the hard-won accomplishments of several generations by preaching this dangerous war whoop of *Paradise NOW!*

Back in Vienna after yet another fabulous Indian summer, a term I am told may be offensive to Native Americans nowadays and certainly to its PC propagators, we realize that Thanksgiving is not all that far away again. This time we are going to celebrate our own, inviting a few close friends and at least one American. Unbelievable, but we just cannot find a whole turkey in all of Vienna. Puzzled why anybody would prefer a big bird to neatly cut slices, several poulterers scoff at yet another American custom "as if that silly Halloween wasn't enough," while others admit that they have had orders for a whole *Indian,* the word still used by old folks in German. After some scouting around, Marianne finds a bird about a third of the size we would need for ten guests. No problem, we'll just get two of them, stuff them with dumplings, dates, apple preserves and then keep roasting them for—how long exactly? Sweet potatoes, not just spuds with sugar sprinkled on them, are equally hard to find, but concocting succotash is easy, its colorful mix of corn, peas, and carrots as appealing as its exotic name. Most of our guests have of course seen king-size turkeys being pardoned by Presidents over the years and have a rough understanding of this holy day in American history. The immediate reason for our own private celebration is copies I made of a document of the first Thanksgiving in 1621 I discovered in the library. Fascinating its quaint language that even our native might have trouble with! Varying the menu of the original diary just a bit, Marianne will help the original frugal pumpkin pie on its feet by crowning it with dollops of whipped cream. That celebrating a Puritan holy day in a Catholic environment calls for red wine instead of the see-through cranberry juice will meet little resistance. At ease around a candle-lit table, we will soon be ready to plow through the historical pages of English arrivals and survivals. Celebrating the fourth Thursdays at our home has become customary over the Novembers, as has getting hold of a whole turkey. Only novices interested enough to celebrate with us have become harder to come by with each news of yet another American foreign policy flop.

Not surprisingly, celebrating the civil portion of our wedding at Peter's downtown hotel turned out to be a party of married couples with their children, a few balding die-hard bachelors and one spinster dear to our hearts. New among my friends over the years was Otto M, who had literally saved my life by isolating the fungus in my lung that I had caught—no, not on my trip to the Ecuadorian jungle, as I had guessed—but from pigeons in our backyard. Already pretty sure of my specific problem, he had asked me to translate a lecture he was about to present. Working my way through the four pages, I began to realize, a bit more each paragraph, that what I was translating was the course of *cryptococcus neoformans* traveling from the lung to disintegrating the central nervous system, *my* nervous system. A loyal friend by now, he popped up at our church wedding three weeks later in an old Gothic church in Marianne's home region, her brother playing a trumpet solo of *Amazing Grace* now that his sister was marrying this America freak. My priest friend Helmut married us, writing the essence of the Old Testament lines of *Kohelet* on his wedding gift, "All is a rush with the wind." Always a fervent believer, he had no problem seeing it all from a much higher perspective. My brother-in-law's speech took the cake, weaving my past close calls into a Greek philosopher's parable. "Asked why he had not married yet, he kept insisting that he was too young until, having crossed a magic line one day, he decided that now he was too old." I had just barely made it.

Tiny Bärnkopf at 3,000 feet could never match the impact that Hardegg still had on my soul. Withdrawing into the larch wood attic with dormers overlooking the stable and pasture for six horses was easy to get used to. So were two Irish tinkers, two palominos, three Noric Austrian draft horses known for their surefootedness and perfect for sleigh rides. During this year's horseback riding festival, they were accompanied by several quarter horses, buggies, and chariots. Interested in my brother-in-law's curiosity about America and his annual horse show featuring races and equine stunts, I brought him a dozen original black and white photos of historical cowboy scenes I had inherited from the US Information Service. Neatly pinned to the boards of his log cabin, they sometimes arouse the curiosity of local rangers, their tall tales getting taller by the pint retrieved from under the floorboards. How amazed they are when I tell them that I had never been to a rodeo, never been to Laredo or Cheyenne, names they recognize from the movies, that I can't even saddle a horse, let alone ride one. Laughing out loud or worrying about my wellbeing, one of them will inevitably ask, "Then, what did you do over there all that time?"—"Oh, learning their language well, studying their literature, their history, just the way they work and play and live and act and eat and think and drink." A lot of headshaking but also congratulations that I married a villager of theirs and could now enjoy my peace and quiet here and not worry about faraway folks and their problems. During a country music festival in the nearby woods one day, a tall American with a deep voice offered me the unexpected opportunity to unravel the secret behind my friend Tennys' memorable introduction in Missouri years ago. "I want you to meet the man who put a knife through Johnny Cash's cheek" he had made us shake hands, leaving me hovering between awkward smiles and the dubious honor of having met a Western outlaw. "No rough stuff at all" the deep voice solved my riddle now, laughing. "I don't know John too well, but I do remember that he had to undergo an operation of his jaw. Your friend must have introduced you to his surgeon!" Western lore deconstructed in the Austrian woods.

UNUSUAL ASSIGNMENTS: TEACHING AMERICAN POETRY TO UKRAINIAN STUDENTS.—TEACHING AMERICAN ENGLISH AT THE IRANIAN EMBASSY IN VIENNA.

It was really Adriana's doing that I could realize my project to teach something America-related in a country interesting enough to visit and to an audience interested enough to accept the idea. A medical student, she had been learning German at the lakeside summer school of the University of Vienna, where we were eager to learn first-hand about her home Galicia. If one could still find remnants of our Austrian imperial past, it was in and around *Lemberg*, now *Lviv*, in Ukraine. Adriana's return home to finish her M.D. and start working as an internal specialist did not sever our friendship, in fact it encouraged me to ponder how I might take advantage of her contacts to realize my idea, not matured beyond a pipe dream yet. She must have done a convincing job backing my project because there were enough English-language natives around to jump at the opportunity. Realizing that teaching even short fiction was not a good idea, considering we had all of five long afternoons, I chose *Emily Dickinson* and *Robert Frost*. Nothing terribly experimental or contemporary, but these students were going for a degree in translation and interpretation, not literature. Surprised by the high level of their English, I was told the course was on a voluntary basis and drew students interested in topics other than their usual. As one of them put it, "Don't worry about questions we have or mistakes we make, all of us are so glad to do something useless like poetry instead of the something economic or technical." Beginning with the most popular poem of them all, one all human beings can easily identify with, I was asking someone to read *The Road Not Taken* out loud. Wonderful, no accent, except an American one, and that's what we needed! "What is *trodden black*?" A reasonable question. "You know *tread, treading* from the tire on your car? Its past participle." Nods, relief. One more minor question, though one attesting to their high level. "Wouldn't it be more American to say *I doubted if I would ever come back*, instead of *should*?"—"I agree with you but *should* here is not exclusively English. Remember we are in New England, and perhaps also because most of Frost's poetry was published in England, where he lived long before he became a household name in the States." Many wanted to hear it read out loud again. "Great, maybe you want to let two or three seconds go by before you read the last stanza, which will make it even easier for you to identify with the poem." Why I liked this poem so much, a student wanted to know, and I told her it was because I spent much of my own life trying to decide which road to take. And I had to do that without knowing I would land here in Ukraine. Smiles, commiserating looks. "Yes, you are right, the old *Robert Frost* read *The Gift Outright*, a much harder and longer poem, at Kennedy's inauguration. I only know the last two lines by heart, '*A golden age of poetry and power / Of which this noonday's the beginning hour.*' As you all know, the shots in Dallas ended those dreams." The next poems were a bit more difficult, but maybe good enough to invite more than one possible interpretation. *Stopping by Woods on a Snowy Evening* seemed to capture them for the simple reason that they could identify with all the winter words that were as much part of life in Galicia as they were in New England. Two groups formed, one asserting that there must be reason for the horse to stop, the other downplaying it as irrelevant. "What about the promises to keep and the miles to go, they can't be irrelevant." The somber mood pervading the poem led a few to bring up the possibility of the horseman approaching death but trying to stop. Maybe to snap out of the overly philosophical mood building up, a fellow wanted to know whether it was true that the word *queer* in its original nonsexual meaning could not be used in America anymore. Trying to evade a discussion about politically correct language, which was beginning to be a subject here as well, I advised them to use *gay,* nowadays used in all European languages. "Not that *gay* is always the appropriate word. We certainly cannot refer to the good old days of waltzing Vienna as *Gay Old Vienna* anymore." Having a heyday with my own favorite poems, we were tackling an easier one to show them that *Frost* was not only a pleasant character but could certainly conjure up sarcasm in *Fire and Ice.* "No semantic questions here, let's have somebody read it who is furious enough about something or somebody to wish the world to hell!" Giggles. "I can see some of you thinking in Ukrainian again! Thank you, I have had a wonderful four hours with this enthusiastic group." Lingering to hear me explain what WASP really means and whether I believed a black candidate would ever become President, two students were busy finding a suitable Ukrainian equivalent for this acronym. A black president? Possible, but unlikely for some time.

Trying to find ever new angles to teaching old *Austrian History* to my American students, Marianne and I spent the mornings and evenings strolling past buildings that could have been in Vienna, Prague, Budapest, or Cracow and deciphering names and dates on stone slabs of the largest Jewish medieval burial ground in Europe, its tombs and domes shrouded in October mist. Indelible her father's descriptions of the horrors committed by the Leninists in the twenties, then the Polish fascists, then the Nazis, then three million by the Soviets again in the early thirties during the *Holodomor,* Ukrainian for "decreed death by starvation." On her forthcoming trip to Vienna to attend a medical symposium, Adriana would talk on all these ethnic, linguistic, historical, and political issues to my American students proud to have met someone from the once easternmost Habsburg province.

Much to my surprise, *Emily Dickinson* received the same warm welcome that *Robert Frost* had. Introducing her as somebody whose geographically and socially limited life had turned her into a bit of a hermit, I made sure they understood that her renaissance in the U.S. was partly part of a general tendency to finally do justice to women's achievements. Asked whether she wrote religious poems, I told the assembled future translators that they should decide after the first two samples. "*Apparently with no surprise / to any happy flower / The frost beheads it at it's play in accidental power. / The blond assassin marches on, / the sun proceeds unmoved / To measure off another day / For an approving God."* The majority agreed that this was not religious at all, one of them adding "*blond assassin* is what we learned the Nazis were!" Not used to thinking in poetic language, some took a while to comprehend *accidental power* and *approving God,* one asking *how a flower* could be *surprised.* "She is cynical, not religious!"—"Are you saying a religious person can never be cynical?" Now I got them going, so here was an altogether different poem. *"I never saw a Moor / I never saw the Sea / Yet know I how the Heather looks / And what a Billow be. / I never spoke with God / Nor visited in Heaven / Yet certain am I of the spot / As if the Charts were given."* Explaining *moor, heather, billow,* and *charts,* I was waiting for the obvious, namely that now Emily would come across as a believer. Only three skeptics doubted whether the charts she used were reliable. Before reverting to Frost the following afternoon, I left them with this thought by Emily, as they noticed I fondly referred to her: "*The sailor cannot see the North but knows the needle can.*" Familiar with trendy lingo, a comment of "*cool, man!*" Having spent a few more hours on topical *Americana*, I left them wondering how they would survive as translators into or from English and hoping that every so often they might think back of the redeeming quality of some of America's best.

Asking whether I would like to teach English at the Iranian embassy, the boss of the *Austro-American Institute of Education* was relieved when I decided to accept. The Iranian embassy had approached him about an elementary course, expressly demanding American English. This would be hard-earned money, I figured, but I agreed for political or cultural reasons. After an interview with the deputy director in flawless American English, which he said he had learned outside America, I began a most unusual interlude in my English teaching life. Seated around an oval table with pitchers of orange juice and cloyingly sweet cookies were five students, all except for one looking businesslike, subdued, possibly a bit nervous. Nobody wore a tie, but how conscious they were of their dress code came out right away when one of them pointed at my bare neck. Deciding on the spur of the moment to tell them the truth, I answered that I simply felt more comfortable without being constricted. The one member of an ethnic minority with a macabre sense of humor showed me his wooden leg when we were alone for a few minutes. "From Saddam Hussein and America. Not good." Unfortunately, he had his facts right. Even if he could have agreed that most of this bloody war was the result of the age-old *Sunni* vs. *Shia* battle, he would probably never have admitted it. "Don't speak Farsi, please" or with a touch of humor, "We all know that your Farsi is perfect" were requests they quickly understood and abided by. Simple questions and even simpler answers had to be our common goal during two double sessions per week, but they were eager to express their ideas in vague approximations of English. Part of my role, as I saw it, was to represent American customs, methods, ways of thinking. Not quite sure whether he himself was wrong, the most severe looking pupil once motioned me into a corner, "You American, you Austrian?" Gesturing all along to make him understand, I said, "The Austrian child spoke German, the Austrian man learned English at school, then got a passport to study in America for five years. He loves both countries." Smiling and signaling *two* the American way by raising index and middle fingers, I went through the motions of cutting myself in half. "Two halves, two identities." Did he really understand? A few cartoons broke the ice, even made them smile, but I never forgot two reactions to *Peanuts.* While they all understood that Charlie Brown was a likeable type, two disgusted faces left no doubt they thought that a real American had to be the opposite of likeable Charlie. Certainly, a signal for me who occasionally brought in snippets of political paragraphs. Once I risked copying portions of an article celebrating the moderate political language of *Khatami,* who had just been elected President. The text was much too hard for them, but the positive bright face of *Khatami's* photo was a good omen. Full of completely novel ideas like working for peace with the West and especially the U.S. while pursuing the interests of the Islamic Republic, the vocabulary they comprehended was rather limited, making us proceed by touch and go. After all, I was teaching in the same building where only six years ago three hit men had received refuge after killing a prominent Kurdish politician in Vienna. Worried about serious consequences or yielding to Iranian threats, the Austrian government had let them fly home to Tehran. My first indispensable visit to the bathroom was a culturally challenging experience. The employee in a black *hijab* who showed me the way was too self-conscious to even look at me and had no way of knowing how jittery I really was only seconds before I might have to tackle the bewildering Iranian system. Once left to myself I realized that the embassy had adjusted to the European toilet seat, and I would not foresee any problem with the hose dangling from my left. *Allahu akbar*, how would I have managed squatting over a floor level pan? Requiring just as much patience as teaching some of my university courses, these sessions were usually full of unexpected verbal, grammatical, cultural, or political surprises. When a second term was turned down for financial reasons, I was toying with the idea of going on for just the experience of it. I was warned by my less naïve colleagues not to do that. Neither would their pride permit it, nor would they understand why a Western professor would volunteer to work without remuneration.

TO RUSSIA WITH ARTAK. BETWEEN HISTORIC MONSTERS, MYSTICAL CHURCHES, POLITICAL REALITIES, AND A SAUNA WITH VODKA.—*AMERICA: THE NEW WORLD IN PICTURES OF THE NINETEENTH CENTURY* IN VIENNA.

Always interested in each other's cultural exploits, my friend Artak had suggested I join him for a week in Russia and to attend his production of Strindberg's play "The Father." Remembering that this was my first time in Moscow, he suddenly pointed to a monument halfway into town, "This is how far the Germans got." Barely time enough to spend a few minutes on this subject, he pointed to a long canal, "And this long canal was built by political prisoners in Tsarist times." Two short introductory remarks on Russian history. Suddenly, he gave me a hard time about my jacket for the play tonight, "You can't show up like this, you are not a student anymore!" Come on! He, the quintessential *bohemian*, insisting I dress appropriately. Was I imagining this, or was I noticing my friend reverting to his "Russian soul," a slight difference in his German with me already, and now this? He had already commented during our trip to the U.S. that "you are not a typical Viennese anymore over here." Maybe there is something to the idea of our hearts and minds ticking to a different rhythm under new conditions elsewhere? Arriving at the small theater I felt like transplanted into the nineteen fifties, the subdued atmosphere of anticipation, visitors in their slightly old-fashioned Sunday's best, the packed hall in stifling heat, an American in short sleeves next to me revealing the information that he had directed this play in Boston.

On our morning walk the exciting view of the big golden dome of the cathedral that Jelzin had erected where the original had been torn down. Strange to see dozens of smokestacks resembling the black and white shots in *Russian* revolutionary films, a reminder of Lenin's famous definition "Communism = Leninism + electricity." Learning more Cyrillic letters by the hour, which did not necessarily yield sensible sentences, I recognized Marshal Zhukov on horseback killing the Nazi dragon. A lingering impression was an orthodox mass with a choir intoning chants in ever new variations, the mysterious depth toward the wall of icons between the nave and the sanctuary, now and then a pope stepping out toward the crowd. Half Armenian, Artak was as overwhelmed as I was. Outside, a group of Communists waving the old red flag and demonstrating "Against those in power now. Return to the Soviet Union!" Carrying portraits of Stalin without the power and the glory now, they were remembering their glorious time in the youth movement. That *krasni* means both red and beautiful was not a surprise seeing the Red Square, Saint Basil's different-colored onion shaped towers and the Lenin Museum below the endless red brick pinnacles of the Kremlin. From up here the members of the *Politburo* used to salute the goose-stepping formations hauling their state-of-the-art weaponry on the annual anniversary of the victorious *Great Patriotic War.* Paradoxically, like a giant Disneyworld, though one begun in the twelfth century, the gold-edged red, blue, and green onion-shaped domes glinting in the icy winter sunlight made for a semblance of magic realism. The dark mystical interior of the Archangel's Church was swallowing us up, dozens of believers pushing toward the icon-studded wall beyond which the congregation was not allowed. Swaying their votive candles, they granted us a look up the walls to the domed ceiling full of medieval icons facing us, the Supreme Creator in the middle. Flickering flames, praying from full pews with choral singing around us, and my friend hands me a yellow wax candle. Fascinated though we both are, we are modern Europeans, right? "Of course, but look at it this way just for a second: how much have we really gained for what we have lost?"

Today, an excursion through the empty corridors of the enormous GUM shopping center, a nineteenth-century steel structure resembling the Eiffel Tower. All these evidently out-of-place logos of *Gucci, Versace, Prada, Calvin Klein* and the like, with only a handful of people around, some with genuine furs slung around their shoulders and the many bored faces of the shop attendants. That used to be different under the more people-oriented Communists, as this joke suggests. *Hundreds of people are lined up and patiently waiting because the word is out that today a shipment of black shoes has come in. After a while, an official comes, asking 'Who is Jewish?' About a third of the hands goes up, "Nothing for you today." Frustrated, they are leaving, the rest keeps waiting. After another while, the same fellow asks, "All Georgians and Armenians, please go home, nothing for you to buy today either!" Grumbling in the crowd, but this group is leaving as well. Those left are still hopeful until the third announcement comes, "Everybody go home, the shipment never came in." Whereupon one of the last disappointed customers cracks, "What really gets me most is that the Jews always come first!"* We talked so much about Austrian anti-Semitism, so my American students should really catch on to this one in a Russian setting.

Having promised his son to bring back a couple of paper place mats from the first Moscow *Macdonald's* that opened only a few weeks ago, Artak talked me into standing in line. No problem, but behind about two dozen teenagers the going looked awfully slow and so my friend suddenly jumped the long noisy line, ran up to the counter but came back right away, laughing out loud. Still out of breath, he said that the girl, neatly uniformed exactly like in the States, had yelled at him in Russian for everybody to hear, "Get back in line, this is not a Russian restaurant, this is an American restaurant, where we stand in line!" The teenagers lined up were learning, and so were we.

Oblomov is the ultimate superfluous character from a nineteenth-century novel, symbol to this day of excessive laziness. Disappointed that the collection of Russian modern painters at the *Tretyakov Gallery* was closed, I returned to the hotel to soothe my anger by taking a bath in a tin tub resembling my grandmother's. Not that I minded the antiquated looks of it, but the fact that the plastic plug, unhinged from its original chain long ago, did not fit the outlet irked me. No way of pressing or pushing it helped, and I quickly dismissed the idea of sharpening it with my jackknife like I once sharpened my pencils at school. Enjoying the hot water slowly emptying itself around my heel playing plug, I now knew that Oblomov was certainly still alive and even kicking.

Flying off to St. Petersburg with Sasha, a Russian sociologist working with Rudi in a Viennese opinion poll institute, included meeting his old parents again. Reading *Yugoslavia and Chechnya* next to me, he shook his head muttering "America with its double standards." Immediately needled by such verdicts, I kept myself from replying. Passengers all around us, no language we spoke well enough for a meaningful discussion referring to an article I had not even read. Calm down, Viennese champion of the New World! Changing the subject, he asked whether there was anti-

Semitism in the States. There certainly was, I replied, our racist nuts in Austria were even receiving propaganda material from neo-Nazi headquarters. There used to be clubs forbidding Jews, blacks, Chinese, and other minority groups to become members, though nowadays this was pretty much impossible. Certainly, ethnic jokes were frowned upon nowadays, at least among the halfway educated.—Great to see his parents again, his old father a retired Antarctic explorer and his wife a convinced Commie of the old school. Their son, running the Russian subsidiary of the Viennese opinion poll institute, had often been to Vienna and given lectures to my American students. Interesting, the post-Communist son of fervently Communist parents, educated according to American and German standards by empirical, utterly un-ideological methods. In a moving tour of the imperial St. Petersburg, a city so different from the organically grown old and shabby Moscow, his father described the year and a half of the German siege of Leningrad with people starving or freezing to death by the tens of thousands. A wise man, cleansed of too much ideology by serious bouts with cancer and old age, he listened to the story of my own father. Suddenly motioning me to quit, he embraced me with words of *mir i drushba, peace and friendship*. Would I like to see the prison cells where Gorki and many other Communists were kept by the Tsarist police, many of them later executed by their Communist rivals? Of course, almost all of them the same appearance, goatees framed by intellectual faces, round metal-rimmed glasses. Some of our European leftist eggheads looked just like them, class consciousness united across decades and boundaries. At the Hermitage, a painting of Ivan the Terrible staring at his son whom he just murdered. Back in the hotel, I was watching the Russian version of *Mississippi Burning*, the name spelled funny and distorted but correctly, as I could tell by the four Cyrillic *i's*, four *s's*, and two *p's*. For the umpteenth time, this time from Russia: where can the average American see Russian films depicting their own national disasters?

Back in Moscow, we were exploring the legendary subway system, some stops with appealing art deco designs and marble walls dating back to the thirties, others in the style of socialist realism with workers hammering, mothers breastfeeding, girls harvesting, and red army guards on alert. Conceived as a giant air-raid shelter for the population, it also used to harbor Stalin´s personal train at the ready down below. The only passengers talking on the subway otherwise shrouded in typical silence, we looked like the foreigners we were.

Confronted with more Russian words than previously, I was headed for Lenin and his consorts on Red Square all by myself. Approaching him without my camera, I heard the guard proclaiming "Lenin is free!" before he gave me a thorough check. Descending toward Uljanov, the real name of "the one from the Lena River," I was yelled at to doff my hat. A uniformed guard in each corner, the next one below the one before and so on down to the Holy Grail. Darting back and forth in my memory between the descent to Dimitroff's corpse in Sofia with my students a few decades ago and the pilgrimage here, Dimitroff's quasi-religious shrine won hands down in eeriness. Shrouded in semidarkness, he made Lenin bedded in bright lights appear like a figure in Madame Tussaud's London wax museum. Walking slowly to absorb the tasteful marble walls with their center stripes of stylized red flags, I was brusquely told to move on. Warm-hearted and cordial though the people I met certainly were, the century-old abyss between *above* and *below* or *uniforms* and *civilians* was noticeable at every step.

Walking along the Kremlin wall in the company of a couple of stocky farmers, their ruddy faces on round heads, was a special treat. Slightly elevated in alphabetical order here they lay, demigods fallen to mortality. Kamenev, hero of the early years, murdered by Stalin, next to a documentary photo of his funeral with his killer carrying the casket. The urn with Gorki's ashes next to that of Kirov, whose murder started the Great Purge in 1935. Podgorny and Kosygin, the last duo before Brezhnev. Andropov, KGB boss and "liberator" of Budapest in 1956. Stepping on two stones to get closer to the plaques, I was immediately called back. What for Lenin's sake did this guard believe I might be plotting? The climax beating Lenin by far, Dzerzhinskij, the Polish aristocrat and founder of the *Cheka*, Lenin's secret police, his ecstatic intellectual face resembling that of an enraptured religious martyr. Able to decipher their names only letter by letter gave me the shivers: Shdanov, the intellectual armchair killer, then Beria, a far more hands-on butcher. Next to him, his bushy moustache well chiseled, Dzhugashvili, nicknamed Stalin, "the steely one." Was I just imagining the spirit of Ivan the Terrible hovering above?

On a long last stroll, we were walking past the brightly lit *Metropol Hotel*, fully aware of its miraculous rise from a refuge for Communists escaping Hitler to a temple of luxury. Not that making it to the *Metropol* meant safety for those comrades accused of "nationalist deviation" or some trumped up charge. Transferred to the torture cellars of the notorious *Lubljanka* across the street, many were the victims of Stalin's paranoia.

It would not have been a real trip to Russia without a sauna in the country. After about an hour of driving east from Moscow, the first old blue, yellow, and grey painted wooden houses of the village where Sasha had his *dasha*. Extensive birch woods conjuring up memories of New Hampshire, I was telling him more about my dual identity, which I could not really expect him to comprehend. Below-zero temperature made it possible for us to arrive at our destination at all. "Gerbert, ven temperature go up, here only mud. You cannot move. Sis is how ve won the var against Gitler." No hard feelings, we agreed on most things except his view of the US. Helping me to throw logs into the fire to the amazement of his sweating neighbor above us who, showing me his tattooed arms and pointing to my spindly and unembellished arms let me know in translation that "Russian woodsman and German city boy, no problem. Vodka on the coals, ha, ha." Whole-souled comradery with herring, cucumbers, slices of pork, lots of beer.—Noticing the gate of the church wide open in the morning, I was about to enter when Sasha caught me, explaining that the main door was dedicated to those for whom prayers would be said today. Much smaller and poorer than the churches in Moscow but still radiating that unmistakable mystical aura, religious or just custom, Sasha suddenly handed me a flickering yellow candle. Strange, but country faces and Russian sounds all around in this poor village suddenly brought back childhood memories of the soldiers straying and bellowing through Hardegg. Between farewell hugs, Sasha's last message was, "Tell dem in Vienna office dat nobody saw bit of real Russia like you."

What remained of this week in another country? Fascinating, but hopeless and probably never part of a distant United Europe. My Russian-Armenian expat friend agreed, adding that he was really looking forward to his Vienna. "Gimme five, brother!"

The exhibit did not only promise to show originals we had never seen in Vienna, but also held out a promise for me, the promise to discover new aspects of the "real America" or at least the rough pictorial equivalents of the American literature I had studied for years. In my mind, James M. Whistler or Winslow Homer could hold their own because they belonged to a common Anglo-Saxon heritage. On the other hand, Mary Cassatt and Childe Hassam were so Impressionist that I, complete amateur, could easily throw them in with the French contemporaries. Interested as always in uncovering the forces once pushing toward developing a distinctly American identity, I set out looking for answers as if they could be obtained for the mere looking within a few hours. The wilderness as the source of American identity used to be a recurring theme in my literature courses, a topic I felt I needed to understand better to escape unscathed these enervating debates about culturally impoverished America. "The Myth of the West," including the unique G. Catlin collection, the last documents of native American life left to posterity. The pictures of the *Ashcan School* dwelling on the roughness of big city life were certainly American enough, whereas G. W. Bellows' brutal boxing scene reminded me of the postcard I had once sent to Peter and which was now pinned over his locker. Full of new impressions from this eye-opening show, I came back for more with a few students open to my debatable influence. How the dazzling red umbrella with just "America" printed across it and sold at the museum shop was supposed to reflect this magnificent exhibit was not clear to us but still interesting enough to talk about. What could it possibly convey to unprepared viewers? It took even me some courage to parade this forceful red around rainy Vienna a few times, but I have not had the courage since. Too splashy, too loud, to kitschy, too American?

Millenarian thinking, whether religious or this-worldly, had always exerted a certain fascination, so what should be more logical than to give some thought to a potential catastrophe ushering in the third millennium? Here we were in *2000* without any immediate danger in sight, except the increasing feeling that the widening gap between the global north and south would sooner or later cause real problems, maybe even sooner than *climate change*, the latest buzzword. With only two more years of teaching English until retirement and my American students continuing to come, my world was not about to be shattered. Not yet.

ICELAND. TURQUOIS GEYSERS BETWEEN REDDISH ROCK, YELLOW SULFUR, AND BLACK LAVA.

2001 Is it really a land full of ice halfway between Europe and America as the English map suggests, or is it just an *Island* spelled like this and easy to confuse with Ireland for the similarity in spelling, size, and northwestern location? Should anybody have problems keeping Iceland apart from Ireland, both islands out in the Atlantic haunted by ghosts and ghouls, here are two sure-fire ways. While the Irish are well known for their "gift of the gab" that includes storytelling, reciting poems, and singing, Icelanders keep pretty much to themselves, are not known for wasting words, or throwing shindigs. While in Ireland liquor of all kinds is available all the time, you better imagine Icelanders indulging at home. Sinewy, big-boned or big-boobed, these outdoor specimens look wholesome enough to vary that old Texan equation to "One Icelander equals three Irish." Pockmarked by hot geysers and active or dormant volcanos, many with gas-puffing fumaroles, Iceland promised to be one ongoing outdoor experience. Joining the two-week camping tour with the feeling of doing something too strenuous to be enjoyable, I spent the first evenings putting my weather-proof tent together to a sleepable ensemble and securing it with stakes without injuring myself. Emergencies at night a foregone conclusion at my age, I spent some time twisting and tying overlapping and extra pieces of tent to a makeshift exit without freezing myself to death at night. Walking up the ravine that marks the line widening the gap between Europe by the fraction of an inch per year meant nothing much to anyone except me. Clowning around by straddling the ravine , I could claim to have stood in two worlds at the same time. Not quite the same painful struggle that ended with the showdown between me and myself on the *Loftleidir* gangway decades ago, but still relics of a lifelong dual identity only gradually on the wane. An old wooden church on the European side of the rift near where the *althing*, the second oldest parliament of the world, met in 930 should remind us that in matters of early democracy Nordic societies always had a lot to offer. Fording streams was almost a daily adventure and on several occasions the driver even got out, prodded the depth of the water, and decided—without ever having heard of Robert Frost—to take the road with fewer ruts in it. The route as such was recognizable only by the driver´s astute exploratory sense or by cairns, rocks piled up for orientation. For hours on end, traversing inland Iceland was quite a rocky undertaking, its holes and stones lulling us asleep or jerking us awake. What a boon the complete absence of traffic, but then the sudden emergence of five buses parked by *Gullfoss,* the first of six spectacular waterfalls. Many dozens of Koreans, Japanese, or Chinese, hard to tell them apart, were swarming all over, each vying for the optimal photo angles. The spectacle of a scintillating rainbow spanning over the gushing water and accompanied by surging waves of excitement was applauded as if performed on stage. Probably because we looked like from somewhere in Europe and presumably because they needed us to share their excitement, two ladies exclaimed "Ooh, rov'ry wata and corors in sky, just rike in Honshu". To avoid a traffic jam in the middle of nowhere, our driver found out that the Polish bus parked next to ours would be leaving in twenty minutes, implying that we should move on to the next cascades worth watching. Pitching tent at campsites next to hot geysers for evening relaxation turned into an almost nightly routine, some sites even equipped with hot showers and water fountains, my favorite American amenities rendering the wilderness so much more pleasant. Reading about restless *Hekla*, known for erupting without much advance warning, I was not surprised that a medieval monk had declared it to be the snow-covered "gateway to hell," the companion of fiery *Etna* in Sicily. Crossing the vast *Odadahraun*, "the lava desert of criminals," we were inching our way over and between solidified lava fields. Easy to see why NASA chose this moonscape for trial landings. No need for extra stories of adventurers putting all their eggs into one jeep or sagas about outcasts escaping into this nowhere land.—Walking through Reykjavik was exciting for the long line of natives bending around a corner, something I had not seen since my childhood postwar days. "They are standing in line to buy some hard stuff in one of the two liquor stores in town. Coming from the States, you should be familiar with this" was an answer I got. "Not quite" I set him right, "lines of this length were food lines in postwar Vienna, and while there are liquor stores and strict rules to go with them in most American states, I have never seen one looking as if Prohibition was back." Another neat surprise for us were the foreign looking tourists in some sort of native costume from Greenland. "We don't mind waiting, we are used to it We love to go abroad, to come south occasionally. No, Icelanders would not understand our Danish here, let alone Inuit. It's English that gets us what we need, after all both Iceland and Greenland are firmly in American hands." Not quite sure what he meant, I suggested referring to the airbases as serving NATO and not just the US. No more politicking with lovely people, it was more interesting to her about "coming south." Hiking along the azure blue ocean in broad sunlight and testing our bird vocabulary by spotting and recognizing the shape, color, and flight pattern of the various specimens landing or taking off from countless nooks and crannies. "This was a gull, but what kind? No way, it was not a laughing gull, I would have heard that!"—"Don't be silly, you can't hear a puffin make any puffin noise either, but you recognize him by his unshapely body on red legs and squashed red beak."—"A tern, I believe, though its plumage does not at all remind me of the *Black Tern,* the name of the freighter that brought us back to Europe decades ago. What's that silly looking bird with a kind of scraggly headgear sitting there?"—"The way it looks and its name sounds, it's got to be a smew!"—"Agreed, that fits! Why are these creatures so much harder to identify than the cormorants with their wide wingspan and long beak?" Later that night, I was buying two ornithological souvenirs, a *No Puffin* sticker with the image of a puffin crossed out by a red line and a multi-lingual poster for the absurd study of seabirds in landlubber Vienna. "Lundi is Icelandic for puffin but the plump sounding tupik is its Russian name."—Skirting several vast glaciers on their perennial slide toward the Atlantic, our driver had us listen to an observation by Nobel Prize winner *Halldór Laxness. "It's a pity we don't whistle at one another like birds. Words are misleading. That's why I contemplate the lilies on the field, but in particular the glacier. If one looks at the glacier long enough, words cease to have any meaning on God's earth."* The pungent smell of dried stockfish spreading over our campsite at supper was nothing compared to the stench of a huge whale gutted earlier that day. A whale of a power shovel was punching blocks of meat out of the body and loading them onto a platform for processing, all amidst hundreds of screaming gulls fighting for their due.—The two weeks with just one rainy day felt like one combination of yellow sulfur, the reddish rock, the black of the lava, the turquois of geysers, and the blue of the sea. A lingering treasure in our minds, but one rapidly vanishing with mass tourism out of bounds since Iceland's surprising show at the Euro Soccer Cup.

THE FASCINATION OF SHIITE MOSQUES, ISLAMIC CALLIGRAPHY, AND THOUSANDS OF YEARS OF HISTORY. DARING TO TALK TO PEOPLE DURING A TRIP ON THE BRINK OF ARMAGEDDON.

Joining Helmut and some of his parishioners on a two-week bus tour through Iran, organized by the decidedly un-Islamic *Biblical Travels,* turned out to be fascinating beyond our expectations, much though Marianne had her doubts about donning the prescribed *hijab* and refraining from wearing short sleeves. In fact, I thoroughly enjoyed her new look just like that of my teenage godchild, also shrouded in black. Descending on pitch dark Tehran meant getting a closer look at the huge Shrine of Ayatollah Khomeini, illuminated in the green color of the Prophet. Moving into the formerly elegant Royal Garden Hotel, now named after one of the many martyrs of the revolution, involved reading about the dress code to be followed. Assuming that numerals are read from right to left as is Farsi, the language written in Arabic, we found out the hard way that this was not so—our room written 489 in Arabic numerals did not switch directions but remained 489. Helmut had arranged for a brief visit to the poor church of the Chaldaic Community, where its bishop briefly told us about the difficult situation of his small congregation but refused to discuss anything the two native ushers might understand or misunderstand. A moving little present for each of us, the Lord's Prayer in Aramaic, the language of Jesus. We would spend more time in Tehran later, but now we were setting out toward the south with our guide Amir, fluent in German after studying in Munich, which meant getting to know him and his political views within a few days. Another pleasant surprise was our driver Hossein, a veritable King of the Road on the excellent highways built by the *shah,* and his young son dividing his attention between watching his dad and us. What was beginning to upset us was that we were arguing among ourselves whether to encourage Amir to tell us about the political situation." No need to argue because bit by bit and more openly each day, Amir let us share his unusual past anyway. As an enemy of the shah and a sympathizer of the religious leadership in exile, his grandfather had sought safety in Germany and invited his grandson to stay there with him. Close to the exiled revolutionary leader in Paris, grandpa had even met the Ayatollah personally and spread his enthusiasm to the teenager. Only after their return to Tehran did they become disillusioned because getting rid of the shah was one thing but executing many of his followers and even nonconformist revolutionaries was something altogether different. *Ahwas*, our southernmost point, was predominantly Arab, that is, *Sunni* Muslim in the largest *Shia* country. Scorching heat and unbearable humidity near the strategic oil and natural gas fields, the flaring visible for miles and miles. Visiting mosques was no problem, just take off your shoes and be respectfully quiet. A surprisingly relaxed atmosphere, people sitting and praying, others just sitting on the large carpets, some even chit-chatting. Whatever the reason, an old clock with its pendulum swinging hung on the wall, an intriguing culture clash, but a peaceful one. Walking under the bridge at sunset, a man with lots of kids was smiling at us. No English, no Farsi. "Austria, Europe." Drawing a rough map in the riverside sand, I was waiting for his reaction. In vain. "Children?" Raising my forefinger to *one*, the short fellow swung bis arm across all these children and proudly raised nine of his fingers. "You win, I lose" was all I could motion to him. A bit enervating for us who were used to pastures and forests was the complete absence of green in favor of a steady mix of shades of yellow, ochre, brown and grey with white 5,000 m peaks of snow in the distance. More than once Hossein stopped in the middle of a village to give us a chance to shake a leg, inhale the clear desert air, and enjoy the strong tea served by villagers popping up out of nowhere and trying to talk to us by sign language and occasional words of English. Women to women, men to men. Pulling out a small rug that he put down two bus lengths away and taking off his shoes, Hossein repeatedly bowed toward Mecca and delivered his prayers kneeling. Signaling him my respect, I followed his invitation to try sitting on my heels, to squat down as he did. No chance. Perhaps piety as authentic as this was something we should try not to look down on in our enlightened Western societies. Surprised that according to the ticket to the mausoleum of Saadi, the famous seventh century poet, we had resurrected him in the thirteenth century, we realized that we had omitted reading *AH, after the Hejira.*

Strictly speaking, we were not in Persia but in Iran, the same stem as in Aryan. Was the closeness of the Shah's Pahlevi dynasty to the Nazis and their obsession with being Aryan a coincidence? Cyrus the Great, Dareus the Great, then our European Alexander, also a Great. As if we had not comprehended the dimension of the empire yet, walking past six huge *bas reliefs* of Sassanid kings of the last dynasty before Islam took over made that clear at the tomb of Kyros, a helpful introduction to our day at Persepolis, the capital since Darius I in the fifth century BCE. Our eyes sweeping over the vast square bounded by several palaces and the Hall of Thirty-six Columns, even these dimensions outdone by the Hall of a Hundred Columns, needed time to absorb what they had just seen. Most intriguing the staggered reliefs of about two dozen ethnic representatives, each wearing his native costume and presenting gifts typical of his region to the king. Medes, Bakhtrians, Cappadocians, and endless others, some characterized by lions on the prowl or goring a bull. Their various hair styles, the conical or round hats, the vegetables or fruits presented, or the supposedly unique way of Persian kings to deal with the vanquished—namely, to walk hand in hand with them. That many of us remembered the Shah's spectacular "2,500 Years of Persepolis" festival made our day here even more spectacular. Musing over this legendary ultimate party on the very square burned down by Alexander the Great in 330 BC, I was wondering what that girl running toward me, her black aba trailing behind her, might have in mind. Coming closer fast and smiling, she asked me in excellent English where I was from. When I said, *"I'm from Austria"* she looked surprised. "But this sounds so *American*!" What a crazy moment to discuss accents! Shocked because of the danger she was putting herself in, I begged her to at least put her scarf back up. "I don't care" she screamed, "all I want is to talk to someone from the outside world for a few minutes and to tell them that the mullahs are terrifying!" Alone on this huge square, the two of us would be an easy target for the dreaded morals squads on the prowl. Probably aware that talking longer to a foreigner might be dangerous after all, she pulled away, turning around several times and leaving me spellbound. Lucky to be here when the regime still limited tourists to a negligible number, we kept crossing the square again from palace to royal gate to monument to those sculptured ethnic delegations and back again. The ancient crossroads *Kerman* topped everything so far with its combination of clay fortifications and pinnacle-serrated walls set off against snow-covered peaks. A desert plateau without a tree in sight to soothe our eyes, its souk on sand and pleasantly unspoiled by anything more modern. Making no bones about what he thought of the ayatollahs, the local guide was not upset at all when some of our women let their headgear slide back to reveal some hair, however tempting. They had to wear their *abaya*, however, "for thus no harm will come to them" (*Quran* 39:55). In the two millennia old oasis of *Bam* we went on a mercilessly hot walk around its huge reddish clay citadel before Helmut invited us to attend Sunday mass in our little hotel room. Not sure whether it was forbidden or just frowned upon, he had brought enough wine from Vienna to last him for two Sundays. Six of us took part in an atmosphere possibly resembling that which early Christians had to go through. An embroidered cloth on the table, a cup shaped like a chalice, a little bowl for the diced bits of bread, another bowl to wash his fingers after holy communion. In his short homily, he simply asked the Lord to reconcile Muslims with Christians and Sunnis with Shiites.—Sincere and overwhelming the curiosity of these simple country folk, always at least one whose English was growing with the challenge of talking to a busload of Westerners, all Christians or perhaps even more suspect, nonbelievers. One of the funnier questions broached to me by sign language "mentioning" my beard, was whether I was Muslim. Ignoring this hairy question, I replied via Amir that Allah and Jesus wanted the same thing, namely respect for each other beyond all boundaries and fulfilment of our lives. At supper the few of us interested in politics had yet another session, this time triggered by the town of Rafsanjan. Even though its famous son, former President Rafsanjani, had been heralded as someone trying to rein in the religious hardliners, he came out for the destruction if Israel just like his predecessors and the Supreme Leader. All of us self-styled *politicos* agreed that we understood why Palestinians had a problem with Israeli politics, some even with the existence of

Israel, but not why Iran had been propagating the annihilation of the "Zionist cancer" all along.

Yazd, a particularly brilliant pearl of the string of historical towns, was the only one not completely dominated by Islam. Visiting the Temple of Fire with the roof top symbol of the turquois eagle, its widespread wings guarding the eternal light, gave us a mild foretaste of the Tower of Silence, where the followers of Zoroaster used to leave their dead to be gobbled up by vultures. Illegal for hygienic as well as religious reasons now, these relics were witnesses of the once powerful rival of Islam. Here it was again in yet another mosque, the grandfather clock ticking away on a wall across the *mihrab*, the prayer niche in the direction of Mecca. Blatantly western and non-Islamic, could it mean that Islam never developed its own gadget measuring time? The geometry on the domed ceilings or the minarets was nothing short of magic, its blue-green-turquois abstract designs occasionally pulling me into what must have been mini trances.. The elaborate calligraphy of holy verses scripted in perfect harmony with the whole made for a vivid discussion over *Fesenjan* tonight, the tasty Iranian pomegranate stew with a choice of lukewarm pseudo beer, mineral water and, judging by its taste, an anti-American imitation of coke. Most of us agreed that our Romanesque and early Gothic art and architecture came closest to expressing that which cannot be expressed, Helmut adding that the abstract art obligatory in Islam was at least as successful in expressing the ineffable. Isfahan with the second-largest square in the world, the *Meidan-e-Imam,* the Kings' Square, meant admiring three more old mosques, this time with a guide particularly open about his view of the ayatollahs. Having asked him whether he thought there was a generally strong anti-American sentiment among the average people, he answered, as they all did, by condemning the American ouster of Mossadegh, who had nationalized the oil fields in the fifties. Beyond that, he put more blame on British politics before that and seemed a bit vague about whether the US should have dropped the shah after supporting him hook line and sinker. "Very dangerous to open door a little to let in air, much air flowing in too quickly opens door too quickly." Curious how he would respond to my limited Farsi, I told him that I sometimes agreed with what the *shaitan bozorg* and the *shaitan kucheki* were doing. Completely floored, he did not look upset but wanted to know where I had picked up "these unspeakables." From my American friend Tom S., a well-traveled specialist in oil and Palestinian-Israeli issues. *Shaitan* was easy enough to figure out, and *bozorg* meaning *great* and *kuchek*i meaning *little* referred to the U. S. and Israel. Staggering in a different sense was the two-level bridge with its thirty-three arches spanning the Euphrates River, a mere trickle over the past years. It was on that same day that out of a clear blue sky a taxi driver turned around to three of us, asking whether we had met the dangerous man yet. Confused what he might have meant, we said "No dangerous man," whereupon he yelled *bang, bang* and, laughing, explained that many tourists did not visit Iran because it was presented as dangerous abroad. Probably only worried about the lack of tourists, would he have relished my half *bozorg shaitan* identity?

Told that the Supreme Leader was on television tonight on the occasion of the annual *Ashura* procession devoted to the martyrdom of Imam Hussein, grandson of Mohammad, I wanted to hear what Farsi sounded like. His avuncular appearance and soothing speech did not at all reflect his hawkish approach on Iran's missile program or loosening the tight grip on people's dress code. The dark *"a"* sound, as in *dawn* or *yawn*, made for a pleasant overall effect, the consonants pronounced softly and scattered unobtrusively over his sentences and his presumable exhortations only slightly harsher. Amazing how long I kept listening to him, a slight up-and-down lilt perhaps making it difficult even for Farsi listeners to doubt his sincerity. The religious holiday that evening ended with a few secret pictures I snapped of believers beating themselves bloody, others just going through the motions, but the whole scene bringing back memories of *penitentes* in action in New Mexico. The cordiality we had met wherever we went received a noticeable dent in the holy city of Qum, the major Shiite pilgrimage center. No curious faces, let alone smiles, just scowling looks from holy men in black.—Visiting yet another museum with a beautiful young woman as our local guide, we were noticing Amir becoming more nervous by the minute and trying to catch her attention. "Marianne, would you be so kind and slip this piece of paper with my name and phone number to her, preferably without being seen?" A bit puzzled at first, she gladly did, Amir observing the moment of delivery from behind a tree. Visibly surprised, the girl was looking around for the possible sender. Would they ever meet?—Suddenly a young couple engaged us in a conversation in fluent English, making it easy to invite them for coffee on the spur of the moment. Students of English, they could not believe their good luck of meeting two Westerners so familiar with English and especially America. The twenty minutes spent together gave us more than a rough idea of what walking the tight rope between staying away from foreigners and too much contact was like. Again my question, whether they thought they might be observed talking to us? Making light of the situation, they said they trusted their good luck, adding that before their marriage they could not have met us because walking hand in hand in public was unthinkable. Never had I promised anyone more sincerely to mail a certain American dictionary, not a risk for them as future English teachers.

Thanking Hossein for having taken us 5,000 km across much of Iran with his by now almost bilingual copilot, we went for a last extended stroll past the famous wall picturing Ayatollah Khomeini's scowling face next to bombs raining down on Iran from each of the stars of the wall-size Star Spangled Banner.—Much to our surprise, though not to Amir's, an official of the tourist board appeared before we left for the airport and asked us to fill out a form with specific questions about the hotels we had stayed in and evaluations of our various regional guides. His businesslike appearance and commanding tone made it easy for us to forget any minor criticism we might have had in favor of checking "excellent" wherever possible.

Lasting insights and impressions? What a potential paradise on earth! Until the discovery of oil in *sunni* Arabia and *shiite* Iran long ago released all kinds of *sheitans,* from western greed and blunders to their own evidently incompatible interpretations of Islam.

IRAQ BETWEEN ME, MYSELF, AND OTHERS. INTELLECTUAL ARROGANCE, SENSIBLE CRITICISM, AND IRRELEVANT COMPARISONS.

The U.S.-led invasion of Iraq to throw Saddam Hussein out of Kuwait was not something I wanted to be against. Finally, I thought, a front where American intervention would not be attacked as "one more imperialist adventure." My criticism was with what the Administration failed to do *after* military victory. Whatever little retired generals and ranking civil servants did to repair the bleeding country was the real scandal. How could such a catastrophic blunder as firing hundreds of thousands from their jobs for being *Baath* party members happen? All it did was raise unemployment even more and unnecessarily create new enemies? Why were not further billions spent on rebuilding the infrastructure, reopening hospitals and schools, and all of it within the shortest time possible? In my estimation, if the suffering population could have experienced quick and determined reconstruction, most Shiites and even a substantial number of Sunni would have joined the pro-American Kurds. In historical disputes it is never possible to prove that whatever did not happen would have been the better option.

Frustrating though it is to defend American policies against unfair, ill-informed, or simply wrong accusations, unmitigated anti-Americanism is even worse because like all -*isms,* it sets mere facts on fire. It cannot be refuted by argument or empirical proof as a leading German theater guru put it: "Culture war? I am all game. I thoroughly loathe everything

American." Recently, a German cartoon showed Jerry Lewis, pulling one of his trademark faces, as the one American most admired by average Germans but most despised by its intellectuals. A famous English writer admitted that her anti-Americanism was "almost running out of control," a mind frame not untypical of intellectuals.

"Why are we using so many English or American words in German, as if we did not have any of our own?"—"I quite agree with you that in many cases, maybe even the majority, there is no need to import Americanisms. But be careful because in many fields, especially scientific ones, there either are no German equivalents and international R&D publications are in English."—"But I can't imagine that all these tens of thousands of words have come in without being engineered by political or commercial agencies, a form of cultural imperialism. The French have understood that and have begun to fight back."—"No need to move America close to Nazi or Soviet intentions. English became the *lingua franca* of our age long ago because it lends itself to the many rapid changes in the world more easily than, say, German or French. What is true, though, is that nobody forces us to import low-class products, including language we could do without, like *der Shitstorm."*—"You mentioned that your son spent four months at Yale. How was it?"- "He summed it up with 'It's another country,' not bothering to explain anything." Would the young man have answered like this, if he had spent time in Sweden or Sicily? Without realizing it, he had expressed the growing belief among Europeans that, whatever may separate our nations or lifestyles, the U.S. is increasingly seen as different, not in degree but in essence. To those interested in politics, it has increasingly morphed into *non-Europe*, maybe even *anti-Europe*. Wisely employed, this growing sentiment of belonging to a common Continental culture might help build up some badly needed cohesion within the EU, but all these points delivered as anti-American jibes are fired away as if against Martians!

THE SHOCK OF *9/11* AND ITS GROTESQUE INTERPRETATION ALONG THE NILE AND IN THE TOMBS OF EGYPT.

Just like we all remember where we were on November 22, 1963, everybody witnessed the inferno of *9/11* from different coordinates. Shocked for weeks on end by this "political statement," I was not alone comprehending that a new dimension in international politics was born. And instantly my young Communist buddy's warning of thirty years ago flashed through my mind, one I had once thought was ridiculous, namely that Islam would be our powerful common enemy. The complexities and pitfalls of Near East politics apart, the rational consistency and fanatic religious zeal of *Mohammad Atta*, who had announced Armageddon in the preface to his dissertation in engineering, should make us shudder at the seeming helplessness of politics and national defense as understood until now. Unbearable the bizarre, far-fetched conspiracy theories, not just a few even from Americans, maintaining that "our politics is responsible" or insinuating that the Israeli secret service or President G. W. Bush was behind it. Shocking the observation of a friend, thoroughly familiar with how Americans act and react, "A tragedy, of course. But isn't it time to stop dwelling on the 3000 plus casualties—we have had millions of people dying in Europe!"

The earliest memory I had of things Egyptian was the shape of a pyramid from my class in *Descriptive Geometry*, my cloven-foot twin brother of mathematics in high school. The base is a square and the four triangles angling at the tip are isosceles or unilateral, okay. But our creative teacher enjoyed slowly rotating the pyramid close to the blackboard, asking us to draw the light rays emanating from a source on the ceiling and to fill in the shadow—not the darker penumbra, that would be too hard, just the lighter dark. Sometimes he would then move either the pyramid or the light bulb and have us start all over again. At the time I knew nothing about the real or imagined secret force of life housed in the center of the giant edifices in Egypt, nor do I now.—It was at the turn of the twenty-eighth millennium after the *Ur*-Pharaoh that we risked a two-week trip to the Land of the Pyramids, my old friend Peter, our friend Eva, and my wife Marianne. Flying to Luxor rather than Cairo to board our ship, we had another snag to cope with after the repercussions of *9/11.* With the downstream stretch to Cairo off limits to ships and the bridge in Luxor under reparation, dozens of ships had piled up. Boarding the *Rose of the Nile* after several hours on the road south was the alternative. The stern looks of some of the submachinegun-toting guards showed they were taking their duty seriously while others radiated the nonchalance of professional welcomers. Traversing the front decks of five parallel-anchored ships to reach ours in mid-stream added up to quite a jaunt over assorted thresholds and mini-bridges but eventually found us taking in the green fertile belt of the *Father of African Rivers.* Exquisite politeness from the benign features of a slightly darker face, a Nubian admixture, as he proudly explained, made us feel at ease right away. Enjoying our first dinner during Ramadan, we were a bit apprehensive about possible after-effects of *9/11.* More than once, we would find that an incredible number of simple, pious folks protested that whoever had committed these acts, could not possibly have been Muslim because "Islam means peace." The penetrating blast of what in northern lands is called a foghorn shattered our concentration, trying to remember the names of the gods and pharaohs we would soon get to know in person. Like thousands of years ago, life on the river appeared to be determined by the rhythm of the seasons, that of *fellahs* working the green banks not different from representations on temple walls. Entranced by the Biblical life sailing past us and lulled into leisure by the breeze and the soft sound of the bow forging its way through the waves, we were trying to grasp what a dreamboat we were really on. Wind-powered *feluccas*, their white sails set off against the bright green of palm trees were meandering between barges and tourist ships, the former not noticeably bound by any rules except *right* and *left.* Dismissing the idea that sharing the river with about fifteen hundred ships might not be all that safe, we were more worried about *Ramses' Revenge*, not just regarding the shits but also real shots. Trying to get the waiter to serve us by the swimming pool, we noticed him pulling faces and vanishing. Not convinced that all was kosher in the land of Allah, Peter returned with our drinks and, roaring with laughter, reported our first intercultural problem. The poor boy did not dare show up because of "the lady in her swimsuit—and during the month of fasting at that!" Ships by the dozens in both directions, peasants working the five percent of fertile land like thousands of years ago but trying to feed a hundred million people, fishermen whipping schools of fish together from different sides. Our first stop at the *Temple of Horus*, the falcon god. Walking through ever more sacred rooms we reached *Isis and Osiris,* the Holy Couple with their Holy Infant. If Isis was not only his wife but also his sister, this could not really faze us with our different interpretation of the virgin birth. Funny that I should think of my ornithology course in Florida decades ago when the professor observed that I was the only student she had ever had who chose to write about the religious significance of falcons and ibises in ancient Egypt rather than about real birds in Florida. Even more spectacular was *Kom Ombo,* where the pre-Christian Ptolemaic kings had celebrated the falcon god and the crocodile god in a double temple with twin gateways, sanctuaries, and a cemetery for the sacred giant lizards. Dwarfed by the enormous columns, each one a single block, we felt under the spell of *Sobek*, the god of crocodiles, his powerful jaws studded with the sharpest set of mangling teeth. Awesome, but in the original meaning of religious *awe, awe-stricken.* Technologically not endowed with profound insights, I hesitated to take sides in the battle erupting between those celebrating the *Aswan High Dam* as the achievement of Soviet engineering and those looking down on it as eventually doomed by the sands. A comment while walking along the huge dam, "The Soviets are smart. They build a big project like this over ten years for little Achmed and Amir to see with their own eyes and marvel at its size. The Americans transfer millions to our Central Bank, and nobody ever sees anything, maybe it never arrived." Locals and our supper guests below deck all seemed to belong to one of these two camps, pro-Nasser or anti-Nasser, the President who had convinced his Communist friends to help him keep the fertile lands flooded all the way to the delta if necessary. Tired of getting roped into politicking, I took to agreeing with all of them or advising them to look behind the scenes. Reaching *Luxor* again on the return, we realized it was neighboring *Karnak* we had come to see, where only twelve years ago a cache of twenty-five statues in perfect condition had been found. Wondering, staring, trying to comprehend without being able to decipher any of the hieroglyphics, we spent more time in the *Great Temple of Amun*, the patron god of Thebes dominating a 250-acre complex of temples and obelisks and 134 columns rising to the largest such structure in the world. No matter how excited our imagination, we could not even begin to imagine Amun' bark floating on the rectangular sacred lake before us, the source of holy water for priestly duties.

Reaching the Necropolis of Thebes across the previously closed bridge, we had the unexpected chance to read the brief description a member of Napoleon's army had left, conveying an idea of the impact these edifices must have exerted. "Without an order being given, the men had formed their ranks and presented arms at their first sight of the temples." Easy to reenact for us because the capital of the New Kingdom was as inspiring today as in 1799 when Napoleon's soldiers snapped to attention. Could we even remotely imagine how we would react if we had never seen pictures and films about ancient Egypt? According to our unique guide, the natural outcrop above the *Temple of Hatshepsut* in the Valley of the Kings had helped the assassins reload between several rounds of shooting over fifty Swiss tourists not too long ago. And here we were, unintimidated infidels in this land rocked by fanatics again. The son of the police chief of Cairo, he told us that he wouldn't ever have to work again but that he loved to show tourists around, especially in a region as fascinating as this one with the site of a crime so close to him personally. Before we knew what he meant, his embittered voice explained. "My American wife, a professional tourist guide, led the group from Switzerland when these maniacs attacked. Badly injured, she spent a year in the hospital but survived. We could talk a long time about why people commit such crimes against obviously innocent tourists, but one thing is certain" and his face darkened as he underwent what we would call cursing, "almost all these assassins come from Pakistan. If not every single one, then surely their spiritual teachers." Robbers had looted many graves before, but luckily for posterity had missed that of the boy-king *Tutankhamun*, including the solid gold mask covering his head, probably the most widely recognized Egyptian treasure. Marianne recounted the story of "lucky sod" Howard Carter, making it more exciting the way she told it. "Of wealthy background like most of these explorers, he was one of the earliest car owners to have an accident in England. Advising the young man to move to a warmer climate, doctors assured him that this was the precondition for any gradual improvement. With plenty of time and money at his hands in Egypt, he made the acquaintance of archaeologists and ended up literally stumbling on a wooden throne sheathed in gold amidst many other treasures in 1922. His other lucky strike after finding the *Temple of Hatshepsut* was the awe-inspiring burial site of *Nacht*, every square foot of this astronomer´s grave covered by the bright-colored hieroglyphics of falcons, ibises, and crocodiles between equally dazzling frescoes of humans. The two tiers of a banquet, the host couple surrounded by guests, closeups of beautiful females, a blind harpist, servants holding pitchers and plates, all represented in the typical two-dimensional Egyptian mode made marveling at *Nacht's* world the most rewarding experience here yet.

El Qâhira, the Victorious, its metropolitan area the home of seventeen million people, roughly a sixth of the country. No chaotic traffic like this since the *go-slow* in Lagos, the only difference being that the smog here was dry rather than muggy. And yet there was something to the definition of the city as a collection of villages rather than of one giant village, the pyramids of *Gîza* proving it. Having triggered our yearning to come here, they were first on our agenda. Walking through sand and dirt piled up inches high, horses, camels, donkeys, motor bikes, taxis, and itinerant tourists vying for a little space to push ahead. Slowly approaching *Cheops*, the biggest pyramid, on a donkey-powered wagon was a new form of excitement. Rocking back and forth in ruts grown hard and deep and shifting sideways over mini dunes, we got stuck on a slight uphill and being good sports, jumped off and helped the asinine cab to get going again. Even Marianne was sure that by keeping all our fingers crossed, we would get to our target without tipping over. Its outlines growing sharper through the haze, this largest stone edifice in the world may once have represented eternal shafts of sunlight or symbolized the mythical mound of creation. Remembering the colossal blocks hewn and moved by pre-Inca in Perú, we realized there was no point in drawing parallels, except the wherewithal of tools. "Look toward *Chephren!* Eva and Peter riding on a one-hump camel or holding on to it anyway! Walking, now waving furiously—that's them alright! More interesting, where do you estimate the geometric middle really is, the point of maximum spiritual force that supposedly contains the remains of a king of the Fourth Dynasty? All sorts of mystical movements have picked up on this idea of magic power radiating from within all pyramids, not just these sacred structures. Even tomatoes pressed into that shape are said to have special nutritional value. Here we are, and we have no clue." Overpopulated like the whole country, figures in the *Egyptian Museum* seemed to be stepping on each other's giant toes, the same pushing and shoving and gawking among the throngs in front of the old glass showcases. Varying an old proverb about a wood and trees, we quickly felt we were unable to see the big mummies for all the sarcophaguses, papyri, and jewelry. Past the bust of Echnathon, the revolutionary who had introduced monotheism until he was forced back into the previous multi-god cosmos by a jealous caste of priests, we found the Royal Mummy Room housing what we were looking for. Here he towered before us, Ramses II, also referred to as *al-Akbar*, the Greatest, a holy word we all knew from crazed assassins rather than the Quran. His famous sharp-edged facial features still remarkably recognizable, he had been removed from the burial place near the Tombs of the Nobles but was also the only pharaoh ever issued a passport to be exhibited in Paris in 1976 shortly after his death over three thousand years ago. A couple of items to comprehend the mere size of the Valley of Kings. While sixty-two tombs are known here, only two have been discovered in the Western Valley running perpendicular to it. Though Ramses' place in history is well documented, it was this tidbit of knowledge I thoroughly enjoyed—that the ruler simply known as "Pharaoh" in *Exodus* was Ramses II. As with all the deceased semi-gods, his internal organs had been removed and placed in special vessels while the embalmed body was wrapped in cloth. Interred in a sarcophagus, a "flesh eater," with everything he might need to travel through the afterlife, such as the *Book of the Dead* including spells with which to gain entrance into the netherworld. None of us had ever heard of *ushabtis*, little statuettes that would come alive to help the dead perform labors for the gods. Even more thrilling, the driedup elongated remains of *Sobek* and two minor giant lizard gods caught our landlubber imaginations. The greyish overlapping scales still as prominent as the posterior teeth betraying power long dead easily beat their live secular relatives in the zoo. Playing jokes on each other for days on end, we passed around nuts in little make-belief *ushabties* or imitated the snapping jaws of Sobek. –

Strolling past the prestigious American University with our guide, we inevitably began discussing the manifold angles of *9/11* and its repercussions again. "No, not seventy percent believe that non-Muslims must be responsible for the attacks, but a hundred percent think so!" Mentioning the political activist *Qutb* (pronounced *katoob*), whose philosophy of sheer holy hatred was bearing fruit, he made no bones about his difficult life between sticking to his American wife and being despised for this very reason. Socialist President *Nasser* had barely escaped an attempt on his life for which he had *Qutb*, the founder of the *Muslim Brotherhood*, hanged.

Led to a rickety old wooden wheel by a little stream, a romantic sight but otherwise unimportant, Marianne spotted a dead dog floating in the water basin. "There's a dog swimming" she reported to the fellow on duty who, shrugging his shoulders, commented "It isn't swimming anymore, it is dead." End of announcement. A day later we saw children playing around the bloated belly of a dead cow floating in the sewage canal next to us walking toward *Gîza.* Shocked by this nonchalance regarding filth or, putting it positively, the absence of concern with cleanliness, we brought this up with two men at hand, their English good enough to make sense. "We have such great respect for your foot-washing ceremonies before entering mosques. How come your concern for spiritual cleanliness does not translate into keeping streets clean and clear of dead bodies?" Curious looks, smiles, comments of "no problem." Just a world innocent of a system.

Alexandria. Founded by its name-giver, the Great. Home of the Lighthouse, one of the seven miracles of antiquity. The intellectual center around the largest library until it burned down during Caesar's reign, destroying the entire corpus of antique knowledge. Destroyed by Muslim expansion and ruled by the Ottomans until invaded by Napoleon in his drive against the British in 1798. Almost conquered by Rommel, the *desert fox,* in 1942.—The oasis of *El-Fayyum.* Jus*t* how long we could stay depended on how clever we were working it out with our two heavily armed security guards following in a jeep. Peter and I the only foreigners in an outdoor café could not resist asking two locals for a few drags of their fancy pipes. Bewildered looks, but no problem while our women were reading that pharaohs had reclaimed this land by regulating the flow of the Nile and that not long ago an American geologist identified a highway dating from 2600 B.C. Nothing special about the name *Krokodilopolis,* though. The city of crocodiles nearby, so what?

More interesting was another local, indulging his hookah across from us and never smiling, never gesturing, let alone uttering a word, just keeping us tuned in. A triangle of this strange fellow, our guards not too happy about our smokes, and us watching the scene. Always the question whether a sudden attack, not by our lone hookah smoker but by a well-organized team, could be fended off by our young protectors. Like the unfortunate Swiss tourists, not the ghost of a chance. Looking for a little gem to keep reminding me of this unfathomable world, I settled for a little round silver receptacle with the hieroglyphic *ankh,* a cross with a loop embossed on its lid. Translated as the *key to life*, it immediately imbued me with enough force to resist buying a comfortable prayer rug or a leather belt once worn by a Nile crocodile. Reading up on my souvenir's guaranteed three thousand year-origin, I was careless enough to order orange juice. Both halves of my identity unable to survive without ice cubes for decades, all of me now surrendered to *Ramses' Revenge* for a couple of days.

We had often returned from other cities, countries, other cultures. This time we arrived at home from another world. What remained? Having tried to convince my American students of the spiritual power it must have taken thousands of *de facto* slaves to complete our medieval churches and monasteries, I could now draw parallels to the spiritual devotion that had fueled the builders of those pyramids and tombs for their pharaohs and gods. Even students appreciating the artistic miracles inside and outside our religious masterpieces tended to make light of the spirituality of those creating them. "They had to work for the Church to survive and hated every day of it, that's all!"— "Why are you so sure that simple workers were incapable of investing the buildings for their gods and demi-gods with meaning beyond making a living, with real meaning?"

THROUGH THE DEEP SOUTH WITH RAMÓN AND A COLLEGEMATE OF DISTANT FSC DAYS.

Recognizing George in the airport crowd was the first step of our trip "down memory lane" we had planned with my Florida collegemate of half a century ago. Five decades heavier than I remembered him but just as curly-haired, he had become a successful dentist living on prestigious Stone Mountain outside Atlanta, where I would soon see the threesome of the Confederate States, Jefferson Davis, Robert E. Lee, and "Stonewall" Jackson chiseled into rock. I had never forgotten the unusual story of his Russian grandfather's arrival in America. Another immigrant on board had lost his only pair of shoes, probably stolen. Approaching Ellis Island, several of the poor fellow's shipmates had collected a little money so that he wouldn't have to begin his new life barefoot. Many years later, a man stopped George's grandfather in Brooklyn, asking whether he had been aboard that ship where so many fellow passengers had chipped in to help him out. After a few nods and hugs, the lucky fellow handed George's grandpa a sizeable amount with "I have done well, my friend, and here's my big *thank you*."

Barely seated and sipping our fruit juices with George and his wife, my buddy Ramón, not known for opening a conversation by mincing his words, fired away with, "Got any guns in the house?"—"Yes, eight."—"Are they loaded?"—George, laughing, "That a typical European question! What good would they do if they weren't?" George´s wife, trying to mediate, "You know, quite frankly, one gun would be good enough for me." Taking us to his practice, George offered to fix or at least polish our teeth, but we got to talking about his customers instead. "No problem with blacks, I have had many black patients. It happened only once that I had to ask one to leave because he came in demanding free treatment as someone whose forefathers had to live through two hundred years of slavery." George and I had a grand time showing Ramón around the spectacular chapel, even running into several black students along the low-roofed esplanades crisscrossing the campus. Memories galore of where I had once collated psychology tests, where I had spent quiet weekends studying by the Hindu temple, where I had hovered by the post office looking for a European airmail envelope, where I had filled my basket with sandwiches to sell in men's dorms. Change and even progress had arrived to stay. On to Clearwater, where I had once seen my first pelicans and Anna Maria Island with memories of my roommates in long American bathing trunks and me in Continental mini length—or was it only the photo I remembered? All these cultural differences, some the result of two worlds steadily interacting and others just of sheer time passing. "The Rough Riders watered their mounts here in 1898" and "Col. 'Teddy' Roosevelt frequently rode by here on his stallion *Texas* followed by his little dog *Cuba"* made us history buffs think of what his "carrot and stick diplomacy" meant and my Catalonian friend not quite sure whether to blast the Spanish colonialists or Teddy Roosevelt for liberating or just "liberating" the island.

"Two mint julips, please," on our flight to New Orleans. Language buffs that we were, was it Orleans or Orleans? Judging by Louis Armstrong's "Do you know what it means to miss New Orleans?" it was clear, but the majority we talked to preferred the accent on the first syllable. Straight to the *Vieux Carré,* to our surprise largely unharmed by *Katrina.* Wrought iron gates and balconies next to the famous *Antoine's*

Restaurant and the "Musical Legends Park" with three jazz greats in bronze and the city's motto above, "Laissez les bons temps rouler!" A white fiacre passing an *azulejo* street sign, explaining that between 1762—1803 New Orleans was the capital of the Spanish province of *Luisiana* that changed its spelling only with Jefferson's *Louisiana Purchase.* A Dominican immigrant rolling tobacco leaves and selling cigars in broad daylight announced that "This is not the United States, this is New Orleans."

Visiting the First Methodist Church in Gulfport, where my life had received a decisive push in the direction it took fifty years ago, was my reason for coming back here. Unfortunately, the mayor who had once made me an honorary citizen for "distinguished services rendered" had passed away only three months ago. The choir was singing under the same neo-Gothic dome where I had once delivered my words of *thank you* in bumpy English. Vivid in my memory, the old black sexton handing me a dollar, "This is from me. God bless you!" Forgetting that half a century had elapsed, I found only one man who could remember the saga of the "live European in Mississippi." At ease to have found a few trustworthy church members, I left an amount for "whoever may need it in your estimation, a tiny fraction of what I had once received here."

What a treat to have my old friend Anne with us for a week, with Ramón, the old charmer, commenting that he had just discovered yet another facet of me. A well-known jazz club turned out to be a tourist trap, the rotund black tuba player gawking at Anne from behind his huge instrument. Crossing *Old Man River* was a highly emotional experience, as was the lovely B&B with an upright between the nineteenth-century portraits of the former owners and lithographs of Natchez chiefs, including a set of arrowheads. An interesting detail about whether gambling is or should be outlawed and how to get around spoilsport laws, we found out it was prohibited on land but perfectly legal once you crossed the wooden pier on to the sternwheeler anchored there. While half of November 12, Veteran's Day, was more than enough for us on the vast memorial premises of the Battle of Vicksburg, parades of differently uniformed veterans from several wars marching under monuments of old oak trees were musically interesting. Bumper stickers surrounded by rebel flags like "I am a proud descendant of a Confederate Soldier" reminded us that the Civil War was still more than history here. An old lady dressed in keeping with her pastime, that of inviting us to the two-room Historical Society of her community, explained details with moving enthusiasm. "It's not the number of years that counts but the degree of identification and the awareness of how quickly today becomes yesterday. And how quickly we forget." Well put, indeed. Pushing my way through a cane sugar plantation just to get the feel, I was stopped in my tracks by *Psalm 9:17.* "The wicked shall be turned into hell." One bit of wisdom for the type of trip you can never plan in detail is to keep your eyes peeled on possible surprises. One such example was the sign, *Angola. Louisiana State Penitentiary.* Why did we choose to visit the place? Obviously not to put us in a better mood. We had read up on how Governor Huey Long had once run Louisiana like a fiefdom, but the prison must have come a long way to invite visitors today. Maybe it was the mere name, for no other country except Congo had ever conveyed all the wildness and wilderness of Africa to me like Angola. Not one of the countries we had been through in West Africa could match the mere sound of the two vowels spun around *-ng-.* Surprised that a prisoner guided us through what described itself as "the once most notorious penitentiary in the South," were admired his calm and the craftsmanship of the woodwork displayed. Tables, chairs, bureaus, the whole gamut of coffins and electric chairs, all manufactured by inmates. Freely admitting that he had been sentenced to forty years, he evidently liked his job. "Without it, we couldn't have met." An astounding relationship of trust and respect building up between us during our forty minutes there, we shied away from asking questions. It had to be more than drugs, we figured. Impressive his faith, "It was here in Angola that I found the Lord." For a while he answered my postcards, announced his wedding in the last one but never replied to my congratulations. Maybe his biggest fear did him in—how to handle freedom after so many years of safety and a structured life.

"Travel through Alligator Land," the one thing we hadn't done yet. Crossing a fenced off breeding ground crawling with gators of all sizes, we moved on a boardwalk with a yellow traffic sign of "mosquito crossing". Saddling us with hearing protection and warning us to "remain seated at all times," the fellow took us through the bayous on a metal johnboat, shattering the peace of water lilies, curtains of Spanish moss, drowned tree trunks, and scaring up long-beaked egrets and satchel-mouth pelicans.

Lunching on gumbo and jambalaya in Mobile, we were facing the *Alabama*, survivor of Pearl Harbor. Wandering about on deck, we had fun watching high school kids clowning around and grown Navy men inspecting the interior of the famous hull. Stopping to tread on the lawns of several spectacular *ante-bellum* mansions, surrounded by archways of huge oaks, we couldn't get enough of those visual wonders. Straight out of "Gone with the Wind." Parking with lots of other *The Heart of Dixie* Alabama license plates to absorb the autumn splendor in a State Park, we encountered yet another linguistic riddle, or was it a legal conundrum? "No open or cold beer allowed in public areas." Because no American would dream of drinking warm beer?

Birmingham is a name everybody shocked by racial violence is familiar with, and so I had a little problem convincing my friend to cut through the black section to find *The Jazz Hall of Fame*. Closed, but that turned out to be our good luck. Introducing himself as "Doc" Adams," this elegant old man in suit, tie, and pocket square showed us through several rooms of documents and photos, going into details about musicians and events he knew well from decades ago. Mentioning that he had played the clarinet with Duke Ellington, he suddenly started playing just for the two of us. A truly moving interlude! He seemed more than happy that two from so far away would take a chance to find the museum and him to take care of us. Learning by taking risks.

"Welcome to Outdoor World in Georgia" lived up to our expectations with a whole section of differently priced raised hides, a whole floor dedicated to fishing gear, a subculture of guns, rifles, and K 47s. The Legend, a color poster of *Marion Michael Morrison*, aka *John Wayne*, fit right in. Celebrating farewell with George and his wife, we already had the memories of a few shared weeks to talk about without resorting to political bickering which could easily destroy the atmosphere around generous hosts and grateful guests. Never had I seen two happier women than the two asking for my plane ticket and getting half of my fifth of gin I could not to take aboard.

While there were of course always quieter hours to reflect about being *On the Road* for weeks on end, it took the many uninterrupted hours on the plane to filter out the indelible impressions and lasting experiences. A journalist by profession, Ramón was of course as interested as I was in everything historical, sociological, economic, and political, and yet he could not really grasp my astonishment with how things had changed. Lakeland, a dreamy southern town in 1957, a half-urbanized electronic center now; Florida Southern, lily white then and a modest black student population now; Gulfport, an attractive small southern town then, badly damaged by hurricanes and a conglomeration of nondescript blocks and Asian eateries now; New Orleans, no European tourist in sight then, a fair share including even Russians now; driving through rural Louisiana, Mississippi, and Alabama meant looking at sugar cane, cotton, and peanut plantations then, driving past Mercedes, BMW, Toyota, and Hyundai plants now. America, the country of cheap labor. Most important, "separate but equal" schools, buses, restaurants, water fountains, rest rooms, etc. then, a distant memory now. Desegregation of all the hearts and minds, not quite yet.

TO ISRAEL WITH BROTHER PAUL AND HIS WIFE. ARCHEOLOGICALLY, RELIGIOUSLY, HISTORICALLY, AND POLITICALLY UNIQUE.

What can I possibly do for my brother and his wife to make their seventieth birthday truly memorable? Having lost their three-year old son to a brain tumor, they have been trying hard to accept that for which there is no explanation beyond the obvious. Clueing them in only a week before departure to the Holy Land, I saw one happy couple beaming with enthusiasm. Touching down in Tel Aviv, the "valley of spring," rows of blue-and-white flags at half-mast on April 21, 1948, the Israeli Fourth of July. *Pochers* with sideburns, rabbis with their much-too-large hats, many with *keppis* in blue and white, in black and white, embroidered, knitted and velvet. A surprising number of people speaking Russian, our guide Michael introducing himself in German Yiddish. "Here's a choke vhat ve have. 'May you grow like an onion, vis the head in de eard and de feets in de air.'" Ah, well done, nothing political yet! On the road to Galilee the first Biblical names in Hebrew, Arabic, and English, the landscape lined with silver-green olive groves and tall eucalyptus. In Haifa long enough to marvel at the golden dome and subtropical gardens of the Bahai, a religion combining key features of all others in nineteenth-century Persia and therefore not tolerated there. After all, no way this almost overly tolerant syncretistic faith could believe in the return of the enraptured prophet, the *Mahdi*. The first Biblical occurrence for Paul to listen to, the community where Saladin annihilated the crusaders in the twelfth century. *Lake Genezareth! Lake Kinneret* sounds similar, Sea of Galilee less so, but this is where everything began! Nazareth, Capernaum, the newly founded Roman Tiberias, which Jesus supposedly never entered. Our hotel a converted *kibbuz,* the early socialist Zionist idealism still in the air without even tipping accepted. Nothing much could have changed in the subtropical landscape, the reedbelt a few yards away and fishing still the hard work it was for the Fisher of Men. Maybe this is why there is a tasty *St. Peter's fish*, also called *angler*? Despite all these religious ideas and Biblical names, none of us even jokingly thinks of walking on the water. Always technically well equipped, Marianne's super gage already indicates 140 below sea level. "This can't be right—oh, I see, these are feet, divide by three!" Scorching heat in Capernaum to see the historical rooms where Simon Peter and his brother Andreas lived. These Biblical lines sure have a different ring here, Marianne's turn to quote from the New Testament today. An octagonal church from the fifth century does makes antiquity come alive easily, the dazzling bougainvillea and the blue-white-collared habits of Carmelite nuns contributing their share. On the spot where Jesus is said to have appeared to the disciples for the third time to confirm the spiritual primate of Peter, Paul is reciting this Sunday's biblical reading during an outdoor mass amidst fig trees, cedars, and the twitter of birds. A stylized stone sculpture of Jesus set off against the gleaming lake behind the altar—if not here, where will the Holy Spirit be hovering above us? Nazareth, the largest Arabic community in Israel, surprises us with its unfortunately logical potential of violence between the fronts. The largest Christian church, that of the Annunciation, where the archangel Gabriel announced his message to Holy Mary, is closed for renovation before the Pope's imminent visit, but we are awed by the inscription Paul is reading out loud in fluent

Latin, *Verbum Caro Factum Est et Habitavit in Nobis.* Dwelling on my brother's reading for linguistic reasons, I must admit I never noticed the Latin aversion toward the letter "*n*" as opposed to the Romance languages and our English *carne, carnal, carnivorous, or carnival.* Our excursion up curvy road to Mount Tabor takes us to colorfully dressed pilgrims from Brazil dancing and others from Ethiopia trilling to curious shouts of "Ah, you know we speak Amharic in Ethiopia!" As if he had not made the point by acting like a *sabra* before, Michael explains that the word, taken from a cactus sweet inside but prickly on the outside, means an Israeli born in the country. Looking down from Mount Tabor we are not surprised to hear that already two thousand years ago the final battle, Armageddon, between the day's superpowers took place at the narrows in the river below. What a perfect spot for any High Noon! Passing Jericho, we are humming the Gospel tune about this battle here before Michael, taking things as lightly as his sense of humor permits, tells us this bit of history. "The Palestinians have always been a problem for us from way back," Bibi Netanjahu complained to Yasser Arafat one day. "How come?"—"Already wanting to wade through the Red Sea ages ago, Moses took off his shoes and put them behind a bush. Noticing that the water level had gone down and he could risk walking, he wanted to put them on again. In vain, they were gone. A Palestinian must have stolen them."—"Impossible! There were no Palestinians around here in those days!"—"Thank you, that's exactly what I wanted to hear from you." A few hours later, Marianne learns from our Palestinian driver that his ancestors were Canaanites who had been here long before the Jews. So, which is the *chutzpah*? Aware of our Austrian pledge to "be perennially neutral" or maybe just to prevent a meaningless discussion, we decide not to tell the likeable cabbie that between King Hussein of Jordan and the old Assad of Syria his Arab brethren have by now killed a lot more Palestinians than did the Jews. Pointing to a blue tank between two palm trees Paul is excited but before he gets to ask questions, Michael explains that this Soviet *T-34* was captured from the Syrians and painted over. Stories and distant memories of *T-34s* rumbling through Hardegg after we children had just seen a German *Tiger* being repaired for the final withdrawal.—Jerusalem! An impressive conglomeration of ancient walls running up and down several hills, tall cedars giving the greyish-ochre stone quality a touch of green. The Golden Gate across from Mount Olive, through which Jesus is said to have entered the city to die a few days later, is the only one directly leading up to the Temple Mount. The crypt of Holy Mary at the foot of Mount Olive survived the destruction of Jerusalem by Saladin only because Maryam is venerated in Islam as the mother of Isa (Jesus), the only woman mentioned in the Quran. Interesting news to us. The seven gold-plated domes of the Russian-Orthodox Mary Magdalen Church, a gift of Tsar Alexander III, are glinting on a hillside even in subdued sunlight. All of us visibly moved by both the holy cobblestones we are treading on, the domes we are struggling to identify correctly, and the quotations brother Paul and other quasi-saints in our group are quoting, we grant ourselves enough time to take in the spirit of Gethsemane. Meaning *oil press* in Hebrew, it is indeed marked by impressive gnarled old olive trees, the knottiest ones not necessarily the oldest as a local Methuselah explains, "It's the ones trying to burrow their way out of old trunks that may well be Biblical." Awe-inspiring, the mere thought of standing next to something still growing since the days of Jesus, according to *Mark 14, 32-34,* where he admonished his disciples to wait for him. A religious and historical highpoint of our wanderings is the stretch between Mt. Olive and the big wall, which our three Abrahamitic religions interpret as the place of the Final Judgment, at least its terrestrial portion. Amazing to see Muslim, Jewish, and Christian stone slabs next to each other here. Not in sight, however, is a bush, a tree, a little recess in the wall, let alone a manmade refuge, and so I am driven to commit what theologians may lightly refer to as a venal sin born of extreme physical displeasure. Also amazing is a barren hill chock full of stone sarcophagi, where Jews already bought themselves a spot in Biblical times to be closer to the world beyond. There are still vacancies. A strange thought, but where is the journey going from here anyway?—Beginning at the Lion's Gate, we are walking the *via dolorosa* through the old Arabic part of *Al-Quds,* "the Holy One," to the *Church of the Holy Sepulchre*, which—an amazing detail—has been opened and closed every day by a Muslim family since the Middle Ages. A veritable battlefield between six religions, the church is no spot for contemplation. "Golgatha, exactly here! Everybody briefly touch the rock under the altar where the cross once stood" a bulletproof guard keeps exhorting the crowd. Clearly visible to the right, the crack that is said to have appeared during Christ's agony. Flashlights, kitschy colored lamps and candles everywhere, gold and silver glinting in the dark, an Orthodox priest alternating between several languages, *"Psst! A holy place! Psst! Terra santa! Heilige Erde!"* Even more pushing and shoving on the way down to the *Holy Sepulchre*. Forty-three lamps, divided up according to a "religious key" dangling from the ceiling. Piety attempted, devotion tried, concentration in vain. What is history, what is an assumption, what is folklore, what is a *schmäh*? Feeling my seventy years of Catholicism shrinking, I am taking the beeline to the exit where I read that Herman Melville once sized up reality in the Holy Land as "disillusioning the traveler by Mammon's perverted activities and overly missionary fuss." Though the basic dignity of the route of Jesus carrying the cross to his death at Golgatha is maintained by all, there is a certain tension. Throughout the day pilgrims from the Philippines carry a cross singing, but our devout friends do better than that by inviting us to walk the entire route without a soul around. Not an old couple afraid of death, nor fanatics, though they have been here twice before, just a farmer and his wife from Marianne's neck of the woods. Reciting a verse out of their prayer book, they stop at each of the fourteen stations. Short quotations at each, No. VI announcing "Veronica offers the veil to Jesus.". Stopping by a Palestinian selling oranges, I am listening to a story as bizarre as any so-called political discussion. Boasting that his father-in-law owns a shop in Florida, where he visits every year, he puts all his political savvy and personal determination into his farewell greeting, *"Hamas* good group, but I don't know. All want peace, but best is Florida." Well, not a visceral hater of America anyway!—Walking toward the Temple Mount in the soft morning glow we are crossing the yard of the Coptic Church with an ancient woman in black surrounded by the monotonous cooing of pigeons. Allowed up here where the Lord had expected Abraham to slaughter his son, we are simply awed by the sheer splendor of the gold-plated aluminum Dome of the Rock, especially the calligraphies reminiscent of the *Shiite* mosques in Iran. Disappointed that we can't even lay our eyes on the footprints of Mohammad's mare, we just accept that it was from the rock *morija* that "he strode toward heaven." *Al Aksa* is closed as well. "You wanna look in?" Accessibility is not a buzzword throughout the Near East, so why should it be here? Sneaking two photos is a bit of a consolation before the grim-looking usher approaches, swinging his bundle of keys. The atmosphere is magic enough to make us walk three complete rounds, a true recovery after all the Christians arguing and pushing. Poking fun at archaeological research in general and particularly at the guide's assertion that the miracle of Pentecost occurred here, our man of the cloth cannot win this round. After all, those inflamed by the descent of the Holy Spirit then allegedly started "speaking in tongues," making any meaningful debate here and now useless.

Men separated from women lining up for passport control to the Wailing Wall, vivid commotion with loud praying, any number of believers in front of us weaving back and forth, bobbing up and down. A few orthodox Jews are carrying around a silver vessel on a kind of cot. Even more bizarre to us, who only understand that there is nothing un-holy happening here, are other groups reading out loud from big books, rhythmically jerking enwrapped Torah scrolls fastened to their foreheads like headlamps. I catch my brother just standing there, bewitched and bewildered, giving me this typical quizzical look of his when he intuitively approves of something without understanding it. Wanting him to share my thoughts, I am whispering "What would our father have said?" Learning that the lower layers of the wall date from Herod's time, we notice believers sticking folded messages between limestones and others already lodged there, written petitions to be removed once a month and buried on Mt. Olive. A bit used to the white keppis by now, Paul and I are debating whether we should leave a message, for we could think of many friends, all *goyim*, who would enjoy the idea. At the entrance to the rebuilt ancient Jewish district the giant heavily guarded seven-arm bulletproof candleholder, the *menorah.* Is it a witness of the seven days of the creation of the world? Of the seven tribes of Israel? Before I know what's happening, a black-kaftaned holy man of sorts is holding on to me, a second one tying a red thread around my wrist, the third holding my hand up to my forehead, mumbling a blessing, "A donation, please" following in perfect German. Michael's dry comment is, "Well-known crooks, the boss and his two employees. Big moneymakers, especially old American ladies are happy to receive a blessing. They are really hated by honest beggars." A slightly more serious matter, Michael tells of the old law of *taqqiya,* allowing Muslims to deceive non-Muslims. "One day when Arafat was negotiating with Israelis, entering compromises with them, he was sharply criticized by fellow Muslims. Soothing his critics, he explained that he had of course done it with *taqqiya* in mind." This communication, Michael adds, was intercepted by *Mossad,* the Israeli secret service. — The afternoon excursion into occupied Bethlehem tells us all we need to see and know. Not allowed into the autonomous birthplace of Jesus, our Israeli guide is waiting for his Palestinian counterpart to take over. Of course, they know each other, have been working together for years. Through a tunnel wrapped in barbed wire we are led across, and nobody has watched me sneaking a few shots. Coincidence or Providence? "Only 20% of us 50,000 Palestinians are Christian, our guide sadly comments. "See this brand-new shiny settlement over there, it's for Russian immigrants. The problem is that this new wall is clearly on Palestinian territory, the dispute lies with the Israeli Supreme Court, but we have been waiting a long time already." Representing the other side, Michael says that the wall costs over a million dollars per kilometer but that the number of assassinations has decreased by a third. Not optimistic that this parable would mellow their standpoints, I am trying anyway.

Eager to get across the Jordan River, a tarantula asked a turtle whether it would carry it across. Replying that this would not be a good idea because, untrustworthy as they are, the tarantula would sting it in the underbelly. "Why should I do that, we would both go under and die." Uneasy yet giving in to the tarantula's pleas, the turtle softened, saying, "All right, hop on, but remember what I said." Sure enough, in the middle of the river, the tarantula swung sideways for a bare second and sank its poison into the soft underbelly." My God, now we'll both drown! why did you do that?" To which the killer answered, "Because we are in the Near East ." Unconvincing smiles, but the two agree that normally anybody with a job in Jerusalem can get to work and back until the slightest provocation brings things to a halt. The difference between Israel and the West bank occupied in the Six Days War of 1967 is clearly visible, everything more improvised and several notches poorer. Being pushed by throngs of noisy tourists through the Grotto of the Nativity, Marianne escapes for a few seconds to crawl down to the silver star marking the exact venue of the Lord's birth. The adoration of the shepherds is supposed to have taken place on a level below, but where is the cradle? Ah, that's been in Rome for some time!—The bus trip to Massada, Herod's summer palace. Camels next to high rises, donkeys passing a stalling tractor, Bedouin encampments sprawled between dunes creeping up to the highway. A first hazy view of something vaguely blue, the Dead Sea. Changing colors from blue via shades of turquois to green, depending on the salt content. Less and less water over the years, Michael explains, adding that in one of these mile-long rock formations shepherds found the rolls of Qumran in 1947. As transmitted by Flavius Josephus, over the years the Romans had come ever closer to the Jewish zealots defending themselves here until the last fanatics decided to commit collective suicide in 73 A.D. Forbidden to do that, they had ordered ten men selected by chance to liquidate their families of which two women and five children survived to tell the story to the Roman historiographer. A national Israeli monument, breathing the idea of "Never again must Massada fall," leads Michael to contradict. "We don't quite see it this way today because when push comes to shove, Israel is not going to go down without a battle." Is history coming full circle? The level of the Dead Sea dropping a meter per year as the result of industrial use has led to advertisements for curing joint and skin problems. "Ten times the salt content of the Mediterranean." Mud-smeared figures stumbling around, aiming at each other with dollops of goo, others trying to force their legs down to get a few clumsy strokes in. Swimming can be fun, acting as if, less so as we quickly realize. Back in the hotel, "candle-lighting" is on, meaning no lights on Sabbath, except if turned on and off by a goi. Another intercultural hurdle I am trying to grasp: the later phase, that of putting out the light, stands before that of turning it on. Yes, of course! I am not used to it yet, but they read from right to left, which doesn't necessarily mean from later to earlier, though. To my left, a Sabbath lift. What is that? It automatically stops on each floor so that an orthodox Jew does not need to push a button. Always interested in political viewpoints, I am asking Michael whether the name of our chancellor Kreisky means anything to him. "Of course, you know that a fair share of Israel's enemies has always come from inside, from Jews themselves." Into the old city past the fully flagged Knesseth and wondering around a grey building, each of its composite blocks numbered, the house in which Theodore Herzl was born in Budapest, brought here and put together piece by piece. "If you will it, it is no dream; and if you do not will it, a dream it is and a dream it will stay" the inventor of Zionism wrote.—The sirens announcing the beginning of the national holiday will start howling in a few minutes, so waiting in front of the hotel seems best. Now, several sirens at once! Everybody is standing up straight, taxis and passenger cars have stopped, their drivers outside. Michael is standing still, his head bent. A compelling wave of solidarity all around. Impressive. Just one fellow squatting on a rock, a pose of studied relaxedness. An Arab who doesn't think too Jewish, an orthodox Jew refusing to accept the existence of Israel, a Peace Now activist, or just an "individualist"? Vad Yashem meaning "One name and one place" from Isaiah is an attempt against forgetting the millions murdered. I am familiar with most of these horror pictures showing German culture so obviously perverted. My first ever film documentation of Jan Karski, parodying FDR in slightly Polish but correct English. The President had assured him that "we shall win the waaar and justice will prevaaiiil, but that minor questions should not stand in the way of defeating Germany now." Questions about the extermination of Jews, of which the escapee Karski had been the first to report in the West. Tracks and barracks, everything clearly visible, but bombs stopped falling 8 km before Auschwitz. Overwhelming the hall here with its eternal flame. Not seeing any, I am reporting it to the flameguard, who is already on his way to rekindle it. All by myself, I have time enough to study the names of the many camps chiseled into stone in Hebrew and English. Solemn, horrible. It is here that one must pray, interdenominationally.—Muslims also believe that Joachim and Anna, Mary's parents, had once lived here in St. Anna, still a beautiful church from the Crusades because it was a mosque for seven centuries. Michael and a few more Jews are here with us Catholics listening to "Amazing Grace" sung by a remarkable choir from Protestant Seattle.—We would love to repeat this journey, preferably with my brother again, and hopefully catching a peaceful phase of an endless conflict again. Soon after our return, there is new hope for peace on the horizon with the election of Barack Obama, young and courageous at that, but can any single politician, however brilliant, stamp out the tingling flames of that tinderbox Near East?

OBAMA ELECTED.—THE ROCKIES AND CANYONS WITH MY RV-DRIVERS. TRYING TO SHOW AND EXPLAIN *MY* AMERICA TO MY NEPHEWS—HALF A CENTURY TOO LATE.

Unable to remember any Presidential debate as high caliber as the one between my Republican favorite John McCain and Barack Obama, I would have been just as happy with the Senator from Arizona except for one thing, the first black President ever. "Just because he is a good speaker does not mean he will be a good President" is a comment I have heard a lot, although the majority in Europe have either show approval or at least grudging admission that the *Land of Liberty* h finally come to this point. For months on end his books have been the party gift number one. "He's got my blessings, and especially those of my kids," Republican Tennys H of Colorado days writes, adding "naïve those who already begin to celebrate the end of racism."

If entering the country in Washington is an indicator of what is awaiting us further west, good night! Already admitted, Otti and I are waiting for our third man who has obviously run into a problem. Returning to find Witi, we spot him in an extra line, his passport showing an ominous "B" attached to it. Alternately smiling and encouraging him to keep cool, we are not worried yet, but the connecting flight to Denver is approaching fast. Picking up the red house phone to find out how long it might take to process W, my "Would you do me a favor..." is brusquely cut off by "We cannot grant any favors, sir." No chance. It has been fifty-five minutes since we last saw him, but then finally and just in time, we have all reached the United Airlines window. Strange, so close to takeoff and we are all by ourselves! The UA man is exceptionally friendly and points to the *computer on duty,* telling us that check-in shut down a few minutes ago. "There are twenty-five minutes to go until takeoff, so where's the problem?" "If plan A doesn`t work, turn to plan B" he says, consoling us to take the next plane in five hours. Turning to me, he says "You lived in the US fifty years ago and have been here several times? You are certainly right, America has changed, o yea, it has *really* changed." What makes me both sad and furious is that the boys have never been to the US and have heard nothing but wonderful stories and memories from me, if not from the media anymore. Trying to chase the blues away, we are ordering clam chowders and hot buffalo steak sandwiches, evoking the spirit of the Wild West at least in the boys' minds. The soups are watery and the sandwiches without the slightest taste. No, America has not changed regarding airport food, I am thinking to myself. Asking W. why he was held up, he recapitulates the Q&A minutes. "Any money on you?"—"No."—"Reason for your trip?"—"Just vacation with two friends."—"You'll still need some money."—"Well, let me see, I have a few dollars here, really only very little."—"But you just said you had no money. Sorry, you will have to line up over there." Was he too soft-spoken and introverted as usual, and if he was too nervous during the interrogation, wasn't the officer an even better example of non-resilient nerves? Lengthy discussions about law and order, exaggerated fears of criminals and foreigners sneaking in. The general tone of welcoming visitors has certainly changed after *9/11,* which is understandable but still enervating. "No, boys, you are wrong, fanatic killers *did* come in the regular way, just like us. One of the *9/11* jihadists arrived via Portland, Maine. Though the customs woman had detected his jackknife, she let the self-professed student through. A bad omen, all this? No, not at all, you have seen Ken Burns' *Lewis and Clark Expedition* on DVD. Do you really think that a small incident like this would have kept them from plowing ahead?" Discovering cardboard full-size images of Obama and Michelle, we shoot photos of ourselves with the first Afro-American Presidential couple and are soon back in our upbeat mood.

A culture shock for breakfast, though a positive one. Choosing between whole wheat, rye, light bread, French toast, rolls, waffles, potatoes, sausages, and bacon is tough, but the waitress asking whether O&W would like to have their eggs scrambled, poached, once over, or sunny side up has them in a bilingual haze. "Please, I would like to just have breakfast!" None of that granola culture here. From now on, W. will settle for hashed browns, and O. will follow me for French toast drowned in maple syrup. Picking up the RV is no problem, surprising to me are *Ziehen* und *Drücken* on the doors as well as German manuals— certainly no necessity fifty years ago. It doesn't take my drivers more than four blocks to be in full control of our *Americruiser,* length 9 m, double clutching. Remembering how fascinated I was by Central City, which we often visited from *Colorado Woman's College* in the "good ole days," we are heading for the old goldminers' town. "Real cool atmosphere" around the original Teller House, seat of the legendary silver millionaire, a scene of Victorian architecture with its old opera house surrounded by saloons with mythical names like *Wells Fargo*, *Annie Oakley,* or *Wyatt Earp.* "You get that at the liquor store, this is Coors country" the funny barkeeper answers O. ordering a microbrew. His genuine looking moustache goes right with his jokes and quotes, but between drafting beers he starts telling us about Central City going downhill. "With the gold rush of 1859 this square mile was probably the richest area in the world for half a century, and what we are looking at now are busloads of retired folks being carted to and from the casino. The rest's a big show for dudes like you," he cracks.—Climbing higher until late into the night, we pitch *Americruiser* at 3,300 m, the two drivers on the double bed behind the wheel, taller O. toward the door to protect his smaller cousin against the cold or bears, and me in a trapezoid-shaped quasi-bed next to the quaint john. Our first camp site is pretty much like all of them, the "Help us preserve our wilderness" sign in action: hot shower in perfect shape, neither water nor paper wasted on the composting toilet, the oiled floor spick and span. What we should have done the night before, we are doing now, namely enter the number of our campsite on a form, put it into the envelope with the $15 fee, and drop it into the metal box at the entrance. Unbelievable, but is this the Wild West we have come to? A $80 pass for all campsites over the next weeks will be well worth it, especially since there is no other way to spend the night.

Heavy fines for parking just anywhere, which is allegedly not true in Alaska and Canada but does not help us now. The wilderness has been tamed, had to be tamed, not against the Indians, but against mass tourism. Driving through the first canyonscape means marveling at spectacular rock formations, its yellow, brown, and reddish shades beyond the sagebrush and occasional tumbleweed rolling in the wind. The three of us agree—this is just the beginning, but the name *Colorado* sure does make sense. Turning south onto Route 128 toward Utah, we are driving along the Colorado River, thin green grass banks against steep red rock walls, too many unique views to capture. Agreeing that this is the landscape we have all seen before in western movies, we also agree that this is the real thing. "There, an eagle tearing a deer to pieces on the roadside!" An unromantic ranger will tell us in a few minutes that it wasn't the bird that killed it, just a driver. It's getting hotter by the hour, black vultures circling above dry skeletons and corroded cables dangling over a forsaken bridge, a man is lugging a tent up to his girlfriend from their rubber dinghy. "This is our third day on the water. Great trip." Unlike everybody else, this fellow doesn't ask where we are from or where we are going. He is completely in tune with the peace of the wilderness. Moab, the Old Testament name pointing to its original Mormon settlers, is a bit of a tourist center now since bikers discovered it about ten years ago. *Dirt shirts*, the latest fad of tie-dyed products combining the rock and sand colors of the land catch our attention at the visitors' center of *Arches National Park.* Remember this name, a great photo of John Muir, who founded the first park *Yellowstone* over a century ago. Creative names like *Three Gossips*, *Tower of Babel,* and *Balanced Rock* reflect the grandeur of the formations. Ascending the *Delicate Arch* along rock cairns in scorching heat, O&W are way ahead of me but our goal, the sunset from the peak, doesn't seem to work out with more and more clouds moving in. A couple at a time, tourists breaking away from their respective flock are huddling under the prominent motif, many of them speaking German to our dismay. "Hey guys, here's a cultural difference for you. We are listening to all those German sounds, Prussian North German at that, but would any one of us even think of yelling *hello*, let alone want to meet them?"—"Not really, but why are you asking?"—"Because nine out of ten Americans meeting their countrymen abroad would make a point, not just of meeting them, but of learning about their itinerary and experiences in the lovely but strange Old World. Mind you, though, this is not a value judgment, just an observation."

Once we have our cameras safely stowed away, we are trying to beat the rain. In vain. Watch out, slipping on the wet sandstone is dangerous! Only last year one of the two-hundred known arches, the spectacular *Wall Arch*, collapsed because of erosion. During an extended jeep tour the self-made outdoors man, knowledgeable and visibly enjoying every bit he is explaining, quickly becomes our hero of the day below his dreadlocks. Witty and spinning tall tales galore, he lives every bit of his job, explaining, showing, touching, picking up—stones, fossils, prehistoric leftovers of plants, "layers of millions of years like in an open book. When uranium was found here sixty years ago, the whole region was contaminated, and endless efforts have been made to clean it up. See the blue lakes glinting in the sun over there? Vast fenced in areas of potash lakes." That much of Utah and Nevada are contaminated is probably not exaggerated. After all, nuclear tests were already made in New Mexico and Arizona nuclear tests were already made during and after the war, with even the civilian use of uranium requiring safe waste deposits. Climbing higher into ever more rugged terrain and windier zones, a certain frontiersman feeling gets ahold of us. Stopping at a particularly spectacular spot, where our guide tells us "Mike Jordan made a famous commercial here, jumping three feet from where we are over to that slightly lower ledge, absolutely nothing in between. Jumping back to his original starting place, he had to jump about three inches higher." Wow, the boys are thrilled at their basketball idol's courage. Of course, the man was secured. The second half of the story makes our blood curdle. "Imitating Mike Jordan, my colleague jumped the same mini distance but not high enough and fell to his death in front of a busload of tourists. The real clincher, he had the bus keys on him, and the shocked tourists had to descend over rough terrain for hours." No tall tale at all! On the way back to our car, a cemetery of sorts. Part of a restaurant, it sports a few funny epitaphs like "Here lies La Sal Sadie, she was a hell of a woman, but not a lady" and "Here lies Dead Horse Dave. Forgot to pack water, wound up in the grave." Stories and History of the old West, what a confounding mix of fact and fiction, so hard to disentangle! Telling the boys what I have told so many of my American students, that in German we have only the word *Geschichte* for the two English words *story* and *history* does not seem to excite them. Doesn't that imply that one cannot ever be fully separated from the other? It is Labor Day weekend and tourists in droves are putting emotional dents into our clear-cut view of what the American West should look like. Somehow, it's all like *The Sound of Music* reversed, with busloads of Americans walking the marked trails from the convent above Salzburg straight into the Alps. Unbelievable, the number of RVs on the road and suddenly five motorcycles, each with the blue cross on white base flag fluttering in the wind—Finns! The yearning to spend a night by an open fire already fueling our imagination, we discard the idea in favor of crawling into our mummy bags in freezing temperature at over 10,000 feet. We know the tune ending with "Deep in the heart of Texas," but never having seen the Big Dipper as big as tonight we are switching to "in the heart of Utahhhh." O. just loves the way they pronounce it here, drawing out the second syllable with each sip of his favorite Corona beer. "The nice woman at the gas station just told me she is Mormon" he reports. "So, what did you expect a Mormon woman to look like?" She tells us that the Mormon State is not run by Mormons anymore, that Brigham Young has lost ground, that drinking came in with the Winter Olympics seven years ago, and that we could now even buy a beer named *Polygamy—Why just one?* Listening to the sonorous voice of *Merle Travis,* a living myth, ties right in with the vastness of the landscape full of Western mythology around *mavericks* and *true grits.* Happy that the boys are thoroughly enjoying it all, including casually returning the high hand of a trucker zooming past us, I am wondering whether this trip can instill at least a fraction of my own fascination, not only with the scenery but also the sundry facets of everyday American life. There is this irredeemable discrepancy between America in the old days, in my five years here, and now in our time, but there are also the totally different backgrounds and expectations they have brought with them. *Bryce Canyon* is our next destination and while the boys are off on a climb down the *Fiery Furnace*, I am spending three hours marveling at the rocks, walls, and turrets changing their shades of red, orange, and brown with the angle of the setting sun. Typical are the *hoodoos,* the whitish caps of salt on top of the columns and spires standing side by side. It has happened to me before, wishing I could inhale all this condensed beauty and keep it stored until needed on a grey day! Plenty of time to recite some of Emily Dickinson to myself. *"Beauty crowds me till I die / Beauty, mercy have on me! / But if I should expire today, / Let it be in sight of thee!"*—Luckily our local radio station announces just in time that today is the birthday of *Colonel Sanders*, the legendary white-goateed founder of *KFC*. "When other babies were still sucking their thumbs, the goodly Colonel was already licking his fingers!" It is the perfect introduction to *Ruby's Inn*, where one family has built an empire round a restaurant and a store of stuffed moose, pumas, black bear and a bookshop is dedicated to the explorers of the region, especially *John Wesley Powell*, probably the first man—certainly the first white man—to go down the Colorado River in a rowboat in 1869. Irresistible for the boys are our evenings in restaurants equipped with two TV sets, one for football in one corner, the second for baseball or basketball in the other, with beer-guzzling tourists glued to the screens. More and more *Kokopeli*, the mythical flutist of the *Ute* people we keep reading about captures O.'s imagination, his nickname for the rest of the West. *Zion National Park* and several villages, peaks, and rivers all reflect the original first

Mormon settlers: *Angel's Landing, West Temple, Altar of Sacrifice, Guardian Angel, The Three Patriarchs (Abraham, Isaac, Jacob),* and *Great White Throne,* a huge white compact limestone. Time to be daring! Eager to finally light a fire in the wilderness, we are pitching our tent in a clearing where dry wood galore will make things easy. Before we know it, the flames are high enough for *Kokopeli* to go for a bucket of water, just t in case. An unbelievably loud concert by cicadas in the still of the night, *Cassiopeia* and the *Big Dipper* brighter than ever. Much to my dismay, my drivers are not too interested in the details of the longest trek ever undertaken in peacetime from New York State to Illinois and from there to the Great Salt Lake in 1847, ending with Brigham Young exclaiming "This is the place." The concept of this new "Promised Land" is hard for them to grasp because they have heard and seen too many discussions and programs dealing with "God's Own Country." Without differentiating much, they begin asking why there were, and still are, so many religious groups and crazy sects like that of Charles Manson in California or the bunch that committed suicide in Texas. They even know about an illegal splinter group of Mormons following the old ways and hiding in the mountains in Utah. Even in Europe we read about the Indian guru who founded a whole village of fanatic followers in the wilderness of Oregon and about the raving and ranting of The Rev. Moon. O. even remembers my obviously vivid description of an evangelical tent meeting I attended as a student in Florida. Why this recurring yen for "religious paradise now"? –"Easy, easy, we need to differentiate a bit. Even if some of these movements were or are out to make fortunes and others have been the sad harvest of maniacs, you cannot understand the founding years of this country without an ongoing search for religious truth. Apart from many Catholics and several Protestant denominations who escaped the persecution by feudal governments or a dictatorial Church in Europe, you had many groups traveling their own roads to new religions or at least new interpretations of old texts."—"Okay, okay. Let's just have a few more Coronas, mine with lime juice, please!"—The next morning the local paper headlines the scary news of a wildfire spreading in the area but adds, much to our surprise, that Congress will have to deal with a bill outlawing not fires, but fighting fires, in protected areas. Ecology carried to its logical conclusion. Lucky, nobody saw our wildfire! Leaving Utahhh past the sparsely populated cemetery of *New Harmony* — "hey guys, have you noticed this name?"—means crossing the scorching desert approaching *Las Vegas.* Hard work for *Kokopeli* at the blackjack table to come out even but no chance at the roulette table with two zeros betting against him here. After a lucky strike of $ 2 at the fortune wheel, the boys are ready to face the scintillating nightlife. We have seen it all on TV, but this is for real! What an incredible mix of imitation Venice and Rome, waterfalls included, the megalomania of several new hotels, the relatively modest old *Caesar's Palace*, and the raw kitsch of *Treasure Island.* Leaving them to themselves, I am wandering back hearing more Russian than I have ever heard since post-war Vienna. Back at the original *Sahara Hotel* where the three of us are residing for all of $26, I am enjoying black-and-white photos of the old days, including some of *Louis Prima.* Ah, for the fifties! Crossing the Colorado River over the technological mega-miracle of the *Hoover Dam* means moving from Nevada into Arizona, the gasoline bills always about half of ours in Europe. Passing *Rattlesnake Wash* with nothing but cactuses along the scorched route goes well with the whining country music, and so does *Kokopeli,* a red bandana around his forehead like Arlo Guthrie in "Alice doesn't live here anymore." The south rim of the *Grand Canyon* in blinding sunshine, flags at half-mast on

September 11. A couple of quick hugs at dawn and the boys are off on their sunrise hike down the canyon, only their headlamps showing their descent for a few minutes. Wandering along the rim, shutterbugs are preparing for the magic moments. This intense beauty of the rocks, turrets and ledges changing colors almost by the minute, shadows of gnarled pines creeping up on spots still shrouded in semi-darkness, how to absorb and store it all! Though aghast at the air-conditioned "hop on, hop off" shuttle bus, I am surrendering to the distances and the heat and by mid-morning am boarding this perfect example of "You can`t have your wilderness and civilize it too." O&W are back within five and a half hours and understandably sick and tired of one more red rock. Driving along the land of the *Navajo Nation,* signposts and the local radio station in *Diné,* their language and name for themselves. Hard to believe, but *Lake Powell,* the huge result of the Colorado River dammed up by the *Glen Canyon Dam,* is surrounded by 1,800 miles of perfectly treeless stratified rock. What a bizarre moonscape! *Coyote's* twenty-second birthday tonight has three highpoints—choosing from among five types of steak, overcoming the shock of the big talkative waitress introducing herself as "Michelle, and twenty-two like you," and following the *Green Bay Packers* against the *Chicago Bears* over more beers than usual. Yet another highpoint is the *Antilope Canyon,* completely different from all others but still crawling with tourists including us. Driving us through raw desert, a heavy-set Diné drops us at the entrance to the narrow canyon, where we are told that our canyons pass is valid "only in the U.S." and that we need to add six dollars to the $25 tour fee. A surprising extra, it leads to a serious little debate between the boys about how autonomous the Navajo really are. Leading us through a tunnel of vertical sandstone, the guide keeps throwing sand up in the air with the dazzling effect of sunlight spraying the grains into sparkling dust and hitting the walls, some still showing the marks of riptides from downpours above. In the supermarket everything is bilingual, not English-Spanish, but English-Diné. The one prototypical Western landscape we have all "seen before" in numerous movies is *Monument Valley.* Lucky to be only the sixth RV, we are parking directly in front of *The Mittens,* probably the most impressive of the giant formations with a rainbow arching above and the ghost of *John Wayne* stalking us. A strange mood has descended on us, part pride to have made it here and part awe before this geological miracle. Driving past the *Three Sisters*, *Elephant Butte* and *Camel Back* easily explains these names, but buying a T-shirt with the native view of American History makes my day. The heads of *Geronimo* and three other famous *Apaches* with *First Homeland Security Since 1492* spelled across it are set against the four Presidential heads hewn into rock in South Dakota. Inspired but confused by so many famous heads, we are soon caught up in another little history lesson. "You have heard the name *Thomas Jefferson* before—no, not *Jefferson Airplane*, stop being sillier than you are. You already know that he supported the first cross-country expedition ever by Lewis and Clark." This finally rallies their attention around the quasi expedition they feel we are on, and when I mention that a coin has just been issued with the image of the Indian woman interpreter through the Pacific Northwest, they are truly excited. *Sacajawea,* probably a *Shoshone,* two names they keep practicing more for days. *Four Corners* is another of those mythical power points, the flags of the *Grand Canyon State*, the *Mormon State*, the *Centennial State*, and the *Land of Enchantment* fluttering in the wind as perfect photo motifs. The three of us and a few Americans alternately standing on each of the four corners makes for a certain communal longing to be part of one great experience. For days on end the boys will be quizzing each other about which state has which flag and which nickname.

Back to another reality in the casino owned by the *Ute* people, its outdoor fresco decorated in stark contrast to the turmoil of hundreds of natives working one-armed bandits. Wrinkled faces of old women with colorful ponchos and weather-beaten features of men, some with heavy bolo ties and huge belt buckles and others with huge Stetsons are part of the scene as are T-shirts like "No Gambling with the Lord." No, this is not my poor eyesight, this is a young mother changing her baby's diapers between two crap shooting tables, next to her the croupier dressed in elegant black. The *Ute* guide is witty but not too careful with the few facts he knows. He does not know how many *Ute* there still are because they are divided into seven bands and his band comprises about nine hundred people, he says. Most are not pure *Ute* anymore, he and his wife are half Navajo, which is why he is learning Diné. "Everything must remain where it has always been" is the one important rule, and we better not pocket a little stone if we want to keep the FBI at bay. During the winter months he works on oil rigs in New Mexico where the work is backbreaking but the money good enough to send his daughter on a trip to Europe. "You are from Venice, you said?" is his parting question. "It's Vienna, but don't worry, many professors have confused that over the years!"—*US 160* takes us up to the forty adobe ruins integrated into *Mesa Verde* National Park. The huge difference between standing in the famous *Cliffs Place* forty years ago and now is that we were four visitors then and one guide. Just for a handful of us, there are now two superbly trained guides, well-equipped to answer questions and eager to preach the gospel of environmental protection. "There are two hundred rooms and twenty-three *kivas* here, most of them to be reached by steep ladders. Around 1300 AD the estimated five thousand inhabitants disappeared, probably because of a drought." Like an impregnable fortress, *Balcony House* below us is aflutter with big black birds, wild turkeys!

Disappointed though I sometimes am that the boys are either too shy or too disinterested to talk to even their peer group, I am happy that after these astounding contrasts we have just been through they have opened up a bit. Weighing the pros and cons, we are debating whether owning their own casinos is a blessing or a curse for the natives. "It's like with the oil found on native land in Oklahoma, those licenses are a mixed blessing at best."—"I guess they should take advantage of those relatively new concessions and make the most of the revenue. Even our guide just mentioned that most of it has been used in a constructive way for their own tribal concerns, especially education."—"I hope he sees it the way it is. I am more upset reading about older tribal members complaining that by focusing on making money and too often wasting it, they are quickly losing the last vestiges of their own culture. Most of their young probably see that differently."—"You are right, they should see it differently! I can't hear that complaining about 'losing our roots' anymore, about how the white man's civilization has brought us ruin."—"Well, but they did, or perhaps we all did."—"Okay, of course on a bigger scale this makes sense, but the only rational choice a young Native American can make today is to take advantage of the opportunities opening up and cherish his tribal ways at home and among his community."—"You are ignoring the centuries of injustice and, even now, of their limited opportunities on the job market."—"Unfortunately, you are right on both counts, but a well-educated *Ute* or *Navajo* will make it if he is good at his job. The alternative is self-pity that leads nowhere. Cultures and languages have vanished all over the world for millenniums, some more quietly and with less pain than others, but it's the way the cookie crumbles, as they say here." From a different background than his cousin, *Kokopeli* is carrying on about our guide's lack of knowledge even about his own *Ute* culture and about what the two women had at *Cliffs Palace*, namely motivation, knowledge, and an interesting way of presenting them. Of course, the two women cannot really be mentioned in one draw of breath with our *Ute*, but I am admonishing him to be fair and take the two vastly different backgrounds into consideration. "Never judge a man until you have walked two miles in his moccasins." College graduates, probably not from poor backgrounds, and a *self-made man* within limits, who maybe not even finished high school. "How do you lift your mug of beer to your mouth, wherever you are from?" is a native's funny reply to my question what *The Elbow* on a pub means. Hearing Austria, he walks down *Silverton's* main road with us, explaining that a hundred years ago it was the embattled zone between "the Italians" on one side and "the Austrians" on the other, all mine workers from impoverished Europe. Now the sign read out loud for us in in slapstick Italian makes sense. "You-a keep-a on de odda side-a of de street-a!" His complaints are that prices are constantly being jacked up by developers from the East, that all kinds of bigshots have bought property, and that over the last five years they have had to lock up everything. *Telluride, Leadville, Ouray, Silverton, Durango*—just pronouncing these names gives us an outdoorsy feeling, the boys pointing out the many offers of climbing, skiing, and wild game hunting. To me gentrification compared to fifty years ago is the one lingering impression, everything is less typically American or putting it in more critical terms, more nondescript. Knowing what enchantment means by now, the boys agree that New Mexico certainly feels warmer than Colorado and more *Hispanic*. A native of Taos implores us not to get lost in the traffic jams of sightseers there. Yes, the characteristic adobe houses are still there, as are several old Spanish mission churches, but the picturesque artists' colony, let alone that which *D.H. Lawrence* depicted in his books, are history. "What's new", she must be teasing us, "is the 100% smoke free Indian-owned *Taos Mountain Casino."* In Santa Fé the *Wheelwright Museum,* built like a *hogan*, a Navajo house, is impressive because it is dedicated to the story of a teacher who encouraged native children in the thirties to draw as much as they could of their own homes and environment, realizing that within a few decades this would be the only way of learning about their native past. Camping on the coolest site yet, spick and span with adjustable shower heads, a closed society around a champagne bar in "the land of enchanting wilderness." Cheers, anyway! In Santa Fé the next morning, we are surprised by the stark native faces in the cloisters of St. Francis Basilica, its neo-Romanesque style reminiscent of Assisi more than of the surrounding natives selling their blankets and jewelry under wooden arcades. Even more surprising is the statue to *Kathi Tetakwitha,* a Mohawk from faraway upstate New York, the first Native American to be canonized. Not at all surprising are the clusters of tourists, especially since Santa Fé has been a regular entry in *Lonely Planet.* Neither of the boys is surprised that the waitresses are from Moldavia. Hurrah for globalization, the excellent Italian coffee included! A nondescript plaque at a street corner catches my attention, the official HQs of the team that once worked on the *Manhattan Project.* If I had to cajole my drivers into visiting the *Georgia O'Keeffe Museum,* I left with two converts to the painter who once left the Big Apple for a simpler life in the desert.

Slowly climbing the Colorado Plateau up to 3000 m, we are arriving in Leadville, another silver mining town with a flair of the Old West. Eager not to miss the deadline at the RV center, we don't even have enough time to visit the Denver campus where I once introduced Jed to Perry, where I learned some American history and poker from Tennys H., and where I filled by VW beetle up to cross the prairies to return home. Memories are made of this. Straight to the airport for a mini photo of Obama adorning a beer tap with Kokopeli smiling back at him, a memorable motif shot exactly three weeks after the one with the cardboard Obamas.—Will my plan for the lobby at Dulles Airport work? Yes, it does. There's Bill, my roommate of half a century ago, holding my name up high and a history student of twenty years ago waiting to meet the four Austrians—*Kokopeli*, *Coyote*, me as a young man, and me three times his age now.

YET ANOTHER TERM WITH *HOPE COLLEGE*. TO TURKEY WITH ITS TRAVEL-SAVVY DIRECTOR.

All these twenty-five odd months of May with Hope College have been wonderful experiences, not merely of delving into *Austrian History* but also of rewarding opportunities to hear and see how twenty-year old Michiganders and Michigeese think and what, as we used to say on campus long ago, *turns them on*. It is with a mix of embarrassed giggles, a few male roars, and the help of some merciful souls that I am learning of the semantic change this phrasal verb has gone through.

As so often, all I need to get started is a flip chart. "You see my family name *Czermak*. Looking at it or listening how it is pronounced, what language background is it?"— "Hungarian?"— "Could be, if it was spelled differently."— "Anybody else want to try?"— "I think it's Slavic because of the *czer*-spelling." —"You are right, it is rather Slavic, though Hungarian has the same sound but isn't Slavic. Any idea which Slavic?"— "Maybe Czech because they are next door."— "Good thinking. Not that I want you to remember this detail, but my intention is to get you excited about history and everything round about it."—"Okay, but what does it mean?"—"I don't speak Czech but know a few words. "*Czern*" means *black* in all Slavic languages and *mak* means *poppyseed*." Within seconds, the only African-American sends the class roaring with laughter. "Well, if it's black, it can't really be all that baad!" We are spending quite some time on getting the basics right because they cannot really understand a text if they confuse geographic with linguistic, or ethnic with political concepts.

"No, John, nobody speaks Bohemian, the majority speak Czech and the small rest, we'll get to that later, speak German. Bohemia was a kingdom in the Middle Ages, and it is the western portion of the Czech Republic now."

Even if we are focusing on the past century and a half, nobody studying history here should leave without having gone through the *Imperial Vault,* where hundreds of Habsburgs lie buried. What is putting this group in a mood funnier than their forthcoming visit is the sign, "Despite repair work, vaults in full operation." I am surprised that so many twenty-year-olds are fascinated by the gem-studded gold crown of the *Holy Roman Empire* donned by Charlemagne almost a thousand years ago. *Awesome!* Trying to avoid discussing why the ten-foot upright narwhal tooth is considered a medieval treasure, we rarely pass it without at least one male shaking his head over this symbol of fertility as well as chastity.

It is encouraging indeed, though rare enough, to have alert minds wonder whether they should not switch to *History* from a major they feel does not do justice to their intellectual curiosity. Then there is the other extreme, sophomores regretting or proudly asserting they have had two *History* courses, one *The History of Michigan* and the other *The History of Mesozoic America.* My worst shock ever was a student breaking out in tears because she had missed all the points, lines, and borders on a midterm map. When she let us know that she had never held an atlas in her hands anywhere, I thought of the many harsh judgments on American secondary education that I usually downplayed. What choice did I have but to encourage her to just look at the maps often enough, consoling her that forty years ago even the Governor of Colorado had put Austria behind the Iron Curtain during his talk. She survived the course unbroken.

Trying to become less demanding over the years is tempting, considering that almost all these students are fulfilling a requirement, that many would never have come to Europe without this program, and that even the slower and lazier ones will be better off having sniffed the air "pregnant with history" and chock full of architecture and art. Reading the definition(s) of *nation, national, nationalism,* and *nationalist* excites them beyond my expectations. "It says in the textbook that Austria is a nation, but if most of the people are German and peak German?"— "Excellent question. In Central Europe *nation* was identified along ethnic lines in the nineteenth century. The present way of defining a nation is *all the people of different ethnic, linguistic, and religious background having lived within one region."*—"You mean it's like in the U.S. We are *one* Federal state and *one* nation because so many different national groups have lived within the same boundaries?"—"Correct, although I wonder if everybody professes to be part of the *American nation* beyond showing his American passport."—"We all would, certainly."—"I am sure you would, but I have met people who said, "Yeah, I am an American citizen, but I am really Puerto Rican or, further away, Yoruba. The Yoruba I knew years ago didn't even give me the name of his state Nigeria but told me "where my soul resides." A simple way for you to comprehend these complexities is to ask yourselves how many *German states* there are, and how many *German nations.* Anybody?"—"Germany and Austria, two."—"You forgot one, though."—"Switzerland, of course."—"No, Switzerland is a well-functioning state, but it does not just include German speakers but almost as many French and fewer Italian speakers." Two students swooping down on a tiny enclave on the Austrian-Swiss border on their maps, "It's this tiny thing, but what's its name?"- "The *Principality of Liechtenstein*! You could win one of those *60,000-dollar question* shows. Are they still on TV? The point is that we have three and a half German states inhabited by one German nation." This hands-on approach, garnished with Viennese *schmäh*, a Yiddish term hard to translate but something like employing subtle satire to the point of bending "objective truth" a wee a bit. That despite decades of bitter battles, the economic and political integration of the fourteen nations within the Austro-Hungarian Monarchy may well have been more successful than that of Europe today is a scary insight to many in class. How the defeated Germans and Austrians were humiliated at the Parisian *Suburb Treaties* after World War I should always serve as a warning to victors everywhere how not to treat losers. "Hitler's ascent to power was to a large part the result of humiliation, and if some think that this is too far-fetched, let's discuss how long you believe it might take the Serbs to forget the Croatian *Ustasha* killer commandos, or the Croats and Bosniaks to forget the recent Serbian massacres. Or closer to our world, you can surely come up with ba few blatant examples of smoldering hatred never letting up."

On the day of reckoning the final exam sometimes produces unheard of interpretations or relationships. "Identify the following ten concepts, one of them being NSDAP." The precious answer deserving an *A+* for honesty and courage, "I have no clue, but Herb's father was in it." Correct, my father had joined the Nazi party out of conviction but primarily for reasons of professional advancement. Grading another exam years later, I was mighty surprised to find that taking a stab in the dark one student had matched the ancient Habsburg widow *Zita* with my classmate *Vranitzky,* chancellor of Austria at the time. We have usually been able to lace the challenges of History with lots of humor, much of it unforced.

Grade inflation has usually made the suffering of the less fortunate ones bearable, though I recall a student arguing that "a *B* is below my standards" and her disappointed classmate driving the point home to me that "I need a better grade for my semester average." Not always easy to prove your point and to stand by your decision and even harder to convince them that they will be much better off in life if they learn to define themselves along lines other than their grades.

Toward the end of the term, questions like this and the answers I try to instill in their minds abound. "Herb, what would you say is the most important thing to pursue or abide by now that we are gradually heading toward a degree?"—"Strange though this may sound to you, the answer is not all that difficult. Let me give you a quick rundown on my own process of elimination when I finished highs school at eighteen. Having flunked math and not really feeling at ease with physics and chemistry, I precluded them right away. Interested in good summer jobs and eventually in a satisfactory position were not enough to egg me on toward fully comprehending economics. Next one crossed out. The mere thought of studying and cutting up corpses, sewing up torn thumbs, or shoving a syringe into a live limb were enough to liquidate medicine from my list. A semester of constitutional law and half-finishing a popular but incredibly dry book on the legal aspects of tackling real life narrowed my option down to the humanities. Languages, history, literature, philosophy, psychology. Then I was lucky because your grandfathers walking and driving around Vienna in their GI uniforms and playing their music awakened my interest in their language and why they were in Europe in the first place. Language and history, you see the connection? Put in a nutshell, *Appetite comes with eating.* Two warnings—*Do not ever go into a field of study or, worse, a position for the only reason that it will fill your bank account*! And secondly, *Just above average isn't good enough, but the top few percent will always make it in the long run!"*

A special course offered has been *Senior Seminar,* featuring Austrians talking about their exceptional lives. "Why do you think God or Providence has chosen to spare only you out of eighty comrades in the American bombing raid you described?"—"Believe me, since that day I have spent many hours trying to find the answer. It has not been easy to shed my guilt feelings. And then there are moments when I believe that it takes as much faith to believe in meaninglessness as it does in some reason beyond me."—A blind American living in Vienna for many years told the class how hard life was for him because during his language studies he had to listen to well-meant but insulting comments like "Why are you working so hard for this degree, you will never be able to be a professional translator." Some students were upset, arguing that nobody in the U.S. would make such an insulting comment, let alone give such horrible advice. A few decades earlier, my American ego-half might have agreed with them, but by now I was ready to believe that brutality was well balanced between our continents. Not only did he get his degree in Vienna, but he also finished a law degree by Braille—where else but in the U.S.?—My old friend Helmut, POW in Colorado and then devoted priest, always eager to convince people of his views as a believer, spent much of his lecture blasting American engagement in Vietnam. "I just cannot understand the willingness of your governments to sacrifice so many lives for no intelligible reason. Accustomed to helping refugees from many countries at our parish, we are now trying to help Vietnamese boat people to begin a new life Europe." The pensive silence following his remarks left all of us thinking, most of us impressed, and only a few angry. Even I, so willing for many years to see America fight evil wherever it raised its head, had become less sure of equating Communism with Nazism. Putting a complex issue in a nutshell, Communism was just as violent in Vietnam as everywhere else, but maybe it could at least nourish its millions?—The mock sparring session good old champ Peter offered in his presentation about "boxing versus brawling," accompanying each explanation with the appropriate bodily move, did not leave us with the slightest sign that within a decade he would be succumbing to Alzheimer's or worse "This God damn boxing!" as he put it toward his end. He was 82, his red boxing gloves in front of his coffin. —

Joseph S., son-in-law of my old friend Maria V., both victims of Nazi rule, had a particularly incredible story to tell. Even by the diabolic standards of what these unfortunates had to go through, his story is more than breathtaking. Hiding in a garbage can at the age of eight, he was detected by a guard and heard him order his gopher "to get rid of this scum by tomorrow." He would have been killed for sure if the bombing of Dresden that same night, February 13, 1945, had not thwarted his torturers' plans. "Something like at least 50,000 civilians died that night so that a handful of us could survive." Not easy to read, but *Slaughterhouse 5* is Kurt Vonnegut's surreal account of the bombings he survived as a POW. Most memorable, asked whether after all these horrors he believed in God, his reply was "No, I do not." And after a few seconds, "But maybe He does in me." With many months to go until next summer, we are trying to find more unusual lives told by life itself.

Exhausted but happy that both summer sessions were literally part of history by now, Prof. Stephen H., Marianne and I went to Turkey. Why Turkey? Two near conquests of Vienna centuries ago, hundreds of thousands of guest workers pushing into Central Europe to improve their lots and fill our rapidly dwindling workforce, several unmistakable improvements of our cooking with spices leading the way. And the proverbially tasty Turkish coffee.—Boarding the bus to Cappadocia from

Ankara, we did not expect much English except for any number of mutilated phrases but were pleasantly surprised to see a T-shirt with a mouth wide open screaming "Fuck Google. Ask me!" When Stephen's suitcase was not unloaded at the terminal, we included all the bus stops *en route* into the search. Drivers, clerks, porters, telephone operators all working hard, especially once it became known that it was the luggage of a professor from the United States that was lost. Sure enough, after a few tense hours the suitcase was brought to our hotel, employees apologizing and visibly glad that the whole thing was the result of rare congenital twin suitcases.

Just for openers, the dozens of appropriately termed "fairy chimneys" hewn into bizarre geological rock beat everything we had imagined. Roughly the shape of cones or mushrooms, many open for us to climb in, one of them even inhabited by a family. In the course of more chimney explorations, we learned that until a few years ago some of these unspoiled dwellings had been for sale for a couple of thousand dollars. More prone to embark on zany adventures than Marianne, Stephen and I spent hours imagining how it would be to withdraw into this chimney-pocked landscape or to stage a seminar here. Reading up on the six millennia-history of this ancient Persian province, we recognized some of the names of ethnic groups we had seen in Persepolis a few decades ago, paying tribute to their supreme overlords. Dareus I and Xerxes: Armenians, Bakhtrians, Lydians, Medes, or Phrygians. Wandering through the cave town of Ürgüp, whose name in context with *büyük bölüm,* meaning *a big part of,* might well be the cradle of all German *umlauts,* we came to a valley known for a tree growing hundreds of blue *evil eyes,* regional charms. In Göreme, known for its ancient churches with partly still recognizable early Christian frescoes and others disfigured during the Muslim expansion, Stephen and I arranged for a balloon ride early next morning. Scary though watching the firing procedure at close range was, we soon enjoyed any number of views over the endless rock desert to the reddish horizon. Now dipping into a side valley for more stratified tuff formations of turrets and crags and torching us up higher again, all in total tranquility. Communicating with the other eight spaceships by "flame thrower" was fun, the Morse code translated into so many shorter and longer hisses and puffs. Watching us landing gently, Marianne was visibly relieved to find us healthy and enjoying the hilarious procedure of shrinking our balloon back to normal.

Istanbul was as fascinating as ever, Topkapi still bursting with unbelievable treasures bar any remnants of the *harem*, the mosques wide open to barefoot tourists. Walking across the Bosphorus from Europe to Asia was intriguing but no match for sauntering over Brooklyn Bridge. And yet, visiting the ancient *Hagia Sophia*, once the orthodox basilica until the Muslim conquest of Byzantium in 1453, then a mosque until the foundation of modern Turkey after World War One, now a museum about to become a mosque again. The famous *Blue Mosque*, a compilation of hand-painted blue tiles inside and drowned in blue light at night, could be taken to be a masterpiece of Cristo, the avantgarde wrapper and packer of houses, bridges, mountain tops, and islands if it were not for the six minarets around it and the fact that no such sacrilege could occur in a country with its religious half on the rise. With eyes wide open and palates alert, Marianne had no problem noticing the obvious shift away from founder *Atatürk's* major commandment of separating church and state. All this was not so easy for our American friend to discern, who ventured into a comparison with evangelical groups at home. The waiter's "No gentlemen, we do not serve beer, this is a Muslim restaurant" signaled the new era in cosmopolitan Istanbul, which did not permit alcohol within 200 m from mosques and schools. My "excellent, we would need that next our schools" surprised the waiter, as did the fact that too tired to look for a more decadent Christian place, we stayed and enjoyed the tasty and healthy local fare with American coke. The overall street scene also appeared a bit less exuberant compared to what we remembered. Pointing at a woman clad in body-length black and her veiled face reduced to a slit for her eyes, Marianne could not get enough of the this stringently dressed tourist from somewhere closer to Mecca and holding her cellphone to where her ear must be and laughing out loud through her hiding. Our *haram* question of "May I take a photo?" sometimes led to instant posing and at other times had to be chalked up as *misfired.* Six women in black sitting cross-legged in a semicircle and listening to a seventh one reading to them made for a picture of seriousness amidst other visitors to the *Suleyman Mosque* just sitting or lounging over carpets in red. The finely sculptured *mighrab*, the prayer niche, in the direction of Mecca and the pendulum of an old-fashioned clock swinging away on the wall appeared as incompatible as ever. Sauntering through various souks and inhaling the fumes and colors of herbs, candies, candles, wools, and enameled plates was as inviting as ever. Inquiring what *bismillah* meant, a word we had seen in both alphabets, we were told it was a holy word uttered before prayers. Represented on a huge scaffolding, 34 times 24 of the same calligraphy, it meant *boundless.*

ENTER WFU, ITS STUDENTS AN EXTRA CATEGORY. DEBATING AN AUSTRIAN'S "WE ARE ALL AMERICANS." FOUNDERING ON THE RUINOUS ROCK OF RACIAL *IDENTITY POLITICS.*

Because his daughter had enjoyed my course at the *Institute of European Studies* several years ago, her father asked me if I would like to teach on a semester-basis for *Wake Forest University* at the villa they own. Located in one of the formerly American-occupied districts, the house was full of beautifully paneled old rooms and furniture with the maps of the Monarchy, modern Austria, and the EU carefully pinned to the walls. The survey course meant making meaningful decisions about which important and fascinating periods and themes to include and which to omit.—"Objective history, literally understood, is humanly impossible even under optimal circumstances, simply because selecting certain materials or aspects and ignoring others is already a form of subjectivity." Ah, this was the type of discussion I was looking forward to, but not to spread myself too thin was even more important now. *The geographic, ethnic, linguistic, religious, economic, and political issues eventually destroying the Austro-Hungarian Monarchy* was the basis. *World War One, the Peace Treaties creating the so-called successor states and their gradual decline into dictatorships* were the logical steps toward World War II. *The history of Austria and the successor states during and after World War Two until their gradual EU membership* would round off our syllabus, only marginally seen through my own set of subjective glasses. The World Cup in skiing underway in Grenoble supplied the stroke of genius that broke the ice. Putting the names of several champs on the flipchart, I was having them tell the country they competed for by looking at their names. Coming from North Carolina, there was a slim chance they would know the racers and spoil the game. *Innerhofer, Marsaglia, Théault, Staudacher, Meillard, Hirscher,* Moelgg "Which of these names sound like the country they are racing for?"— "They are almost all German names, but since there are a lot more Austrian than German super skiers, most are probably Austrian."—"Good thinking, so who are all Austrians?"— "*Innerhofer, Staudacher,* and the last three."— "Sorry to say so as an Austrian, but the two you named and the last one are Italian."—One of the students knew why this was so—her ancestors were from *Meran,* which she called *Merano,* and she knew about the highly controversial partition of Tirol after WW One. "*Théault* has got to be French, with this 'thing' on the *é,* the same for *Meillard,"* another student was sure.— *"Good,* except *Meillard* is Swiss. Remember, half their population speaks French and they have more of the highest mountains, too. *Hirscher* is a German name but luckily he is Austrian. Whose name in the list is the only one as Italian as *spaghetti?"*—"That's easy, *Marsaglia.* My granny is from around Napoli."—"This sort of knowledge sounds like just a game, but believe me, linguistic and ethnic differences have wrought loads of problems over here for centuries. Come to think of it, you didn't have to leave your shores to learn about that, right? While we are at this, nobody ever spoke Yugoslav, which is a purely political concept founded after World War I and defended against the Nazis by Tito. As long as Yugoslavia survived, they spoke Serbo-Croatian officially, his political coinage to downplay age-old ethnic and linguistic battles. Moving back to square one, two decades after his death, the

Serbs speak Serbian again, the Croats Croatian, and the Slovenes Slovenian. All this is eminently important and played a major role in the Balkan wars over the last hundred-odd years but it is also ridiculous, for there is hardly any difference between Serbian and Croatian, except of course the Serbian Cyrillic alphabet. “Can we say it’s like German and Austrian?”—“Yes, although here too, there are people so afraid of anything German since the catastrophe of World War II and as a result so gung-ho Austrian that they talk about the *Austrian language.* No, there is only *Austrian German*, *Viennese German,* or *Swiss German*, and naturally *Bavarian* or *Berlin German* if we start talking about regional variants.”—“I am an *Art History* major, so I know what a *bohemian* is, but I doubt that they speak Bohemian.”— “You are right, not just your *bohemien* can’t speak Bohemian, but nobody does. In Bohemia, which is the western Czech Republic with Prague as the capital, the majority speak Czech and the rest of the three million ethnic Germans still living there speak German.” Having read the pages on how many began to sympathize with Hitler in the twenties, joined him in the thirties, and were summarily expelled in 1945, they began a lively discussion about revenge and its limits. “Sir, you said that your own childhood memories of old women and children starving by the roadside at the Czech border are still with you. They sure would be with me, too, but what about many more Czech women and children dying at the hands of the Nazis?”—“The question is excellent because it gives us the opportunity to stop comparing things that should not be compared. Czech civilians killed by the Nazis were clearly victims of crimes or casualties of the war, unless we declare any war to be a crime anyway. Most of the expulsions or killings of people in 1945 happened *after* the war. Besides, they were all Czech citizens, and just because they were ethnic Germans did not necessarily prove they had actively joined Hitler's world."— "You mean they should have been tried in court, but in our textbook the only trials mentioned are those against some of their own leading Communists." These students sent over on the Wake Forest program were certainly above average, one semester standing out in particular because, excepting one student, the best fifty percent were Chinese-American, Korean-American, and Indian-American (from India). One African-American of that group was excellent to the point of being a sensation. Brilliant and blessed with a great sense of humor, he asked me one morning whether it would be o.k. to miss class for two days because he needed to fly to New York for a job interview. "Come again?" was my bewildered question. "Yeah, it looks good for me, but they want a decision now."— "Good God, Jasper! Thanks for even asking. Good luck!" He was back in class Monday morning, with a top job in electronics, a black country boy, all of twenty-one years. For weeks we were discussing whether Marxism-Leninism-Stalinism or National Socialism was responsible for more deaths until I advised them to plow through Timothy Snyder's *Bloodlands* for details, adding that if they go on comparing these insanities long enough, they'll end up with a tie. Often tempted to end endless discussions, I summed it up like this. "Everything else being equal, there are still the beautiful ideas of an economically and socially improved world left by Marx, at least the so-called early Marx without resorting to Lenin's killing squads. What better world, however, did Hitler and his consorts have in mind except one without Jews and other inferior races?" Most of them not History majors, they were sensitive enough to tackle even quasi-philosophical issues, and so we scheduled a poll one day, asking how many believed that "Those who cannot remember history are doomed to repeat it." "That's *George Santayana*" our American Lit major recognized the quote. The vote came out a tie, the pessimists slightly ahead.

"History never repeats itself."—"Of course, its details never repeat themselves but perhaps similar constellations do, benefiting from better ways of dealing with them."—Sensing their argumentative mood, I asked "So, what does it mean to you to read that in Greek mythology *Mnemosyne*, the goddess of Memory, had two children, *Klio*, the muse of History, and *Kalliope*, the muse of Epic Literature?"—"I can't even pronounce the name of that goddess, but I guess it's a more amusing way of saying that her one child is something real or exact and the other something fictitious and vague."—"You are right on track, and maybe this definition will make it even clearer. 'History is that novel which actually happened,' a brilliant aphorism by French nineteenth-century novelist *Goncourt*." Roaring laughter, some claiming that it was simply a clever paradox, that *history* and *novel* mutually exclude each other by definition. "No, come on, no brilliant French novelist would have risked his reputation by giving you a simple little paradox. That's the whole point—there cannot ever be any such a thing as *pure facts* because the minute you collect or interpret them you have already altered them. This is why the truth contained in great literature is the result of facts, though facts polished to a degree of artistic perfection." It was for quite a few sessions that we went on like this and at the end pretty much agreed that great literature can indeed, or at least should try to, penetrate to Truth by transcending the mere facts provided.

When Uncle Sam's world-wide decline in power conjured up by America baiters for as long as I can remember but also predicted by experts at ever shorter intervals became hard to ignore, an Austrian political scientist wrote "We are all Americans," a title that must have caught America scoffers on the wrong foot. Not questioning the relative loss of world-wide political and economic influence, he argues that too many of us either refuse to accept, or have lost track of, our eagerness to follow American ideas, expressions, trends, gadgets of everyday life, and how Americanized we have become in the process. That English, especially its American variant, became the preferred and sometimes only way of communicating is old hat, and paranoia about terms for which German has no or only rough equivalents is uncalled for. *Schönen Tag noch* for *Have a Nice Day*, one of dozens of literal translations, sounded funny only a decade ago and *Kaffee To Go* is the latest cool acquisition. That a whole subculture of American dirty words, not at all limited to four letters, has made it on the walls of public buildings has enriched the vocabulary of teenagers learning the language. This is not so because scribbling the German would naturally take up more space but because the American originals guarantee more peer group prestige. How casually American to hear our newscasters calling each other by their first names! More importantly, who deserves to be known as our first American-style anchorman? Making life easier for people in wheelchairs by not calling them invalids is a good idea, but would they not benefit a lot more if all buildings were made accessible to wheelchairs and more curbs were level with sidewalks like in the US? Not only have we followed the American invention of political correctness, but too many have gone the whole hog, often rendering this well-meaning philosophy useless or even counterproductive. Gendering grammar is particularly cumbersome in German, simply because its basic rule of using the masculine and feminine endings of each noun separately makes a sentence longer, piling up quite a few extra lines or minutes. In so many ways *We are All Americans,* as this title suggests, but over the decades my Austrian half has offered more resistance. With pubs and restaurants complaining that they would lose half their customers without offering the amenity of puffing away in separate rooms, innkeepers only haltingly accepted the

American *absolutely smoke free* but criticized it as violating minority rights. Not really faulty thinking, is it? Strange also that the idea of wrapping up leftovers which your stomach can't handle in one sitting for later treatment at home was not born during our post-war years of hunger but came in with American students much later. Only a few years after the first Boston Marathon was run, its Vienna version followed most successfully, making those unable to participate or not having worked out enough feel almost guilty of a sin of omission. When half a century ago the early celebrity of women's rights was invited by Chancellor Kreisky to beat the drum for women's equality, companies with less than half their board members women went public and promised remedy. There is hardly an opportunity missed to jump on the Central European *MeToo* wagon these days, the instances of fighting serious cases of sexual harassment or assault hopefully outnumbering those of sheer *chuzpah*. Nor does condemning highly celebrated paintings as *disgusting* help women's rights because they supposedly "violate my rights as a modern woman." The words of a good American friend who had studied art history! As is so often the case, "the opposite of good is well intentioned."

"Many of your America skeptics around the world send their children to our top U.S. universities," is a statement often heard, but at this point in my and the nation's life I would reply, "Correct, but what does this prove about the level of general education?" Celebrating the accomplishments of American medical, technological, or economic research institutions is a good thing, but realizing that they don´t easily translate into benefits for the average citizen is quite another. No other country has spent anywhere near the millions on research in psychology, but would I conclude that Americans are more balanced or content with themselves or the world than non-Americans? Nowhere has R&D developed more insights, systems, and equipment to advance language learning than in America, but how many fractions of a percent in the U.S. can claim to be bilingual, other than most Hispanics? Having grown older and maybe even a wee bit wiser, I have found so many of my viewpoints of half a century ago much harder to defend, sometimes not at all. Nothing particularly unusual and easily summed up in the ancient Roman lines (Ovid), "The times are changing, and so are we with them." Yet everything else being equal, it is emotionally still easier for me to listen to and to accept American criticism of things Austrian, German, or even European than the other way around.

What happened during and after my last History class with only five rather than the usual dozen plus students was as far beyond the pale as was the pandemic paralyzing us all only a few months later. Warned that our unusual mix of one Jewish and two African-American women plus two Chinese from Shanghai already in the U.S. for two years could easily lead to controversial discussions in a course focusing on ethnicity, nationalism, racism, and fascism, my premonitions turned out to be justified in midcourse. The two blacks were excellent students, one more uncompromising and aggressive than her classmate when it came to the inevitable discussion of why controversial monuments should—no, had to be—torn down. "Of course, I understand your viewpoint, but couldn't you settle for a compromise acceptable to all, like adding a corrective state-of-the art explanation and leave the monument intact, which several black voices have also suggested?" My plea not to jeopardize the tremendous achievements their parents and grandparents had made might have been the straw that broke the camel's back, in this case mine. "No compromises anymore, those days are over!" Shocked by her icy tone, I went on talking about how crystal-clear the huge differences were to me as a foreigner in the South of 1957 and sixty years later now."—

"What counts is that we don't see it like that" and "Beauty is in the eyes of the beholder" her friend joined in, putting me down as yet another *old white male.*

All this time, Fang and Fong kept quiet except when we touched upon the millions starved or killed by Mao and the Kim dynasty. "But those millions killed were dying for progress." Of course, just a thought, China was not on our syllabus. Even more of an eye-opener was their failure to even begin to understand what western thinking meant with its insistence on personal liberty and individual rights. "We just spent a weekend in Paris" they told the class and what did we see other than burning cars and smashed windows? The heritage of 1789, if we understand you correctly. For thousands of years we have taught, lived, and achieved many a miracle by thinking communally and collectively. Individualism is a concept we have great problems even underanding." The yellow of the egg was that Fang and Fong warned me of a plot, simultaneously ridiculing the black students′ arguments with complaints like "that's all we ever hear about on campus, minority rights, the poor blacks." Fascinating indeed, two Chinese playing down the fate of Tibetans and Uigurs and accusing blacks of being overly sensitive!—A tense farewell boat trip up the Danube, some interracial picture taking, and lasting impressions of one kind or another for different pairs of eyes.

With the rumors of a plot against me on my mind, I learned that the university "expected me to leave." Despite repeated pleading with the local director, I could not find out anything at all about the case against me and eventually turned to the home campus. Complaining that I was being treated like a derelict without even learning about my crimes, I received this devastating reply. "You should realize, as all of us had to, that progress was continuously being made in education, some of it by coopting students into our decision-making processes, and that Europe should try to keep up with these developments. You are entitled to your belief that the students are too fragile and coddled, but when you are on a WFU-affiliated program, they should and do expect their faculty to behave according to our guidelines." *Wokeness* the new panacea, "the need to search for more knowledge and truth to fight injustice." Brand new idea. Big deal. Holy *Xi Chi Ping*, Fang and Fong had really tipped me off in mid-stream! All of this was of course also part and parcel of rising racial tension on the home campus, news of which had infiltrated the Vienna faculty. A semblance of good luck thanks to *Corona*, I would not have wanted to go on teaching without real-life students around anyway.

Learning by experiencing identity politics.

AFTERTHOUGHTS

By now the thought of returning to UNH was like that of returning to Hardegg, except even more painful. The latter is all childhood memories and recurring visits with history students, two highpoints being the nine-hundredth anniversary of its elevation to township and a decade later the removal of the barbed wire fences separating us from the land of my ancestors. UNH, however, was the place of my awakening in so many ways. With its faculty and former classmates gone, what would there be to return to? What would be the point of rewinding my inner clock to zoom in on "Sweet Diana" once more? Of slurping a craft beer sitting on the *Theta Xi* wall looking for faces I might remember as much younger while ignoring the many strange ones? Of looking forward to a piano recital by Donald S? Or the hardest of such imagined efforts, the point of finding myself*?* Put in *Durham* for *Siena* in these gripping lines by Austrian writer K. M. Gauss, and you will have an idea of the search I mean.

"I stayed on for two more days because I knew Siena from a visit thirty years ago and was hoping to meet myself in the streets after so many years. Myself, that is the one I was thirty years ago, including the part of me I did not become."

Had I been brought up in the British or French occupation zone, I might well have responded with the same enthusiasm to their soldiers and their ways of presenting themselves, Scottish kilts and blue French berets marching to the *Union Jack* and the *tricolore.* A moot point, though intriguing enough considering that our impressionable teens set us on tracks leading into directions we could not be aware of until much later. Growing up with the same pool of genes my father did in decades of devastating unemployment and a dictatorship with zero access to the outside world, could I have resisted joining the faith he did? Ah, "the blessings of those born late!"

Now that my race is run, I am grateful that my Maker always let me pursue my dreams with great longing.

Made in the USA
Middletown, DE
22 July 2024

57823238R00201